INNER PATHS

TO

OUTER SPACE

Journeys to Alien Worlds through Psychedelics and Other Spiritual Technologies

RICK STRASSMAN, M.D.

SLAWEK WOJTOWICZ, M.D.

LUIS EDUARDO LUNA, PH.D.

EDE FRECSKA, M.D.

Park Street Press
Rochester, Vermont

Park Street Press
One Park Street
Rochester, Vermont 05767
www.ParkStPress.com

Park Street Press is a division of Inner Traditions International

The Library of Congress Cataloging-in-Publication Data
Inner Paths to outer space : journeys to alien worlds through psychedelics and other spiritual technologies / Rick Strassman . . . [et al.] .
   p. cm.
   Summary: "An investigation into experiences of other realms of existence and contact with otherworldly beings"—Provided by publisher.
   Includes bibliographical references and index.
   ISBN: 978-1-59477-224-5
1. Hallucinogenic drugs and religious experience. I. Strassman, Rick, 1952–
   BL65.D7I56 2008
   154.4—dc22

                                   2007049373
Printed and bound in the United States by Lake Book Manufacturing, Inc.

10 9 8 7 6 5

Text design by Jon Desautels, layout by Jon Desautels and Rachel Goldberg
This book was typeset in Garamond Premier Pro, with Percolator as display typeface.

To send correspondence to the authors of this book, mail a first-class letter to the authors c/o Inner Traditions • Bear & Company, One Park Street, Rochester, VT 05767, and we will forward the communication.

contents

Foreword

Stephen Hickman

To those who are close observers of what's happening around them and who have reasonably sharp powers of analysis, it is apparent that there are fascinating things that science, as it currently stands, tends to ignore. Dr. C. G. Jung referred to these events, such as telepathy and precognition, as *synchronous phenomena*. I am morally certain that attitudes toward these phenomena will change in the foreseeable future, but at the moment any ideas that have the slightest breath of being paranormal or synchronous are highly charged and emotional issues that have a mystical or superstitious connotation.

As I understand from my reading and conversations on quantum theory, we exist in what I visualize as a sort of quantum soup, wherein what we experience as solid matter is actually the binding energies at an extreme end of the electromagnetic spectrum, the opposite end to the more familiar energies such as light and heat. If we were to venture into this end of the spectrum, thoughts would have the same validity or reality as solid matter. The Brooklyn Bridge is real; no one would dispute that. But its design had its inception in thought, didn't it?

The paranormal is so inherently fascinating that for any valid conclusions to be reached from investigation, a searching and objective skepticism must leaven the desire to discover wonders. The greatest obstacle to a clearer understanding of these matters is the overly naive willingness to believe virtually any "authority" on esoteric matters. This in turn has generated hordes of fraudulent exploitation that has done much damage to the validity of investigation into these subjects.

As a hardwired survival characteristic, the human mind has a highly developed pattern-recognition system built into it. However, like any other tool, the results of its use are limited to the skill of the user—in this case, the objectivity of the searcher and observer. Wisdom is where you find it, no question about that. But if you look in the usual places, you are only likely to find someone at the end of a psychic hotline whose pattern-recognition skills have shown him or her how to profit from your search for answers.

This is much like the semi-mystical hysteria that clouded even trained scientific minds when dealing with the issue of powered manned flight—issues that were solved by the triumph of a rational engineering approach over what can only be described as a superstitious alchemical approach. These two issues, mechanical flight and what might be called mental flight, are closely parallel in that the symbolic as well as the practical implications are of such tremendous significance that the emotional aspect tends to cloud public perception of them. Just look at the muddle-headed mistakes that were made by the early experimenters in human flight: Samuel Pierpont Langley, a trained astronomer whose catapult-launched Great Aerodrome nearly drowned his test pilot Charles Manley; Hiram Maxim, an otherwise competent engineer and inventor whose overly large aircraft designs never succeeded in getting off the ground; and Octave Chanute, a trained and successful civil engineer whose hang gliders never flew. Unbelievable stuff, from our modern viewpoint, isn't it?

The value of this book is that it takes a rational and scientific approach to esoteric subjects, opening a valid door to an avenue of wonder and the most fascinating implications. This it does in plain words—one sure way of spotting the opportunist and the fraud is by their employment of a specialized esoteric vocabulary, deliberately obscure phraseology, and defensive or arrogant attitudes in the presentation of their material. This book is blessedly free of any taint of this. Please note that I do not think of technical terms as esoteric.

Survival is observation, pattern recognition, and objective analysis, whereas blind faith is walking blindly to destruction. Yet survival at its barest level is merely scraping along at its pragmatic best. Even scientific intuition has a strong element of what can be called faith. Certainly many of the greatest minds in the history of science, both past and present, have seen no conflict between a sense of the Divine and scientific thought.

In fact, the closer you look at things, great or small, the more miraculous they are (observation was in fact the original basis for all the world's religious beliefs). If you do the research, you will see that this is literally true—organic life, star formation, the vast and the unimaginably small, all are bound together in an infinitely beautiful magical pattern.

So the illusory conflict between survival (which is closely related to scientific thought) and Divine faith is evidently not a simple division of the practical and the mystical. Mythology, as defined by Joseph Campbell, is the mechanism by which the human psyche relates to the chaos of an infinite environment. The various types of human mythos are composed of what Jung called the archetypes, symbols with the power to release the stored energy of the human psyche. Sounds like quantum physics, doesn't it?

Inner Paths to Outer Space shows a direct path into the realm of these archetypes and provides access to the energies inherent to your mind. My own creative experiences and profession are closely related to the investigations and speculations in this book. My job is to paint visionary pictures, from my own vision quest as well as from the interpretation of the visions of others. The art I produce is a practical form of magic that provides physical access to the imaginary realm. This book would have formed the basis for my own vision quest had it only been written earlier, but it shines with fascination to minds of all ages. It is a signpost to avenues by which the mind can see into the magical workings of creation in ways beyond the everyday human experience.

To me, though, the most fascinating aspect of this book is the implications that this research material has on what I think of as the *psychic* component of the evolutionary process. The *physical* process has gone quite far enough—so far, in fact, that human geopolitical affairs have reached a stage that can only be described as critical. By this I mean that the human intellect (as distinguished from what I might call the psychic intellect), which has evolved with the rest of our physical selves, has by itself created grave problems of such complexity that they now constitute a crisis similar in magnitude to those that in past epochs have served to trigger physical evolutionary changes. This is no longer the type of regional pressure that previously initiated evolutionary development, but rather a global crisis of a magnitude such that further physical changes are no longer sufficient to deal with it. These are problems that only a *psychic* evolution will be able to unravel. The human mind has created these problems for us with its vaulting advances in technology, and it lies with the heretofore-untapped component of our minds to find solutions to these problems. The way to these solutions lies ahead of us, not back to some childish pre-technical primitivism.

When you consider the astounding adaptability that Nature displays everywhere we look, the notion of psychic evolution is not as fanciful as it might at first seem. If you carefully consider how the human body has evolved to adjust to every aspect of its surroundings, it is certainly not farfetched to wonder how far beyond the purely physical that the human mind is equipped to go.

I can easily see that the implications of the ideas and results discussed in this book will be the starting point for some of the most rewarding psychophysical discoveries this century will produce.

✧

Stephen Hickman has been illustrating science fiction and fantasy since 1977. His painting, sculpture, and writing has earned him a World Science Fiction Convention's Hugo Award and six Chesley Awards. In 1988 Hickman wrote *The Lemurian Stone,* which formed the basis for his *Pharazar Mythos* illustrations. The results of his own vision quest can be seen at stephenhickman.com.

introduction

We have been building spaceships and space stations, pointing our telescopes toward the heavens, and hoping that someday, in a not-too-distant future, we'll get lucky and discover alien civilizations out there. The Search for Extra-Terrestrial Intelligence (SETI) program has been listening to the sky for more than forty years—a significant time period during which Earth's population has doubled—and the heavens appear to be hopelessly silent. . . . Perhaps we have been looking in the wrong places or in the wrong direction or using inappropriate methods. Perhaps, instead of searching for aliens in the sky, we should look much closer—inside ourselves, in those places from which we have been receiving messages of alien intelligence for millennia, though few of us have ever paid attention.

Our universe is beautiful, complex, and full of delightful surprises. The most astounding secrets are often hidden in plain sight. What if the supermarket tabloids ("the best investigative journalism on the planet," according to Tommy Lee Jones's character in the film *Men in Black*) are right on target and aliens indeed live right next to us?

There is an old story that after Creation, God was wondering where to hide the ultimate secrets of the universe. The Almighty contemplated: Should I hide them deep in the oceans? No; humans can invent submarines and these secrets can fall into unworthy hands. Should I hide them in the remote corners of the universe? Not good either; humans can develop spaceships and the secrets can get into wrong hands. Then an idea occurred to God: The secrets of the universe can be hidden at the bottom of humans' minds, deep in their souls. Then, only the worthy can find them.

If you are already capable of listening to the inner voice or are on the way inward toward that goal, then surely you will become worthy to discover the secrets of the universe. This book not only aims to show you the inner paths to the outer space, but it also attempts to explain to the rationally minded why and how these paths work.

Astronomers are still trying to locate and identify dark matter and dark energy. More than 80 percent of the mass in the universe is unaccounted for and is effectively invisible to our most sophisticated instruments. New theories posit that dark matter and energy are hidden in the six, ten, or more additional spatial dimensions predicted by string theory, though some physicists argue that dark matter is simply difficult-to-observe particles in our universe. Physicists such as Michio Kaku tell us that parallel universes may be hiding in the higher dimensions, and experiments are in progress to prove their existence. Is it possible to access parallel universes by any means? Is it possible to perceive extra dimensions?

Physical laws as we know them are restrictive in this regard. Electromagnetic waves—as far as we know—cannot carry information between dimensions. Some speculate that gravitons can travel between multiple universes, but coherent light cannot reach us from these places; we can only feel the gravitational force of our neighboring universes. In *Psychedelic Shamanism* Jim DeKorne postulates: "[F]or human beings, spatial dimensions of three and less are external, and dimensions higher than three are internal. Hence, for us, all spatial dimensions higher than three are mental or psychic. It follows from this that a four-dimensional being would be experienced subjectively by a three-dimensional being as an inner voice or hallucination, as an interior phenomenon."[1]

Some claim that people have been venturing into alien worlds for thousands of years. Most of these people have not necessarily been

NASA astronauts, scientists working for SETI project, or even science-fiction fans. Many of these explorers have not been prepared for what they have experienced, and most of them have never heard about First Contact manuals. Instead, they have been spiritual seekers, shamans, religious ascetics, medical research subjects, psychiatric patients, drug abusers, and common people who, accidentally and sometimes against their will, have been forced to become our planetary ambassadors to alien worlds.

One notable exception: science-fiction writers who have traveled through these gateways in search of inspiration. There is more science-fiction literature, art, and film that may have been inspired by mind-expanding experiences than most of us suspect, from Lewis Carroll's *Alice in Wonderland* to Philip K. Dick's brilliant novels such as *Valis, Ubik,* and *The Divine Invasion.* Movies such as *Total Recall, Dark City, The Matrix, Renegade, eXistenZ, Vanilla Sky, The Fountain, The Waking Life, The Truman Show, The X-Files, The Lord of the Rings,* and even *Star Wars* may owe their inspiration to these same sources, the altered states of consciousness experienced by their authors.

Why is it that most science-fiction fans, the very people who are probably best prepared for contact with aliens, are not the ones who have visited alien worlds and traveled in time to call on the lost cities of Atlantis? Most of our fellow humans still don't have the faintest idea that the universe is teeming with life. It may be surprising to many that the secret gateways to alien worlds may be hidden inside our own minds and that humans already have been traveling in space and time and making contact with alien species.

Where do shamans actually travel when they go to the underworld or fly to the upperworld looking for spirits, arguing, bargaining, negotiating, or even fighting with those they find? Who are these entities who give shamanic healers advice and powers to use upon returning to their tribe? What is the source of that otherworldly information, that immense energy these shamans tap in to in their travels? Does it originate in the shaman's mind or does it come from external powers that reside in some invisible realm?

Another important, fundamental question: Can information bypass the five senses to enter the brain? The power of intuition and mind-expanding experiences may explain why almost every important idea introduced by science-fiction writers has entered mainstream science eventually. Academic articles on hyperspace, time travel, supraluminal speed, teleportation, and parallel universes once belonged solely to the realm of science fiction, but are published nowadays in journals of theoretical physics. Some of these ideas have even reached an experimental stage. This may be shocking to skeptics, even though skeptics are rather difficult to surprise.

Most of us have heard about the ideas of Erich von Däniken and Zecharia Sitchin. Perhaps these authors have a point: Humankind has had visitors—but they may have come to visit us through inner space, rather than outer space. It is possible, however, that the people whom we consider instrumental in the sudden growth of civilization experienced some sort of naturally occurring psychedelic visions as a source of their inspiration and ingenious inventions. Perhaps the culture we are so proud of was shaped many thousand of years ago by the influence of an endogenous hallucinogen. Perhaps mystical traditions are correct in teaching that there is an infinite world inside of us and that this infinite world merges with or is established upon the same fundamental principles as the world outside. Surprisingly, contemporary physics has a great deal to say about all of these suppositions.

The idea for this book came from research conducted on human volunteers who were administered intravenous DMT, or dimethyltryptamine. DMT, a compound found in the human brain, produces extraordinary changes in consciousness: dreams, religious exaltation, psychosis, and near-death experiences. Substances such as DMT are known as *psychedelics* or *hallucinogens*. They appear to work as keys to locks inside the mind, allowing entry into different realities. Each key (hallucinogen) opens a different door, but all of these doors lead to realms that differ from our consensus reality.

DMT and related compounds are present in numerous species of plants growing in temperate and tropical regions. DMT has been used by shamans in South America and the Caribbean for millennia as a main component of snuff and in a decoction called *ayahuasca*—a plant extract that combines DMT, which is inactive when taken orally, with the beta-carbolines that potently inhibit the enzyme responsible for very rapid degradation of DMT in our gut and liver, which therefore allows DMT to reach and exercise its effects on the central nervous system.

Shamanic use of sacred plants such as peyote, mushrooms, and ayahuasca serves to free the soul from corporeal confinement, facilitate access to realms of alternate reality, and allow communication with the spiritual world. These plants are also used to diagnose and treat a wide variety of illnesses, both psychological and physical. Ingestion of traditional sacred plants in connection with shamanic rituals often results in spiritual experiences. We can argue that some of these experiences qualify as travel into realms belonging to certain genres of science fiction such as horror, fantasy, and ghost stories. Participants in these rituals frequently report encounters with spiritual beings—some of them benevolent, some of them scary and threatening. Others experience time travel, telepathy, or merging with God.

DMT often induces experiences that belong to hard science fiction or space opera. Almost 50 percent of the subjects participating in a clinical study conducted by Rick Strassman claimed to remain totally lucid while visiting absolutely alien realms. Some of them described seeing vast, orbital structures around unknown planets or meeting and interacting with peculiar alien beings. These contacts ranged from various attempts at communication to bizarre surgical procedures and even intercourse with aliens! Many of these reports parallel those of "alien abduction" literature, leading us to speculate about a relationship between endogenous DMT and such encounters.

It is interesting to note that subjects who have been hypnotized for a variety of purposes have reported similar experiences. These experiences may also be explained by the effects of endogenous DMT. But are such experiences real? Can hallucinations be true? Did these people actually meet aliens and visit distant planets? Read on and judge for yourself.

1

The psychedelics
Overview of a Controversial Drug Type
Rick Strassman, M.D.

Consciousness is a mystery, and the association of consciousness with matter is even more mysterious. How does a particular collection of molecules and energy combine to create awareness? Further, what determines the quality and content of consciousness? These are some of the general questions facing us as conscious beings. In the context of this book, we address particular questions regarding unusual states of consciousness in which we perceive things that are not normally perceivable.

Consciousness contains an unlimited number of states, several of which humans access in their lives. Wakefulness, deep sleep, meditation, and psychosis are some of these general categories. We may enter these states via built-in biological rhythms, such as the sleep–wake cycle. Perturbations of normal physiology—for example, fever, illness, sleep deprivation, starvation, and fasting—also produce different states of consciousness. In addition, a variety of natural substances contained in plants as well as certain synthetic drugs affect consciousness.[1]

Many nonhuman animals consume plants or plant products for their consciousness-altering effects. Examples include fermented fruit–swilling elephants, dazed and confused bees that return repeatedly to wallow in the flowers of psychoactive datura plants, and catnip-intoxicated felines. Some authors suggest that animals possess an innate drive for intoxication.[2] We can assume that in the mists of pre-history, early hominids, imitating the animals with which they shared their ecosystem, also partook of plants to enter altered states.

In some of Andrew Weil's early work, he suggests a specifically human drive to experience altered states of consciousness.[3] Some of the methods employed are modifying our biology through environmental or behavioral means, such as sweat lodges, spinning in circles, and prolonged chanting. Another way to experience altered consciousness is by ingesting psychoactive plants.

Throughout the world and at all times, humans have consumed a dizzying array of plants and plant products for their mind-altering effects. We have been drinking wine; chewing coca leaves; smoking opium; drinking coffee; and chewing, smoking, or snuffing tobacco. Chemical compounds in certain plants are the most proximate causes of these effects: In wine, this compound is ethanol; in coca leaves, it is cocaine; in opium, morphine; in coffee, caffeine; in tobacco, it is nicotine.*

↑s, ↓s, AND ★s

According to nature-based religious traditions, plants possess intelligence. Many modern Westerners who have undergone a deep experience with ayahuasca (a psychedelic botanical brew from the Amazon) can vouch for the apparent presence of a "personality" in this botanical brew with which they communicate under the influence.

While such phenomena strain the credulity of disciples of materialist science, they nevertheless point toward realms of consciousness containing nonhuman intelligence that we may find useful in our struggle to continue existing on Earth.

---

*It is appropriate to discuss, although difficult to keep that discussion within scientific confines, why plants produce these psychoactive substances. Even more, what does this relationship between man and mind-altering plants say about the biological and biochemical matrix in which we and the plants exist on this planet?

As thinking creatures, we construct categories for things we encounter. In this manner, we can note different categories of drug effects. How can we best classify mind-altering drugs? Many years ago, I attended a lecture by Dr. Alexander Shulgin on the chemistry of psychedelic drugs. Dr. Shulgin is a San Francisco Bay Area medicinal chemist and the creator of hundreds of novel psychoactive compounds.[4] He is a dynamic speaker—a fount of information, opinions, and first-hand experience. Doing his best to put the nonchemist members of his audience at ease, he began the lecture by sharing with us a simple model in which all psychoactive drugs belong to either the ↑s, the ↓s, or the ★s.

We usually call drugs in the ↑ family stimulants, or "uppers," hence the arrow-up symbol. The member of this category with which we are most familiar is caffeine, found in coffee, tea, and soft drinks. Other members of this family are nicotine in tobacco; cocaine in the coca plant; synthetic amphetamine and methamphetamine; the cathinone-containing khat plant of the Middle East and northern Africa; Ritalin (methylphenidate), the commonly prescribed medication for attention deficit disorders; and arecoline-containing betel nuts, chewed in Asian and Pacific regions.

The effects of ↑s are relatively easy to describe: In most of us, most of the time, typical doses of these drugs used in a controlled manner elicit a magnification or amplification of various psychobiological functions, including attention, thinking rate and accuracy, wakefulness, level of anxiety, and motor activity. Taking too much of a ↑, however, pushes us beyond our limits, and leads to effects such as seizures from nervous system toxicity and potentially lethal arrhythmias from cardiac toxicity.

We call ↓ agents sedatives, or "downers." We refer to them as hypnotic drugs when their primary purpose is to induce sleep, anxiolytic drugs when we need to reduce overall arousal but maintain wakefulness, and anesthetic drugs in cases that require an unresponsive, inert state.

Alcohol, benzodiazepines such as Xanax and Valium, opiate narcotics, kava found in Polynesia and Hawaii, and general anesthetics belong to this category.

Their effects, relatively easy to describe, are essentially opposite those of ↑s. With their use, attention drifts, thinking slows, and sleep approaches; we are calmer and less anxious and we move more slowly and clumsily. At toxic doses, coma and respiratory and cardiovascular collapse may occur.

The effects of the ★ group, the focus of this book and those that may provide an inner path to outer space, are more difficult to characterize—but not because their effects are more subtle, for they are anything but subtle at effective doses. Instead, these substances seem to modify the quality of consciousness, rather than produce the general enhancement or reduction of mental process that we observe with ↑s and ↓s, respectively. The ★ substances affect those aspects of consciousness that we identify most closely with our sense of being human—that is, particular ways of thinking, feeling, perceiving, and willing.

We usually call the effects of the ★s psychedelic or hallucinogenic. These drugs occupy a unique position in the superfamily of mind-altering chemicals. The highly charged nature of discussions of these drugs relates to the extraordinary nature of these psychological effects.[5]

The difficulty in describing accurately or consistently the effects of psychedelic drugs has led to a bewildering profusion of names for them: hallucinogen or illusogen (producing hallucinations or illusions, respectively), psychedelic (mind-manifesting), entheogen (generating the divine within), mysticomimetic (mimicking the mystical state), oneirogen (generating dreams), phanerothyme (making feelings visible), phantasticant (eliciting fantasy), psychodysleptic (distorting or disrupting the mind), psychotomimetic (mimicking psychosis), psychotogen (generating psychosis), psychotoxin (toxic to the mind), schizotoxin (toxic in a way that causes schizophrenia), and deliriant (causing delirium). Each name captures a certain element of the intoxication and the manner in which we interpret those effects—what they mean, and how the drugs produce them.[6]

Hallucinogen is the preferred medical-legal term for these substances. Although hallucinations do occur in psychedelic drug intoxication, they are not invariant. Neither do all of us agree, particularly across cultures, regarding the "unreal" nature of the perceived visions and voices that the term *hallucination* suggests. This perhaps unintended implication of the term *hallucinogen* probably reflects more or less conscious materialistic skepticism regarding nonvisible realities. Note I use the term *materialistic* rather than *scientific,* because we may indeed apply the tools and models of science just as easily to nonmaterial data as we do to material data.

While the term *psychedelic* evokes memories of and reactions to a particular political and sociocultural phenomenon harkening back to the turbulent 1960s, I prefer it over the other terms currently in use. This philologically incorrect amalgam of Greek and Latin roots refers to the most basic property of these drugs—that is, they are mind-manifesting. They show us our mind—its contents and its processes—from a very different perspective. Beyond that level of abstraction, however, I believe all the other terms become either too value-laden or restrictively particular in their labeling of what we experience under the influence of these drugs.

EARLY HUMAN HISTORY OF PSYCHEDELIC USE

There are anthropological and art historical data suggesting humans have used psychedelic plants for thousands or perhaps tens of thousands of years. Terence McKenna, a psychedelic philosopher, gazing back at man's preverbal African ancestors, speculates that protohominids used psychedelic mushrooms for their unique visual effects to aid hunting. An unexpected side effect of this use was the stimulation of language development, perhaps through the unique property of psychedelics to blend and merge the senses of sight and sound. Our ancestors may have seen the sounds they were making, which provided them with an unprecedented additional level of abstraction with which they could manipulate communication.[7]

We can add to this the speculations of Gordon Wasson, a New York banker and amateur mycologist. In the 1950s, Wasson discovered and reported on psilocybin mushroom ceremonies in Mexico that most anthropologists believed had been extinct for hundreds of years. After experiencing firsthand the ineffability, ecstasy, and visions induced by the mushroom intoxication, he proposed that psychedelic plants were responsible for the first glimmerings of religious sensibilities in man: such experiences were evidence that invisible, freestanding, portentous realities exist beyond the veil of everyday life.[8]

Thus, we have theories suggesting that plant-based psychedelics are responsible for two of humanity's most unique creations: language and religion. Why, then, is it so difficult to come by information about psychedelics? Pendulums swing; perhaps the shift from a primarily matriarchal worldview to a more patriarchal one caused the banishment of psychedelic plants from mainstream religious and social use. A more matriarchal, nature- and earth-based civilization with a panoply of divinely imbued entities probably perceived little conflict between using plant-based psychedelics to commune with spiritual realities and a philosophy that emphasized humans' inseparability from nature. Patriarchal religions, in both the East and the West, on the other hand, developed a more dichotomous view of humans relative to the rest of nature, and more often than not assumed a frankly antagonistic attitude toward the spiritual significance of all things material.[9] This was not the original teaching of those who founded these religions, yet the priestly classes eventually established hegemony over doctrine and practice. These clerics adopted a worldview that extracted from nature any spiritual relevance, and succeeded eventually in driving psychedelic plant use underground. Those in positions of religious authority considered psychedelic, plant-induced experiences ill-informed or degenerate at best; at worst, they condemned the use of these plants as an evil that required extermination.*

The only significant human institution that, from its earliest origins, has regarded plant-based psychedelics as a fundamental component of religious and spiritual activity is shamanism. Later in this book we will discuss the relevance of a shamanic approach to the use of psychedelic plants and drugs.

RECENT HISTORY OF PSYCHEDELICS IN THE WEST

Within traditional Western academic settings, anthropology is the field that has focused attention on psychedelic plant use and the role of these plants in the societies that use them. More than any other field, it has maintained the flame of interest in these plants and drugs over several hundred years of Western suppression of all information about them.[10] Within the last sixty to seventy years, however, it has been within the medical-scientific framework, primarily psychiatry, psychology, and the neurosciences, that our culture has viewed and understood psychedelic drugs.

In the 1890s, the German chemist Arthur Heffter isolated mescaline from the peyote cactus and, in a series of self-experiments, determined its psychoactivity. Over the next twenty to thirty years, this drug attracted some scientific attention;[11] however, mescaline's pronounced side effects of nausea and vomiting, as well as the lack of a cogent psychological and biological context within which to understand its effects, limited its study.

From the viewpoint of biology, very little data existed regarding how drugs affected the brain. From the viewpoint of psychology,

---

*I nevertheless continue to puzzle over why no mainstream Eastern or Western religious tradition has even attempted to incorporate psychedelic plants or drugs into its practice and teachings, at least so that these are available to the few members who may utilize their effects.

Freudian systems, dominant at the time, took a dim view of what were viewed as religious or spiritual states, considering them infantile or regressed. The exception to the Freudian school's disdain of altered states of consciousness was the use of free association, a variant of hypnosis, in psychoanalytic practice.

The Swiss psychiatrist Carl Jung, at one time Freud's closest disciple, took a broader view of religious and spiritual experience in human psychological development, yet it appears that discussions of plant-based or synthetic psychedelics are absent from his writings. This is surprising inasmuch as the synthesis and first use of LSD occurred in Switzerland more than a decade before Jung's death.

In the mid-1940s, all this changed when the Swiss chemist Albert Hofmann synthesized LSD and soon thereafter described its profound psychological effects.[12]

LSD's properties and the biological and psychological contexts in which its discovery took place were much more propitious than those of mescaline. Psychology was beginning to question the all-encompassing power of psychoanalysis to explain and treat every psychological condition. In addition, the rest of medicine was going through a period of great expansion via the discoveries of many basic pathobiological processes: for example, the efficacy of antibiotics in treating infections. Psychiatry began looking at biology as a way to join once again the larger field of medicine, healing the breach that an overreliance upon Freudian psychoanalysis had created.

LSD did not have many invariant physiological effects, particularly the unpleasant gastrointestinal ones of mescaline. Even more striking was its potency, which is thousands of times greater than mescaline. LSD is active in doses of millionths of grams, rather than mescaline's thousandths of grams. In addition to LSD's more benign side-effect profile and startling potency, developments in the nascent field of psychopharmacology provided a strong impetus for LSD's research use.

In 1948, scientists discovered that serotonin (5-hydroxytryptamine, or 5-HT) is involved in the mechanism by which blood vessels constrict in response to injury. Soon thereafter, researchers discovered 5-HT in the brain. Studies then demonstrated its behavioral effects in laboratory animals. As a result of these latter two findings, 5-HT was labeled as the first known *neurotransmitter,* a naturally occurring chemical modifying brain function through its effects on nerve cells. Eventually, research revealed that LSD produces its effects by modifying serotonin function in the brain,[13] a theory that has only become more refined and sophisticated over the last sixty years.

The use of chlorpromazine (Thorazine) in the early 1950s as the first specific antipsychotic medication provided another cause for excitement in the young field of "biological psychiatry." For the first time, a medication could selectively block the delusions and hallucinations of psychotic patients without putting them to sleep, which occurred regularly with the use of barbiturates, the only previously available drugs for these conditions.

These three agents—serotonin, LSD, and Thorazine—affecting the mind through the aegis of knowable biological processes ushered in a new era of scientific inquiry, that of *psychopharmacology*—the study of how drugs affect the psyche. Serotonin is a naturally occurring, behaviorally active neurotransmitter; LSD is a drug affecting serotonin and producing what appeared to be a bona fide psychosis; and Thorazine blocks psychotic symptoms in patients with endogenous psychoses such as schizophrenia. These three were the original scientific legs of the tripod supporting the birth of this new field.

It is striking that our society has forgotten how critical LSD was in the early stages of the development of psychopharmacology, and that it continues to be a seminal contributor to the field today. It is reminiscent of the patriarchy "forgetting" the role of psychedelic plants in spiritual and religious settings. During the late 1940s through the late 1960s, hundreds of scientific papers and dozens of books, monographs, and scientific meetings discussed the latest in psychedelic drug research. Many of the key figures of academic psychiatry and pharmacology began their career in this field. Presidents of the American Psychiatric

Association, chairmen of psychiatry departments, advisers to and members of the U.S. Food and Drug Administration (FDA)—all cut their teeth in the psychedelic research field. It was an exciting, well-funded, and creative time.

There were several approaches to the study and application of psychedelics within psychiatry. One group focused on the brain–mind relationships that these drugs could illuminate (structure–activity studies)—that is, how does the structure of an individual drug affect its pharmacology? What is the relationship between the pharmacology of a particular compound and its effects on the brain, and how do those effects relate to behavioral and subjective effects?

Scientists used several more-or-less proximate outcome measures to assess how these drugs affect the brain. The most proximate included variables such as the localization and characterization of changes LSD produced in the living brain. For example, scientists might attach a radioactive atom to LSD and then inject it into an animal. Using radiation-measuring photography, they could then determine where in the brain this LSD ended up by locating the "lighted" sites. Researchers also determined effects of a psychedelic drug on electrical activity within individual nerve cells.

Farther downstream, reflecting a closer link between pharmacology and organismal biology, were physiological reactions to these drugs, such as fluctuations in temperature, blood pressure, and blood hormone levels. By knowing which neurotransmitter systems mediated these biological effects and then comparing a psychedelic's effects on these parameters, scientists could deduce which brain systems psychedelics modified.

The least proximate but most relevant outcome measures were behavioral effects in animals and psychological effects in humans. For example, a drug somewhat like LSD in structure might produce in laboratory animals behavioral effects that were more or less like those produced by LSD. And, in humans, for example, this "LSD-like" drug might produce more emotional but fewer visual effects than those produced by LSD. Once researchers knew the basic receptor or electro-physiological pharmacology of this new drug, they could hypothesize regarding the link between pharmacology and animal behavior and/or human subjective response. It is important to keep in mind, however, that no matter how sophisticated our behavioral models in nonhuman animals are, nothing replaces human data in establishing subjective effects.

Other researchers believed psychedelic drugs were useful tools for studying psychosis. By producing a "model" psychosis in normal volunteers and assessing it carefully, they hoped to understand the nature of the endogenous illnesses that these drug intoxications resembled. In addition, if scientists could find pharmacological antidotes to a model psychosis, they could apply these treatments to endogenous psychotic illnesses: a drug that blocked the LSD effect in humans might prove beneficial in treating schizophrenia, if indeed LSD-induced states and schizophrenia had the same features.

A logical outgrowth of the model-psychosis approach focused on searching for an endogenous psychedelic chemical. If scientists could identify an LSD-like compound in the human body, they could then characterize its properties and develop ways to block the production of, or responses to, this schizotoxin. As a result, we would have a formidable tool in treating naturally occurring psychosis.

Indeed, in the 1960s several reports described the existence in the human body of the powerful, short-acting tryptamine psychedelics DMT and 5-methoxy-DMT. These compounds attained great prominence at that time. Later, we will address the history of endogenous tryptamine research in more detail.

A variant of the model-psychosis approach was that of self-experimentation with these drugs by researchers and other psychiatrists. They believed it was possible to obtain a firsthand experience of psychosis and thereby enhance their empathy in dealing with patients afflicted with this disorder.

Researchers also noticed that human volunteers reported profound changes in emotional and psychological processes akin to those occurring in the course of psychotherapy as a result of the use of psychedelic drugs. For example, these "psychedelic psychotherapy" researchers hoped to apply the increased suggestibility of psychedelic drug intoxication in order to strengthen the therapeutic alliance between patient and therapist. They believed that it might be possible to use the enhanced visual symbolization of thoughts and feelings to delve deeper into presumed unconscious conflicts. Novel and more-creative associations among thoughts, memories, and feelings might also provide the ability to perform deeper psychological work than any that could occur with drug-free psychotherapy, and could therefore allow for better resolution of conflicts.

The reports describing enhanced creativity under the influence of psychedelics are related to the psychotherapeutic model. Much of what occurs in effective psychotherapy is essentially creative in nature and involves attaining and applying new, more conscious ways of relating to mental structures and processes. Psychedelic drug-induced modifying of mental processes in "the service of the ego" in healthy, creative individuals might be useful in developing new approaches to problem solving.

There were a great many psychotherapy studies during the boom years of psychedelic research, enrolling hundreds of patients with a wide variety of disorders. These projects generated encouraging data that suggested efficacy in treating otherwise intractable conditions: neurotic, psychotic, and personality disorders, as well as substance abuse and dependence. Early studies often were positive, but also were difficult to generalize from research site to site. The abrupt discontinuation of research in the early 1970s precluded the fine-tuning of procedures and patient selection that naturally evolve to optimize any new treatment method.

The similarities between psychedelic drug effects and less pathological, highly altered states of consciousness, such as mystical and near-death experiences, were the focus of inquiry for a small but vocal group of researchers. They believed that the more reliable, consistently attainable psychedelic drug state could shed light on some of these naturally occurring psychedelic states. They hoped to understand better the nature of these states and to exploit their potential beneficial properties free of the accompanying religious discipline and dogmatic overlay of any particular tradition. These researchers were responsible for establishing *transpersonal* psychology, a field that continues to thrive.

Military and domestic intelligence agencies also carried out a covert research agenda during those years. The U.S. Central Intelligence Agency (CIA) and the military funded and performed these projects, due partly to similar efforts that took place in countries whose aims we considered hostile to ours (e.g., China and the Soviet Union). Investigators attempted to use psychedelics as brainwashing or truth-serum agents. The lack of reliability of these drugs to produce these effects led to the cessation of these pernicious projects. Though informed consent in aboveboard research at the time left something to be desired, these covert operations were surreptitious to the extreme.[14]

A generation of human psychedelic research came to an end almost as quickly as it began after the enactment of the Controlled Substances Act (CSA) in the United States in 1970. Similar legislation followed throughout the world, primarily through U.S.-driven United Nations enactments. The CSA effectively shut off academic research by placing these drugs behind a nearly impenetrable wall of bureaucracy and permits. This law passed because of fears in the academic, law enforcement, and public health communities that these drugs were too dangerous for anyone to use in any setting. In addition, legislators believed academic researchers were incapable of preventing unacceptable diversion of drug supplies to the street. Timothy Leary's behavior and pronouncements while he performed bona fide psilocybin research at Harvard University did much to fuel these anxieties.

It is also likely that the political upheavals in the United States over the Vietnam War and the media's promulgating the perception that these drugs led to a libertine and anarchist lifestyle contributed to enacting what now appears to be hastily conceived legislation. Human research with psychedelics thus ceased for twenty years, but basic research using nonhuman species continued apace. The next two decades saw great advances in a fundamental understanding of how psychedelics affect the brain.

In addition, though government-licensed and government-funded psychotherapy studies ended at this time, psychotherapeutic use of psychedelics continued, albeit underground. Participants used a number of different approaches to optimize drug effects on the therapeutic process: Jungian, Freudian, gestalt, and neoshamanic orientations. These activities were poorly documented and difficult to discuss in any manner of public discourse, but were enormously widespread.

In addition, field or street use of psychedelic drugs never dropped off seriously, even with the newly restricted status of these substances. Individual use of these drugs for pleasure, psychological insights, and spiritual practice remained and continues to be popular. So has their use in groups to enhance social bonding at rock concerts, raves, and similar gatherings.

It should be clear that we are dealing with an extraordinarily complex family of drugs—or, more accurately, with an extraordinarily complex experience into which these drugs seem to allow entry. We must look more closely at the various psychedelics and their effects, how they produce these effects, what these effects may say about human consciousness, and how we can best utilize these drugs for the greater good and with the least harm.

CHEMISTRY

Let us begin with the basic objective molecules—that is, the chemistry of these drugs. For our purposes, we are concerned with the "classical" psychedelics—LSD, psilocybin, DMT, and mescaline. The two chemical groups into which we classify these drugs are the tryptamines and the phenethylamines.

Tryptamine psychedelics possess a tryptamine core—a hexagonal six-carbon ring joined to a four-carbon plus one-nitrogen pentagonal ring. A two-carbon chain with a nitrogen atom at the end then attaches to the pentagonal ring. The body easily synthesizes the tryptamine building block from tryptophan, an amino acid contained in all of our diets.

The prototypical tryptamine psychedelic is N,N-dimethyltryptamine, or DMT, in which two carbons attach to the nitrogen at the end of tryptamine. A large number of plants contain DMT, as does every mammalian species whose tissues researchers have analyzed. It has been detected in human blood, urine, spinal fluid, and brain and lung tissue. Scientists have identified and cloned the human gene that makes the enzymes catalyzing the final step in DMT synthesis. Further, DMT is the visionary component of the psychedelic Amazon brew known as ayahuasca. The federal judiciaries of the United States and other countries have upheld the legality of the use of DMT in ayahuasca by specific churches, such as O Centro Espirita Beneficiente União do Vegetal.

A closely related tryptamine is 5-methoxy-DMT (or 5-MeO-DMT). Many of the same plants and animals that contain DMT also contain this compound. A better-known tryptamine is psilocybin, the active ingredient in magic mushrooms. The structure of psilocybin is essentially the same as that of a DMT molecule with a phosphate group—a phosphorus atom plus four oxygen atoms—attached to the six-carbon ring of the DMT.

More "complex" tryptamine derivatives include the signature psychedelic drug LSD, or lysergic acid diethylamide-25, also known simply as acid. Its "lysergamide" backbone contains the basic tryptamine building block. Another complex tryptamine is the African psychedelic ibogaine, found in the plant *Tabernanthe iboga,* which reputedly possesses profound antiaddictive properties.

The other major chemical family of classical psychedelics is the phenethylamines. These contain a phenethylamine core—a six-carbon hexagonal ring with a side chain of two carbons and nitrogen. Though amphetamine and methamphetamine, two powerful ↑s, are phenethyl-amines, we are more interested here in those with typical psychedelic effects, the best known of which is mescaline.

Mescaline is the primary active ingredient in the peyote cactus, *Lophophora williamsii,* found in the U.S. Southwest and in northern Mexico. The Native American Church, extant among North American indigenous populations, uses peyote in its ceremonies. U.S. and Canadian law protects this use.

Alexander Shulgin has created a vast array of phenethylamine ana-logs, chemical cousins of mescaline, with varying degrees of pharmaco-logical and psychological similarities to mescaline and amphetamine.[15]

There are other drugs, both synthetic and found in plants, with psychedelic properties, yet we do not usually consider them classical psychedelics. These compounds, however, possess psychological and pharmacological properties more or less like those of the classical drugs. Some examples are salvinorin A, found in *Salvia divinorum* (diviner's sage); 3,4-methylene-dioxy-methamphetamine (MDMA, also known as Ecstasy); ketamine; phencyclidine (PCP, also known as angel dust); dextromethorphan (DXM); and perhaps high-dose marijuana.

PHARMACOLOGY

We understand relatively well the pharmacology of the classical hal-lucinogens. Researchers continue to fine-tune hypotheses regarding mechanisms of action of these substances, but have established the basic outline in some detail. Most drugs act in the body by attaching to receptors on target cells. These receptors, composed of protein and fat, are produced by nature to receive chemical information from both within and without. Hormones attach to specific receptors located on different cell types in the body: for example, insulin attaches to recep-tors on fat cells to modify metabolism, and thyroid hormone attaches to receptors on heart cells.

In the brain, receptors exist for the large number of neurotransmitters synthesized either in the brain itself or in other tissues (particularly the gut). These chemicals provide a vector for information transfer and communication between and among the cells in the brain. A tiny space called the synapse separates adjacent nerve cells. Neurons propagate information within their own cell bodies via electric currents. When this current reaches the end of the neuron, it releases into the synapse packets of neurotransmitters, which it previously synthesized. These neurotransmitters attach to receptors on adjacent cells. Examples of neurotransmitters are serotonin (5-HT), acetylcholine, dopamine, norepinephrine, gamma amino butyric acid (GABA), and glutamate.[16]

Though serotonin exists throughout the body, particularly in the gut and blood, for the most part it is not abundant in the brain, except perhaps in the pineal gland, a quasi–nervous system organ. Nevertheless, 5-HT has diverse effects on multiple brain functions, which include control of physiological systems such as cardiovascular and endocrine systems as well as temperature regulation. It also affects areas of the brain that mediate emotional, cognitive, and sensory functions.

Scientists quickly determined that LSD and other classical psychedelics modify 5-HT systems by interacting with 5-HT receptors, usually activating the cells possessing those receptors.[17] Occasionally, however, depending upon the biochemical milieu of the relevant neurons, LSD could elicit antiserotonin effects.

In the last several decades, the model of classical psychedelics interacting with 5-HT receptors as the means by which they produce their effects remains undisputed. Further refinements have detailed the importance of particular types of 5-HT receptors, their location, and the nature of the cascading effects begun by the initial interaction of the drugs with those receptors.[18] Classical psychedelics affect serotonin systems in brain areas that we know relate to the particular mental functions modified by these drugs: for example, the frontal lobes, in terms of the effects of these psychedelics on thinking; the limbic system, in terms of their effects on emotional states; and visual and auditory cortices, in terms of their visual and auditory effects.

Other neurotransmitter systems are more relevant to the effects of the atypical psychedelics. For example, MDMA causes neurons to release serotonin and dopamine, rather than attaching directly to serotonin receptors on downstream cells. Salvinorin A affects a particular type of opiate receptor that normally mediates effects of opiate painkillers and naturally occurring opioids—the endorphins. Dextromethorphan, phencyclidine, and ketamine modify glutamate and opiate systems in a complex, interactive manner.

While we understand a great deal about the pharmacology of these drugs, it is important to remember the existence of the "explanatory gap" in psychopharmacology—that is, our inability to relate directly, in any particular case, the relationship between subjective experience and changes in brain chemistry. People under the influence of LSD do not feel it modifying their serotonin receptor function; instead, they feel bliss or terror, and they see and hear things that other people do not. This explanatory gap operates even in cases of drugs with less-dramatic effects, such as antidepressants, antianxiety agents, and stimulants. People on fluoxetine (Prozac), for example, feel less depressed; they do not feel their serotonin levels rise or their receptors decrease in number.

In the case of the relationship between the brain and consciousness, we may be able to pinpoint the location and nature of the relevant physiological changes, but how they play out in the mind of any particular individual at any particular moment remains an absolute mystery.

TIME COURSE

In addition to the chemical and pharmacological properties of psychedelics, it also is possible to characterize their time courses—how quickly effects ensue and how long those effects last. Intravenous and smoked DMT effects begin within seconds and conclude in about thirty minutes. In the case of ibogaine, an hour or more may pass between oral ingestion and the onset of effects, and its effects last for at least twelve to fourteen hours. Oral LSD and mescaline begin exerting their effects within thirty to forty minutes of ingestion, and these last eight to twelve hours. Oral psilocybin and ayahuasca effects begin within twenty to thirty minutes of ingestion and are barely perceptible after six to eight hours.

SUBJECTIVE EFFECTS

It is probably as difficult to describe the effects of psychedelic drugs on consciousness as it is to describe consciousness itself. These drugs affect all components of consciousness: self-awareness, sensation, thinking, volition, emotion, perception, and relatedness. One of the challenges wrought by the psychedelics is just this concatenation of consciousness-altering properties. Because so many functions change under their influence, they force us to examine more closely the very nature of consciousness—its basic properties and normal operation.

Sensory effects often predominate in psychedelic drug intoxication and are responsible for the common term *hallucinogen*. Visual changes are striking and may include the presence of a visible, buzzing, vibrating field around physical objects and a melting of the boundaries of those objects. There may be magnification, diminution, or alteration of color intensity and hue. Sometimes colors generate auditory impressions, a blending of sense information called *synesthesia*. Those who take psychedelics may see things others do not, either with eyes closed or open. In addition, what they see with eyes closed may be superimposed upon the outside world when they open their eyes.

They may see relatively simple geometric swirls in space or on an object, or more detailed images. Some of these visions are extraordinarily complex and may consist of quite well-formed and recognizable objects—for example, living creatures, machinery, and landscapes. Those experiencing psychedelics' effects may even perceive a white light that mystics claim to be divine or spiritual revelation.

Sounds become either mellower or painfully harsh. In another form of synethesia, individuals may see sounds. Previously unheard rhythms—pulsating, rushing, or mechanical—may manifest, or one or several voices may be heard. In some instances, individuals might not hear anything at all; they might be in a state of functional deafness.

Effects on tactile and gravitational senses can be pronounced. These range from feeling a dissociation of consciousness from the body to extreme hypersensitivity to inner and outer physical stimuli.

Emotional changes are also quite striking and can vacillate between abject terror and indescribable bliss. Tremendous fluidity of emotion may exist, with rapid shifts between extremes of joy, anger, passion, hatred, shame, and grandiosity. At other times, a person may feel nothing at all—that is, no human emotions—or may feel the emotions of another being, either real or imagined, as one's own.

The process of thinking may speed up, slow down, or qualitatively change. It may seem to these individuals as if they experience a different perspective or filter on both thought processes and thought content itself. Those undergoing psychedelics' effects might experience new personal or philosophical insights, or find themselves devoid of thought and unable to process any cognitive information. They may be able to unite opposites or see striking differences within some previously perceived unity. In addition, there may be an effect on the sense of reality: what they experience may feel "more real than real" or may feel totally unreal. Information arises from novel sources—a flower or cloud may impart new insights and reveal hidden meanings in nature. The beings or entities in their visions may communicate—about themselves, the person in the drug state, or the nature of reality.

Those under the influence of psychedelics may experience a change in relationship to the "other." Usually, there is increased suggestibility: it is easier to be affected or swayed by others. Sensitivity to interpersonal cues and body language impart previously unappreciated features of those who are "other"—strengths, conflicts, relatedness, and emotional states. Further, their own personality may change in directions they don't expect or anticipate. Perhaps they may gain more voluntary control over their reactions to people. They might also experience an expanded sense of empathy with nonhuman entities such as animals, plants, rocks, and even machines.

SET AND SETTING

In addition to qualitatively unique effects on consciousness, experiences induced by psychedelic drugs are exquisitely sensitive to matters of set and setting. Researchers developed the concepts of set and setting, discussed in further detail below, to help explain the extraordinarily variable effects of psychedelics regardless of whether the same dose is given to different people or the same dose is given to the same person at different times.[19] This variance is in contrast to the ↑s and ↓s, which usually produce similar effects among different people and within the same person even at different times.

In the case of psychedelics, we must pay special attention to the inner and outer environments of the individual taking them, because these may have profound effects on the psychedelic drug reaction. In some ways, set and setting color a taker's reaction to a psychedelic drug as much as the dose of the drug itself.

Set usually refers to who a person is at the time of ingesting and experiencing the effects of the drug. It contains both an individual's state at that time and his or her more enduring biological and psychological traits. The state includes both psychological and physiological factors such as present mood, current health or illness, food recently eaten or drunk, level of anxiety, and attitude toward and previous experiences with psychedelics. Traits take into account more pervasive, long-standing psychological and biological qualities, such as generosity or stinginess, acceptance or rejection of novelty, and being trusting or suspicious of human warmth. We also must include the hard-wiring of the person, such as the number and sensitivity of certain receptors in the brain and other organs.

Setting refers to the external environment in which a person takes the drug. If the psychedelic experience takes place outdoors, is the environment pleasant, safe, and comfortable or unpleasantly rainy, windy, loud, dangerous, or chaotically urban? If a drug is taken indoors, is the environment warm, safe, dry, and homey or high-tech, sterile, and filled with machines and testing implements?

Just as important, setting also refers to those around the taker. Are they supportive or hostile to the person or to the nature of the psychedelic drug experience? Have they taken a psychedelic themselves? This latter question has to do with basic issues of empathy and informed consent; in other words, can those nearby truly empathize with what the taker is experiencing, and how well have they explained or can they explain what to expect under the influence? Did they give the drug to the taker—and if so, why? Did they do so for research and data-gathering purposes? Was their intent psychotherapeutic, shamanic, or religious? Did they simply desire to party or to take advantage of the taker's heightened suggestibility and passivity? It is also important to learn if they believe psychedelics cause insanity or a mystical experience. Other considerations are how they are dressed, how they smell, and how they move around the space.

We should note that much of the conflicting data from the first generation of studies with psychedelics resulted from a lack of attention to and reporting of set and setting—particularly the latter. The fundamental assessment of a psychedelic experience as either good or bad depends to a large degree upon paying careful attention to comfort and safety issues, and how those in the taker's proximity deal with his or her anxiety when it arises.

ADVERSE EFFECTS

Psychedelics may have either physical or psychological adverse effects—or both. The classical psychedelic drugs are physically safe; I have been unable to locate any reports of deaths from overdoses directly attributable to their ingestion. Yet under these drugs' influence, people may engage in behavior that can result in significant morbidity or mortality, such as jumping from a rooftop because they believe they can fly.

In the mid-1960s to early-1970s, much media attention highlighted reports of chromosome damage and birth defects in children born to mothers who had taken LSD during pregnancy.[20] Later, more-rigorous and better-controlled research studies refuted the earlier alarmist ones, though they garnered much less attention.[21]

As for adverse psychological effects, these include those that occur during the acute psychedelic drug intoxication, such as paranoia, confusion, and disordered self-control. These are time-limited phenomena. These time-limited effects, in fact, were cited to support the proposition that psychedelic drugs were useful in producing a clinically relevant, discrete episode of psychosis in the psychotomimetic model. When these frightened, disorganized individuals need treatment, the first response is to provide a quiet, nonstimulating, supportive, and reassuring environment—the "talking down" approach. More-severe reactions of anxiety or potentially dangerous levels of agitation may require antianxiety or antipsychotic medication.

The potentially traumatic nature of a full-blown psychedelic experience can lead to significant psychiatric morbidity after acute drug effects have worn off. Yet early research investigators found that these "psychedelic casualties" were rare. The low incidence of such outcomes was the result of carefully screening volunteers, closely monitoring their sessions, and providing supportive follow-up as indicated. When disturbed psychological functioning did persist beyond twenty-four hours, it appeared that the particular syndrome was a psychedelic-precipitated event, rather than a specific LSD psychosis. Distressing, intense psychological effects of a psychedelic drug experience could therefore trigger manic, depressive, anxiety, or psychotic disorders. In other words, the psychedelic drug effect may be akin to other psychic traumas such as rape, a natural disaster, and battle shock.

Case studies of emergency room visits and psychiatric hospitalizations in people who have taken LSD or similar psychedelics usually revealed previously existing psychological instability or actual mental illness in most of the individuals. In addition, these patients often used other drugs in combination with psychedelics, such as alcohol, amphetamine, and PCP. Finally, the impact of set and setting variables limited the ability to generalize to a supervised environment the effects of these drugs as described in these psychedelic casualty reports.

Longer-term or delayed symptoms attributed to LSD and other psychedelics include flashbacks and posthallucinogen perceptual disorder. Flashbacks are episodes of reexperiencing certain sensory, cognitive, or emotional features of the psychedelic experience after an intervening drug-free period. Most people who have these experiences do not report them to clinicians, because they find them interesting, enjoyable, or time-limited. Only when flashbacks interfere with ordinary function and cause distress do people report such symptoms to care providers.

Flashbacks appear to be a generalization phenomenon—that is, certain internal or external cues remind the person of his or her psychedelic experience and bring on other associated features of the intoxication. For example, an individual might feel anxiety of a certain nature or pertaining to a certain conflict that is similar to anxiety experienced in the psychedelic state, or a person might return to where he or she had the initial experience or meet with someone with whom the experience was shared. By virtue of the mind's associative capacities, these triggers may elicit other features of the psychedelic intoxication such as visual or cognitive effects. Treatment of flashbacks usually involves reassurance and advice to strictly avoid any mind-altering drugs. In more severe or persistent cases, relaxation training, cognitive-behavioral approaches, or antianxiety medications may be useful.[22]

There also exists a rare syndrome that may cause more subjective distress in an individual than flashbacks. This posthallucinogen perceptual disorder (PHPD) is a troubling and at times debilitating disorder of mostly visual perception. Its etiology is uncertain, and it is difficult to treat. PHPD may relate to kindling, a quasi-seizurelike phenomenon in visual pathways in the brain. Psychedelic drugs may have somehow overstimulated those pathways or the visual system may have been especially sensitive to their effects originally.[23]

Nevertheless, despite real risks to mental health that psychedelics pose for the user and the continued great popularity of these drugs over the last thirty to forty years, psychedelic casualties have remained quite low for several decades. It appears that people are taking lower doses, at least in their initial exposure to these agents, and there exists a much greater awareness of the set and setting issues involved in minimizing adverse effects.

THE SECOND GENERATION OF PSYCHEDELIC RESEARCH

Human studies with psychedelic drugs resumed in Europe in the late 1980s with mescaline and in the United States in the early 1990s with DMT. These new investigations, rather modest in scope, have focused upon careful characterization of drug effects using modern psychopharmacological techniques. To a large extent, these methodologies are the result of advances in nonhuman animal research that clinical investigators are now seeking to confirm or refute in humans.

The conservative nature of this initial resumption of research is probably at least partly the result of extreme sensitivity to the political nature of such studies in humans, particularly in the context of the "war on drugs," and unpleasant associations with the seemingly drug-fueled youth movement of the 1960s. Current research is progressing steadily in the United States and Europe. It has branched out into experiments using psilocybin to treat obsessive-compulsive disorder, to investigate the nature of the mystical experience, and to help the pain and suffering associated with terminal cancer and post-traumatic stress disorder. It is interesting to note that no new LSD studies have begun.

In addition, social scientists in anthropology, education, and religious studies continue to develop new theories and approaches to the optimal use of psychedelics based upon their fieldwork and their analyses of the historical use of these agents within other cultures.

Two websites that provide current information regarding ongoing and anticipated research studies with classical and atypical psychedelics (such as ketamine and MDMA) are www.heffter.org (the Heffter Research Institute) and www.maps.org (Multidisciplinary Association for Psychedelic Studies).

2

DMT

The Brain's Own Psychedelic

Rick Strassman, M.D.

We have known about the psychedelic effects produced by plants containing DMT, particularly from Latin America, much longer than we have known about DMT itself.

In the 1600s, priest-ethnographers from Spain described Latin American indigenous people's use of DMT-containing psychedelic snuffs and smoking mixtures made from the genus *Anadenanthera*. Intrepid nineteenth-century European explorers of the Amazon, such as Spruce, von Humboldt, and Koch-Grünberg, observed the preparation and use of ayahuasca containing DMT-rich plants, particularly *Psychotria viridis* in combination with *Banisteriopsis caapi,* which contains the enzyme inhibitors that allow DMT to become active orally. In the last century, the late Richard Schultes was instrumental in carrying on this tradition of documenting the vibrant use of psychedelic plants in Latin America.[1]

The Canadian chemist Richard Manske first synthesized DMT in his laboratory in 1931, as one of a series of tryptamine derivatives related to his research on a toxic North American shrub.[2] There is no evidence, however, that he was familiar with DMT's psychoactivity, and we assume he never used it himself.

A 1946 Spanish-language scientific paper first described the presence of DMT in South American psychedelic snuffs,[3] and in 1955 a comparable paper appeared in the English-language literature.[4] While the presence of DMT in these plants was now established, its psychoactivity was not. In 1955, Hungarian psychiatrist and chemist Stephen Szára, stymied in his attempts to obtain LSD for research behind the Iron Curtain, decided to synthesize DMT based upon the papers documenting its presence in psychedelic plants. As so many research scientists before him had done, Szára experimented on himself, swallowing ever-increasing doses of the drug. Failing to note an effect through the oral route, he injected himself intramuscularly, and thus discovered the profound psychedelic activity of DMT: "In three or four minutes I started to experience visual sensations that were very similar to what I had read in descriptions by Hofmann [about LSD] and Huxley [about mescaline]. . . . I got very, very excited. It was obvious this was the secret."[5] Szára soon thereafter recruited thirty volunteers, mostly physician colleagues, to receive fully psychedelic doses of DMT.

One of these physicians described his experience: "The whole world is brilliant. . . . The whole room is filled with spirits. It makes me dizzy. . . . Now it is too much! . . . I feel exactly as if I were flying. . . . I have the feeling this is above everything, above the earth." As effects wore off, he continued: "It is comforting to know I am back on earth again. . . . Everything has a spiritual tinge, but is so real. . . . I feel that I have landed. . . ."[6]

Szára soon thereafter immigrated to the United States, where he spent a distinguished career spanning more than three decades at the National Institute on Drug Abuse, finally retiring in 1991. His research group in Hungary continued with some additional DMT studies, as did several U.S. groups, but within the academic literature, no one was as thorough as Szára in documenting the subjective effects of DMT. For example, the premier U.S. psychedelic research site at the time, the federal prison in Lexington, Kentucky, published reports on DMT used in its prisoner volunteers that described effects simply as ". . . anxiety, hallucinations (usually visual), and perceptual distortions."[7] Nevertheless, there were some tantalizing reports generated by European and U.S. labs that fall particularly within the context of this book's focus, namely outlining contact with seemingly autonomous, sentient, and interactive beings.

For example, Szára's former Hungarian colleagues noted the experience of one schizophrenic patient on DMT: "I saw such a strange dream, but at the beginning only. . . . I saw strange creatures, dwarves or something; they were black and moved about."[8] An American team also studying the effects of DMT in psychotic patients reported one volunteer's experience: "I was in a big place, and they were hurting me. They were not human. . . . They were horrible! I was living in a world of orange people."[9]

These reports of DMT effects, both from the late 1950s, are the only ones I have found in the peer-reviewed academic scientific literature that describe contact with beings, despite the vastly greater number of studies describing effects of LSD and other better-known psychedelics.

DMT garnered a rather negative reputation on the street based upon some popular literature describing its effects. *Naked Lunch,* by William Burroughs, is probably the most widely read account of the tendency of DMT to overwhelm its users with its rapid onset and disorienting "rush."

DMT emerged from its relative scientific obscurity, especially relative to LSD, when scientists discovered that both it and the necessary enzymes for its synthesis were present in laboratory animals. In 1965, German scientists demonstrated that DMT is present in human blood and urine.[10] Soon thereafter, brain and cerebrospinal fluid (which bathes both the brain and the spinal cord) were also found to contain DMT. The requisite enzymes, similar to those in nonhumans, were also found in brain and lung cells and red blood cells. Thus, the endogenous nature of DMT, its short duration of action, and its possible role in psychosis made it the object of substantial scientific inquiry.

Nevertheless, DMT suffered a fate both similar to and, in some ways, even more tragic than that which befell LSD during the antipsychedelic furor of the late 1960s and early 1970s. The relevance of its unique endogenicity was limited to being a possible cause of mental illness, primarily schizophrenia. When studies measuring its presence in various human body fluids failed to demonstrate significant differences between normal volunteers and those with psychotic illness, enthusiasm waned. Rather than refine the assay technology for DMT to measure more accurately the very low endogenous levels found in human body fluids or the diagnostic criteria by which to parse research subjects, the studies lost momentum. The most quoted paper in this field remains a British report that describes fluctuations in DMT levels in psychotic patients correlating with their level of psychosis.[11]

By limiting the importance of endogenous DMT to mental illness, psychiatry lost an opportunity to study the more general topic of human consciousness and its perturbations. Even if DMT was ultimately not found to be involved in psychosis, it may have been shown that it was involved in nonpsychotic altered states of consciousness such as mystical, spiritual, and near-death.

This, however, was more than psychiatry wished to undertake at the time. Psychedelic drugs were high-risk as a reputable research agenda, as was any attempt to relate them to religious sensibilities. Though there existed psychiatric research groups that tackled thorny religious issues with psychedelics, such as the University of Maryland[12] and Johns Hopkins University,[13] the relationship between endogenous DMT and endogenous spiritual experiences seems to have been overlooked.

WHAT IS DMT?

N,N-dimethyltryptamine, the prototypical tryptamine psychedelic, is first and foremost a chemical entity. It contains twelve carbon atoms, sixteen hydrogens, and two nitrogens. Its molecular weight—the combined value of the weights of all its elements, relative to the 1 of hydrogen—is 188. This is only slightly more than that of glucose, the simple sugar providing all of our body's energy, which is 180. The weight of DMT is only ten times greater than that of water, which is 18. Thus, we are dealing with a relatively small, simple molecule.

Pure DMT is a waxy or crystalline substance at room temperature and usually has a slightly orange-pink tinge. It may smell slightly like mothballs due to its indole ring. DMT's pharmacological profile is fairly well understood. It binds to the same subtypes of serotonin receptors as do the other classical psychedelics such as LSD: the 5-HT2A and 5-HT1A sites.[14]

A unique pharmacological property of DMT—different from the nonendogenous psychedelics such as LSD, psilocybin, and mescaline—is the lack of tolerance that develops after repeated dosing of the drug. If it is given daily at the same dose, LSD becomes less effective.[15] Even if it is given more frequently in lower animals, however, DMT does not elicit behavioral tolerance.[16] In our human DMT research, giving the drug several times at half-hour intervals in one sitting, we also demonstrated a lack of tolerance development.[17] Our data confirmed and extended previous comparable human findings using less frequent dosing of DMT.[18]

Another unique feature of DMT is its active transport into the brain across the blood–brain barrier. Cells that are tightly glued together line the brain's blood vessels, preventing movement of most blood-borne chemicals into the brain's confines, yet the brain sometimes expends energy to acquire some crucial molecules via active transport across the blood–brain barrier. Examples of such molecules are glucose, the brain's fuel source, and certain amino acids that the brain is unable to synthesize on its own. DMT is one of these select compounds,[19] though why the brain expends energy to bring DMT into its confines remains a mystery. It is tempting to postulate, however, that just as glucose is necessary for the brain's function, so in some mysterious way is DMT.

HOW DO PEOPLE CONSUME DMT?

Most street use of DMT involves vaporizing and then inhaling pure DMT in the free-base form—that is, the DMT is not chemically combined with an acid to form a water-soluble salt. This is similar to cocaine free base, which is smoked, as compared to cocaine hydrochloride, which is cocaine free base dissolved in hydrochloric acid, which therefore makes the salt (cocaine hydrochloride) water soluble, because a water-soluble salt provides more efficient uptake orally, nasally, or by injection. In our studies, the acid providing the most water-soluble form of DMT was fumaric acid. Therefore, we gave people DMT fumarate by injection. When smoking DMT, however, the free-base form is most efficient. It is vaporized in a glass pipe and then inhaled, or it is placed onto combustible vegetable matter (such as inactive mint, parsley, mullein, or marijuana) and inhaled along with the combusted plant material.

When a person swallows DMT, digestive enzymes—the monoamine oxidases (MAOs)—break it down nearly instantly, and negligible DMT enters the bloodstream and thus the brain. Latin American indigenous cultures discovered centuries ago that mixing plants containing DMT with other plants containing digestive enzyme blockers allows for very good transport of DMT through the gut. These enzyme blockers are the monoamine oxidase inhibitors (MAOIs), specifically the beta-carboline compounds harmine, harmaline, and tetra-hydro-harmine. Only relatively recently has this pharmacology been well understood, having been elucidated primarily by Dennis McKenna while he worked at the University of British Columbia, in Canada.[20]

WHERE IS DMT FOUND?

DMT exists in our bodies and in the bodies of all mammals in which scientists have searched for its presence. In addition, an enormous number of plants from both temperate and tropical climes contain DMT. Marine sponges contain water-soluble salts of DMT, as may some corals. Magic mushrooms contain psilocin (4-hydroxy-DMT—that is, DMT with an extra oxygen and hydrogen attached to one of its carbons), but the presence of DMT itself in these mushrooms remains difficult to establish. While DMT is not thought to be present in fish, serotonin does exist in this family, as do the subtypes of serotonin receptors necessary for DMT effects. The venom of the Sonora Desert toad, *Bufo alvarius,* contain 5-methoxy-DMT, a close psychedelic relative of DMT.[21]

DMT is present in the brain of lower mammals at birth, and levels rise in the brain of these animals in response to stress.[22] As previously mentioned, dozens of studies cite that DMT has been found in human blood, urine, and spinal fluid. Scientists have isolated the gene that synthesizes the DMT-forming enzyme in humans and have inserted this gene into a virus. After they infect mammalian cells with this virus, the cells produce DMT in the test tube.[23]

A DMT–PINEAL GLAND CONNECTION?

Early on, my attention was drawn to the pineal gland as a sort of spirit gland, a physical organ whose function might be associated with spiritual or other highly altered states of consciousness. There are several lines of circumstantial evidence linking the pineal gland and endogenous psychedelic states. Some of these are metaphysical or metaphorical, others are more firmly rooted in biology but are nevertheless still speculative. The pineal gland's long history of association with consciousness and spirit intrigued me. The location of this gland is mirrored by the location of the highest Hindu chakra, as well as Jewish sephira, and is associated with the highest level of spiritual development in esoteric physiology systems.

Over the centuries, the pineal gland's unpaired status in the brain has also drawn the interest of philosophers, including Descartes. He noticed that parts of the brain exist in pairs—two amygdalas, two hippocampuses, and so forth. He believed that the pineal's unpaired status supported his hypothesis that it mediated the phenomenon of our being able to think of only one thing at a time. Through some admittedly highly speculative reasoning, Descartes proposed that the pineal gland's unpaired status was supporting evidence for it providing the most direct avenue of this one-thought-at-a-time communication between divinity (the source of our intellect) and our brain.[24]

The pineal gland functions as a third eye in amphibians and certain reptiles from its position on the surface of the top of the skull, complete with lens, cornea, and retina. It receives light information, which is used to regulate skin color and body temperature. In mammals, the pineal has moved deeper into the brain, but indirectly, through the eyes, it continues to receive information about ambient lighting conditions. In mammals, the most studied pineal product has been melatonin, which appears to have a role in reproduction, alertness, and temperature regulation.

When melatonin did not prove especially psychoactive in our studies of its physiology in normal humans,[25] I looked more carefully into the possibility that the pineal gland might synthesize DMT. While this has never been established, the necessary precursors and enzymes for DMT synthesis exist in high concentrations in the pineal gland. It is located quite fortuitously near crucial sensory relay stations in the brain, so if indeed the pineal gland does secrete DMT at certain times, its proximity to these brain centers could explain the highly visual and auditory nature of many mystical and other endogenous psychedelic experiences.

Furthermore, it is extraordinarily difficult to stimulate the pineal gland to produce melatonin. Highly efficient sumps near the pineal gland form a nearly impregnable barrier to stimulation by the neurotransmitters that normally regulate melatonin production. Melatonin's psychological and biological effects are rather subtle, and require a relatively long period of time to exert their effects. Because of this, we must wonder what other pineal products require such tight regulation. The pineal gland's potential production of DMT would help explain the need for such pineal gland protection, for widely fluctuating levels of DMT would not be in an individual's best survival interests. It is worth noting, in this regard, that of all the biological parameters we measured that showed extremely robust elevations in response to a high dose of DMT, the only one that did not rise at all was melatonin![26]

At this point, the pineal gland–DMT connection must remain speculative. Yet there are plenty of other organs that do produce DMT—including brain, blood cells, and lungs—and its endogenicity remains a fact we must contend with. It raises the obvious and compelling question: Why do we possess DMT in our bodies?

UNIVERSITY OF NEW MEXICO DMT RESEARCH

There were several reasons driving my decision to begin psychedelic research with DMT, rather than with better-known drugs such as LSD, mescaline, and psilocybin.

1. DMT is short-acting. I knew that the clinical research center environment in which I needed to begin such studies would most likely be rather onerous and unpleasant. It was a setup for potential bad trips or panic reactions. I also realized I had no experience administering psychedelic drugs to people. Thus, I did not have a great deal of confidence in dealing with adverse reactions, should they develop.

I believed that DMT's short duration of action would work to our benefit on both counts. Adverse reactions, should they occur, would likely be short-lived. In addition, I would have less opportunity to make the wrong intervention in an attempt to help our volunteers if my time to intervene was so limited. I could rely more upon the volunteers' intrinsic restorative resources than my own uncertain ability to modify the course of a bad trip.

2. DMT is relatively obscure. I believed there might be tremendous curiosity on the part of the public and media regarding the resumption of psychedelic research in the United States after such a lengthy hiatus. I also believed that curiosity, and perhaps hostility and sensationalistic coverage, would be that much greater if drugs with 1960s-associated notoriety were the objects of our study. Research with LSD (acid), psilocybin (magic mushrooms), or mescaline (peyote buttons) would be potentially prone to much more scrutiny and perhaps even resistance on the part of regulatory, licensing, and funding bodies than that with a relatively unknown drug.

3. DMT is endogenous. This cut both ways in my mind: one being a support for its study within a traditional psychiatric research framework and the other within my own, less well-articulated agenda. From the psychiatric research perspective, I argued that DMT remained the most suitable candidate for the role of an endogenous psychotomimetic compound. Understanding its effects, and the mechanisms of action by which it exerted those effects, would shed light on the etiology of endogenous psychoses such as mania and schizophrenia. In addition to helping us understand the causes of such illnesses, to the extent that endogenous DMT contributed to endogenous psychoses, drugs that demonstrated efficacy in blocking the effects of exogenous DMT might also prove therapeutic by reducing endogenous DMT-related psychotic symptoms.

Regarding some of my deeper reasons for investigating DMT, I was interested in the biological bases of naturally occurring psychedelic experiences, such as mystical and near-death states. If exogenous DMT reliably replicated all or part of such experiences, this would bolster my theory that endogenous DMT played a role in their occurrence. Somewhat straddling the more- and less-overt reasons for my work with DMT was a consideration of the therapeutic properties of DMT in particular and of psychedelics in general. I wanted to see firsthand the effects of DMT, as a representative of the psychedelic family of drugs, on some of the processes important to psychotherapy. For example, I wanted to observe the effects of DMT on nonverbal behavior, on the feelings and thoughts of the intoxicated individual toward the outside world (including myself), and on the transformation and representation of psychological conflicts into more symbolic currencies, such as visions.

I also wanted to gain experience with people to whom I was providing a highly altered psychedelic state. By doing this, I hoped to develop and hone my own empathetic and supportive skills in order to understand and, when needed, to direct complex and confusing drug-induced mental states. These sorts of factors would come into play in any future attempts to articulate a research plan and develop a psychotherapeutic approach that utilized deep psychedelic states.

One of the most important lessons I learned in my clinical research training as well as from my previous melatonin research is the importance of asking simple questions, no matter how abstract, complex, or poorly formed my ultimate research questions might be. I learned that when I ask simple, one-step questions, I don't need an especially complicated experimental design to answer them. I can develop experience and expertise in the field, which will mean that any subsequent questions I have are that much more sophisticated and answerable.

In the case of my proposed DMT work, the additional burden imposed by its controversial nature and complex regulatory logistics made even more important the design of a study that could generate solid, irrefutable results—objective data within a short time frame and with the least risk. Additionally, the twenty-five-year hiatus in U.S. research, and the underlying reasons for this hiatus, compounded our burden of developing a research protocol with a high likelihood of approval and funding. In a way, we needed to reinvent the wheel: in addition to our basic clinical research design, we needed to build in to our studies mechanisms by which we could allay regulators' inherent anxiety about reopening what had become a Pandora's box during the first phase of psychiatric research with psychedelics.

Therefore, we needed to clearly state that one of our research goals was the carefully considered recruitment of suitable volunteers. At this delicate stage of early negotiations, psychedelic-naive volunteers were not an option. We could not risk giving DMT to people who had no idea what to expect, and who were incapable of truly giving informed consent. *Informed consent* depends upon a volunteer having some familiarity with the expected effects of their participation in a study—for example, nausea and a pounding pulse. In the case of DMT, which was most likely guaranteed to elicit intensely novel and unexpected thoughts, feelings, and perceptions, psychedelic-naïve prospective volunteers were at a disadvantage by not really knowing what we were talking about. Even the most experienced psychedelic veteran knows that it is impossible to predict how any particular trip will turn out. As Terence McKenna was fond of saying regarding smoking DMT, "One's hands always shake lighting the pipe." Thus, the issue of whom we chose as volunteers was crucial. I thought we must study only experienced psychedelic users, and they needed to be psychologically and physically healthy.

One factor that played into this decision was that of adverse effects. I believed that those with previous psychedelic experience would be less likely to panic in our study because of their familiarity with the strangeness of the psychedelic experience, even if they had not actually taken DMT previously. In fact, one of the most important questions I asked prospective volunteers was not how much they had enjoyed their previous psychedelic experiences, but rather how bad any of their previous trips had been. I needed to know that a volunteer could articulate fears, ask for help, and take advantage of any assistance offered. For example, one prospective volunteer told me that whenever he took a high dose of psilocybin mushrooms, he regularly found himself on top of a building's roof, without knowing how he got there. Clearly, he was an unsuitable subject for a study in which all subjects would be strictly confined to a hospital bed for several hours, with various tubes, wires, and the like attached to their bodies!

The nature of the subjective reports—the information our volunteers would provide—was another important consideration in my decision to use experienced subjects. I believed experienced subjects would give more discerning and nuanced descriptions of drug effects, and could compare DMT to other psychedelics with which they were familiar. Another, more liability-based reason was the university lawyers' concern that we avoid having any psychedelic-naïve individual become a psychedelic "addict" and then blame us for this development.

We also had to establish, in this first project, that we could administer various doses of DMT in a safe manner. In order to begin this process, we needed to learn the best way to administer DMT and the optimal doses that would produce the desired effects.

All but one previous scientific study with DMT used the intramuscular (IM) route. While allowing for relatively rapid absorption of a drug relative to the oral route, it is not as rapid as the smoked, intravenous (IV) or intranasal (snorted) route. We began by giving a moderately high dose of IM DMT to two volunteers who had smoked DMT free base in the past and who were also familiar with the effects of oral DMT from their experiences with ayahuasca. We believed these two volunteers were ideal subjects with whom to begin preliminary dose-finding and an optimal route of administration. Our two seasoned DMT volunteers reported that the rush—the rapidly developing wave of effects characteristic of smoked DMT—did not occur with the IM route. Neither was the intensity of the peak effects comparable to that of smoked DMT. Because our funding came primarily from the National Institute on Drug Abuse, we had to make our studies as relevant as possible to the institute's charge of understanding effects and mechanisms of actions of drugs of abuse in the manner in which they are normally taken.

Smoking, however, was not an option because of the potential for lung toxicity from combustion by-products. In addition, it is very difficult technically to reliably inhale a drug while at the same time trying to negotiate its early, often disorienting effects. Therefore, we switched to the IV route, which proved to be a little more rapid and intense than even the smoked route. After some trial-and-error work, we settled on a range of IV DMT doses from very low (0.05 mg/kg) to very high (0.4 mg/kg), with two intermediate doses (0.1 and 0.2 mg/kg), encompassing the full range of DMT effects. There are about 2.2 pounds in a kilogram, so there are about 73 kg in a 160-pound person. A high (0.4 mg/kg) dose of IV DMT in that sized person is slightly more than 29 mg.

The variables we decided to measure in response to these doses covered a wide array of those employed in classical psychopharmacology studies, particularly those we believed DMT would stimulate by virtue of its effects on serotonergic systems. These included pupil diameter, blood pressure, heart rate, body temperature, and a host of pituitary-gland hormones and other hormones controlled by brain regions rich in serotonin receptors: prolactin; growth hormone; adrenocorticotrophic hormone (ACTH), which stimulates the adrenal gland; beta-endorphin; and cortisol from the adrenals. We also looked at melatonin levels, presumably of pineal gland origin. We also needed to measure blood levels of DMT after each dose so that we could establish relationships between dose of drug and resultant blood level and between DMT blood levels and outcome measures.

Measuring all of the hormones for our study involved purchasing assay kits that our highly trained laboratory technicians could use. However, there were no assays currently available for DMT, which meant we needed to consult with several senior scientists at other sites who had worked with their own assays in the past. We were lucky to find an assay whose developer generously helped us establish it at the University of New Mexico (UNM). Within six months, we were able to measure DMT levels down to the millionth of a gram (a nanogram) per milliliter—not sensitive enough to measure endogenous levels, but quite adequate for our purposes of measuring the much higher levels that occurred when we injected our volunteers with the drug.

Finally, I set as a goal the development of a new rating scale for DMT effects: a paper-and-pencil questionnaire, filled out by the volunteers themselves directly after drug effects had worn off. I hoped our scale would be a theoretical and practical improvement over previous rating scales, which quantified these effects in order to facilitate statistical manipulation of subjective data. These earlier scales had several inherent flaws. Some emphasized unpleasant over pleasant effects of the drugs—

which might steer a subject's subsequent drug sessions toward a more negative outcome. More important, however, is that such an emphasis on unpleasant effects ignored the positive or reinforcing properties of psychedelics—those effects that led people to use them. In other words, people take psychedelics for their uniquely positive—not negative—effects. Another drawback of older rating scales was their use of penitentiary inmates serving time for federal narcotics violations as the normative sample. These individuals hoped their participation would assist in obtaining either an early release or preferential treatment in prison. In addition, few if any had previous experience with psychedelic drugs. Therefore, they were not a representative sample from which to generalize to the rest of the population.

I interviewed nineteen experienced DMT users who also had substantial experience with other psychedelics in order to both prepare a first draft of the rating scale and to anticipate issues that would arise in supervising each DMT session. In drafting the Hallucinogen Rating Scale, or HRS, I chose the Buddhist psychological system, the Abhidharma, as a model for the psychology of the psychedelic experience. I appreciated the Abhidharma's relatively objective, phenomenological, and value-free approach to mental contents and processes. The essence of its classification approach is to parse mental experience into five categories, those related to: emotions; thought and thought processes; perceptions (visual, auditory, taste, and smell); bodily sensations; and volition (the ability to interact willfully with external and internal realities). To these five I added a sixth, a general measure of intensity.

While not going into any further detail regarding the development of the HRS and the data generated by it, it is worth noting that it has held up quite well against older, and even some newer, rating scales. In addition, in our own studies, it proved more sensitive to effects of various doses of DMT than did any of our multiple biological variables.[27] Many research groups, both in the United States and in Canada, Europe, and South America, have used it successfully in their own projects involving the study of a diverse range of psychedelic and other psychoactive drugs.

It took two years of lobbying of local university, state, and federal regulatory agencies before I obtained permission to begin the DMT research. A grant from a branch of the Masons, the Scottish Rite Foundation for Schizophrenia Research, helped establish the merit of my study a year before I actually began it. Why the Masons had an interest in schizophrenia in general, and DMT in particular, I do not know, but I believe that garnering such support enhanced the esteem of my study in the eyes of the relevant regulatory and funding agencies. The final hurdle to overcome was to locate a source of pharmaceutical-grade DMT that was pure enough for approval for human administration by the U.S. Food and Drug Administration. Professor David E. Nichols, of Purdue University, agreed to synthesize a batch for our studies, and we began our research soon thereafter, in late 1990.[28]

Before wrapping up the first phase of research five years later, in mid-1995, we had given four hundred doses of DMT in various strengths to more than sixty volunteers in seven DMT studies. We had also begun some dose-finding pilot work with psilocybin, the active ingredient in magic mushrooms. Whereas the clinical research center environment, onerous as it was, seemed to assuage the anxiety of our DMT volunteers, who sometimes feared they were dying and were relieved to recall that a hospital-based resuscitation team was readily available, it quickly proved intolerable for the longer-acting effects of psilocybin. Thus, we cut short our psilocybin study and never began an LSD project for which we had funding, approval, and drug on hand.

NOTES ON PROTOCOL

Using three levels of examination, I screened all potential volunteers carefully before they received any drug. The first level was an interview that was structured loosely and revolved around a potential subject's interest in participation and previous psychedelic drug experience—particularly with respect to how he or she managed disturbing or frightening effects as well as how "far out" he had gone in his psychedelic journeys. In this latter case, I wanted to know if any had experienced a near-death or mystical state or the feeling that his consciousness and body had separated—all effects I thought might be relatively common during our studies. I also inquired about the support system prospective volunteers had at their disposal, for I knew the psychological demands of the study required more social and emotional support than just our research team would likely be able to provide. At that time, I gave a general overview of my research interest in these drugs and in DMT in particular and described the theory behind and protocol involved in the particular study for which I was recruiting. I warned prospective subjects of the intrusive, rigorous, clinical nature of their participation, and was clear about its absolutely voluntary nature, adding that they could withdraw from participation at any time with no undue consequences. We would provide whatever follow-up they needed, including making appropriate referrals.

The next step in screening was a standardized psychiatric interview to exclude any individual with a current psychiatric diagnosis, and if it was determined that a prior psychiatric diagnosis had existed, to ascertain the severity of the previous problem and the adequacy of treatment, and to determine that a sufficiently long period had elapsed between the present time and its resolution.

The last stage involved a physical examination, laboratory blood tests, and electrocardiogram to ensure that a prospective volunteer was healthy enough to manage the physically demanding nature of the DMT infusions, particularly the heart rate and blood pressure effects.

After passing these three layers of screening, the volunteer received a low 0.05 mg/kg dose of DMT and high 0.4 mg/kg dose of the drug on consecutive days, at which time only blood pressure, heart rate, and psychological responses were monitored. These screening doses were intended to familiarize volunteers with the mechanics of the DMT infusion in the clinical research environment and with the most powerful and intense experience they would encounter during their participation.

If any volunteer found either the hospital setting or the high dose of DMT too unpleasant, he or she could drop out before we had spent the time, energy, and funds involved in any of the full-scale studies. These days also allowed us to get a sense of how people reacted to the research environment and to the effects of DMT.

For all the sessions, volunteers lay prone in a hospital bed, in a slightly more cheery, informal, and comfortably furnished room in the University of New Mexico Hospital's fifth-floor General Clinical Research Center. An IV line was inserted into a subject's forearm vein, and a cuff leading to an automated blood pressure and heart rate monitor was attached to the other arm. We gave the DMT solution over a thirty-second infusion through plastic tubing into the forearm vein and then flushed the tubing with sterile salt water for fifteen seconds. After this, we checked blood pressure and heart rate for the next thirty minutes, and discussed the experience starting at about fifteen to twenty minutes after the injection. Once any pressing issues were dealt with, the volunteer filled out the rating scale, after which we discussed at length his or her just completed experience. The subject then ate a snack or light meal, napped as he or she wished, and went home.

For actual full-scale study days, a second IV line was placed in the other arm of each subject to provide access for drawing blood samples throughout the session. A thin, flexible rectal temperature monitor was inserted in order to record temperature automatically every minute and send this information to a device from which we downloaded data after the session's completion. In our first study, we also asked volunteers to open their eyes at prearranged times so that I could measure pupil diameter using a reference card with black circles. For all other studies, however, because of the intensely visual and disorienting effects of the drug, particularly during its onset, we no longer measured pupil diameter, and had volunteers wear comfortable black eyeshades for their sessions. In chapter 3, we will discuss the actual trip reports of the volunteers who participated in our studies.

3

The Varieties of the DMT Experience

Rick Strassman, M.D.

SITTING FOR SESSIONS

Supervising psychedelic drug sessions is often referred to as *sitting*—as in babysitting or sitting in meditation. Regarding the first comparison, people under the influence of a high dose of a psychedelic drug often are relatively regressed: helpless, suggestible, and dependent. They may have lost control of bodily, emotional, and thinking functions, and are unable to communicate effectively. They may project all kinds of positive or negative feelings upon the sitter that would be more appropriately placed on important, powerful people from other times or places in their lives—usually their parents or comparable figures. At the same time, their behavior can stir up in the observer very powerful and sometimes confusing feelings. To watch over a psychedelicized person in your care, then, you must manifest great tact, loving firmness and consistency, support, education, and attentiveness—all in the proper dose and at the proper time.

The term *sitting* also refers to the importance of an observer staying as focused and centered as possible while psychedelic chaos is breaking loose all around. The intensity of energy in the room of a person on psychedelic drugs can be palpable, and it may require great effort for a sitter

51

to maintain equanimity. During our research, I found it useful to enter into a light meditative state elicited by the simple practice of feeling my breath pass in and out through my nostrils as my eyes were half-open and gazing slightly downward. This take on sitting provided our research volunteers with the necessary combination of freedom and support to have their own trip without the imposition of unnecessary structure, suggestions, or distractions. It also provided them with a sense that we were readily available, and willing and able to help whenever the need arose.

GENERAL OUTLINE OF DMT EFFECTS

Volunteers described the two lower doses of DMT as not particularly psychedelic. The 0.05 mg/kg dose was relaxing and slightly euphoric, and the 0.1 mg/kg dose was somewhat unpleasantly stimulating. Most volunteers found the 0.2 mg/kg dose caused them to break through a threshold into more typical psychedelic effects. The 0.4 mg/kg dose was even more intensely psychedelic, and seemed to elicit some qualitatively unique experiences.

A 0.4 mg/kg dose of DMT began exerting its effects within several heartbeats, well before completion of the thirty-second drug infusion. By the sixty-second point, when I was withdrawing the syringe that had just flushed the IV with sterile saltwater, volunteers were usually no longer aware of their physical surroundings. Effects peaked at two minutes postinjection, began fading within three to five minutes, and were usually nearly completely resolved by thirty minutes. Some volunteers were able to speak within ten minutes, but I encouraged them to remain silent for another five to ten minutes, so that they could continue carefully observing the latter part of the drug experience. This extra time also allowed for a smoother reentry into normal consciousness. The initial rush of a high dose of DMT was intense, developed at startling speed, and could not help but be disorienting, at least temporarily. Some expressions describing this rush: "a nuclear cannon," "ground zero," and "a freight train."

A tremendous sense of inner tension developed in the subjects—to a degree that volunteers did not believe their bodies were capable of containing it. This buildup of inner tension was accompanied most often by a similarly building high-pitched whining, ringing, or crackling sound. While the rush and sound were developing, there was a concomitant display of rapidly emerging fluid and morphing kaleidoscopic visual patterns. Finally, for most volunteers, this culminated in an abrupt separation of consciousness from the body. It was as if their consciousness could not remain attached to the body because of the internal pressure generated by the rush.

We regularly heard comments such as "My body dissolved; I was pure awareness" and "I no longer had a body." Often the movement of consciousness took either an upward direction or that of the body falling downward. Once set loose or freed from the distracting and frankly intolerable physical tension of the rush, volunteers were now able, in a less encumbered manner, to observe what was going on around them. Visual effects were profound and nearly always began with the kaleidoscopic display of patterns, which took on "Mayan," "Aztec," or "Islamic" qualities and sometimes qualities of pixilation, "like being an inch from a TV screen." Usually in response to the higher doses, however, more formed, recognizable, and discrete visual images emerged.

Early on in our studies, as drug effects took hold, most volunteers opened their eyes nearly involuntarily to deal with the astonishment of the rush and visual effects as much as to look around the room to see if what they were visualizing was "real." An overlaying of their visions onto the outside room added to their confusion, however, and placing eyeshades over the volunteers' eyes before drug injection reduced disorientation and provided an impetus for a deeper involvement with the experience. When their eyes were open, subjects described objects in the room appearing to undulate or shine with an intrinsic brightness and a living, breathing quality. Some volunteers also reported a disarticulation in the perception of the normal fluidity of movements of others in the room. Movements seemed "robotic," "jerky," or "mechanical."

Though it was difficult, most volunteers—familiar as they were with high-dose psychedelic experiences—were able to maintain awareness during the early tumultuous moments of their high-dose session. They did an admirable job of hanging on—that is, observing, and remembering the experience.

Intense, rapidly shifting mood states were also a hallmark of the high dose, although a few volunteers reported a marked flatness or paucity of feelings. Nevertheless, most found these sessions extremely pleasurable—ecstatic and euphoric. One of the most striking aspects of the intoxication was how much experience was packed into a short period of time, including a sense of timelessness. A common feature of a high-dose psychedelic experience (as occurs in non-drug-induced mystical states) is that time feels eternal—the "eternal now." In other words, time no longer seems to pass, at least not as we normally experience it. Thus, the occasion of a tremendous amount of activity taking place in a relatively short span of real time usually led to our volunteers gasping in surprise when they learned how much time had actually elapsed between drug injection and the beginning of our subsequent conversation.

DMT NONRESPONDERS

It is interesting to note that three of our sixty volunteers had little or no reaction to a high dose of DMT. One of these three was a former monastic who had a meditation-induced mystical experience, but the other two—one of whom had absolutely no reaction to DMT—were otherwise ostensibly unremarkable in their background, experiences, and personal characteristics.* The former monastic's experience was tentative support for a corollary of my hypothesis that endogenous DMT is involved in spontaneous mystical experiences—that is, once

---

*In a personal communication, Terence McKenna, who introduced many hundreds of people to DMT, shared with me that he also found "about 5 percent" of them to have little or no response to the drug.

subjects gain familiarity with their own, endogenous, high-dose DMT states, additional exogenous DMT has little further impact. This is not a case of drug tolerance as such, but rather suggests learning to negotiate within the state of consciousness brought on by the drug (known in pharmacology as *behavioral tolerance*). The unremarkable characteristics of the other two volunteers, however, makes this explanation less likely.

Perhaps it is easier to explain this resistance to DMT as something that occurs in people whose relevant receptor mechanisms exist on the far end of the spectrum of responsiveness. Perhaps there are too few receptors or the "stickiness" of the receptors to DMT is very low. Another explanation could be that some people metabolize DMT particularly efficiently.

TYPES OF SESSIONS

We parsed the volunteers' DMT experiences into three general categories:

- **Personal.** These were psychologically oriented sessions in which volunteers dealt primarily with their own lives, histories, circumstances, and feelings, whether these were conscious or unconscious. Often these sessions would yield deeper awareness and acceptance of difficult personal issues.
- **Transpersonal.** These sessions went beyond the individual's historical life experience, but continued to manifest within their own personal field of particulars: Though the state was novel in intensity and quality, it still consisted of the familiar building blocks from the subject's previous experience. Mystical and near-death experiences fall into this category.
- **Invisible worlds.** These comprised encounters with what seemed to be freestanding, autonomous realities that coexisted with our reality. Sometimes such realms appeared inhabited by alien beings

that were more or less aware of the volunteers and were able to interact with them to varying degrees.

Usually, sessions were not solely one type or another, but rather combined elements of different categories. For example, a psychotherapeutically helpful session for the subject may have been experienced as occurring through the aegis of beings or entities. A mystical or near-death experience may have been preceded by encounters with beings. A deeply personal, psychologically cathartic session might have led to mystical or spiritual insights or experiences.

PERSONAL SESSIONS

Psychological sessions often became psychotherapeutic. It is difficult to be psychedelicized in the presence of a psychiatrist, which can lead to a discussion of deeply felt concerns, and not have these concerns at least reflected back in a way that provides support and possibly further explication and understanding of the issues at hand.

Marsha, an African American fund-raiser for nonprofit organizations, was an example of someone who underwent a high-dose session that consisted mostly of personal insights, even though its content shared features with being contact. In her case, the issue of concern was her denial of the anger she felt at her husband's lack of acceptance of her own deeply ingrained, culturally valued body image. This seemed to be played out in a vision of lifeless though beautiful Anglo dolls that pirouetted mindlessly on a merry-go-round.

Cassandra was a young, bisexual woman with interpersonal and psychosomatic features of post-traumatic stress disorder brought on by a neglectful mother and a sexually predatory stepfather. In her sessions, she was able to feel love, warmth, and comfort in parts of her body that had been numb to her for many years. She also felt a sense of peace, serenity, and completeness that was wholly unknown to her previously: "Something took my hand and yanked me. It seemed to say, 'Let's go!'

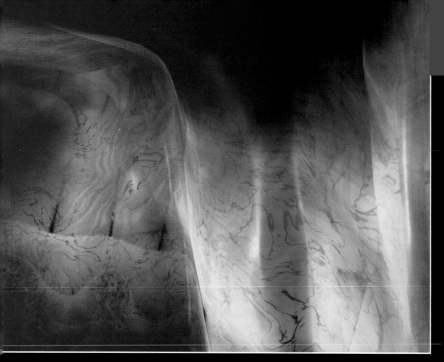

Out of the Fog

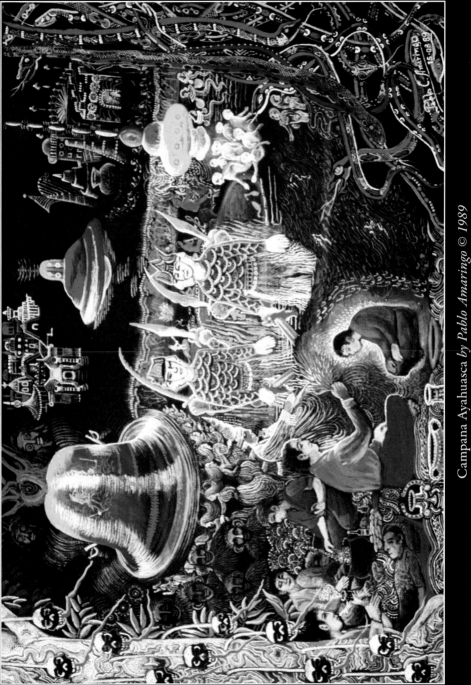

Campana Ayahuasca *by Pablo Amaringo* © 1989

Noron City *by Karl Kofoed* © 2007

We went through a maze at an incredibly fast pace. I say *we* because it seemed like I was being accompanied. . . . They looked like jokers performing for me, [with] funny-looking bells on their hats, big noses. However, I had the feeling they could turn on me, [that they were] a little less than completely friendly."

As her session progressed, the beings began to effect a healing: "I definitely felt the presence of others. They were kind to me, nice and caring. They seemed small, as if they could enter my body and mind in that space. There was a total sense of losing my body, but the little presences knew how to enter it, somehow. I was loved by the entities, or whatever they are. It was pleasant and very comforting. . . . I feel like I have a new body. It's so much more aware."

TRANSPERSONAL SESSIONS

The transpersonal states brought on by DMT were those most sought after by our volunteers and the ones I also hoped would be relatively common and effective, "sticking to the ribs," psychologically, of our volunteers. We have known for quite some time that psychedelics, either in plant form or in their isolated state, can elicit these types of experiences. There are cases from the psychiatric literature documenting such effects with LSD, psilocybin, and DPT (a synthetic derivative of DMT), and historical and anthropological literature from the recent and more distant past is full of reports of such enlightening experiences with a wide variety of drugs and plants.

Near-death experiences (NDEs) include a sense of rapid movement, often through a tunnel, together with music, singing, or voices. There may be a feeling of being accompanied by others—living or dead relatives or friends—and a dawning awareness of "being dead." Also taking place is a life review, the rapid sequential display of more or less highly charged events in an individual's life. While most people report a great sense of calm and peacefulness, some undergo great terror and fear. Sometimes an NDE climaxes with a mystical experience. In all cases, those who have had an NDE describe it as "more real than real," and in cases of highly positive NDEs, it is difficult for the subject to return to this "world of trials" after he or she has just begun to taste the pleasures of the "world of reward."

Mystical experiences are sometimes the culmination of NDEs. Even if such experiences do not take place at the actual border of life and death, they may require what feels like a battle to the end with a subject's own inner demons; the death of a version of the self that depends upon separation rather than community; domination rather than cooperation; an end to the "me-and-mine" way of relating to existence. At other times, however, less struggle is necessary to attain a mystical state, which may occur by what appears to be a fortuitous descent of grace. The mystical state relates to extreme alterations in the fundamental components of our experience—namely, time, space, and self. Paradox abounds: The infinitesimal coexists with the vast without friction or conflict. Likewise, the eternal coexists with the instantaneous and the sense of no self coexists with the notion of self containing all of creation.

Time no longer passes in its normal manner, but instead seems suspended or subsumed in an eternity containing past, present, and future. Space is no longer limited, but at the same time, all existence rests in the smallest possible unit of space. The self can now hold and feel at utter peace with life, good and evil are seen in their deepest reality, and the nature of free will is clearly perceived. In a mystical experience, individuals are certain of the soul's existence without a body and are thus sure of its existence after the body's death. It is known as a certainty that there exists an unimaginably powerful creator and sustainer of reality, and of you in particular. This creator is unborn, uncreated, undying, and unchanging. The ecstasy and searing bliss accompanying such experiences, though previously unequaled in intensity, is nevertheless less striking than the peace and equanimity that supports and underlies this bliss.

I was particularly interested in transpersonal experiences being induced by DMT because I believed that endogenous NDEs and mystical states were accompanied by or associated with high levels of naturally produced DMT. To the extent that our administering exogenous DMT elicited experiences that shared features with these naturally occurring states, my hypothesis would be strengthened. Indeed, several volunteers had these types of experiences, but generally not as many as perhaps we all had thought likely.

Willow, a psychiatric social worker, had many visual effects after her first low dose of DMT, leading us to believe her high-dose sessions might be profound. They resembled, in many respects, a classical NDE:

First, I saw a tunnel or channel of light off to the right. I had to turn to go into it. Then the whole process repeated on the left. It was intentional that way. It was as if it had a source, further away; like a funnel, bright and pulsating. There was a sound, like music, like a score, but unfamiliar to me, supporting the emotional tone of the events, and drawing me in. I was very small; it was very large. There were large beings in the tunnel. Things were flashing by, flashing by, as if from a different perspective. Everything was unimportant relative to this. It was so much more real than life.

There were gremlins, small, with wings and tails. I paid them little attention. The larger beings were there to sustain and support me—a sort of good vs. evil thing. Something rushed through me, out of me. I remember thinking, "Here comes the separation." I felt my body only when I swallowed or breathed, and that wasn't really a physical feeling as much as a way of setting ripples through the experience. I felt strongly that this is dying and it is okay. . . . The other side is very different. There are no words, body, or sounds there to limit things. I first saw deep space, white with stars. Then there was this multidimensional experience starting. It was alive. It was the aliveness I heard. My body was trying to say "Remember the body" as I was going into that place—not a desperate cry, but an attempt to keep it real from the point of view of the senses. I thought I could see light down below, the world's light, like a little flap was lifted, like a simultaneous alternate reality.

Several other volunteers had experiences similar or identical to mystical and spiritual states. During her low-dose session, Cleo, a legally blind massage therapist and counselor, noted "some eyes looking at me, friendly. They wanted to see who was there, and seemed to say that I would follow them later."

Her high doses took her above and beyond, following the eyes:

> I had the expectation I would go out, but I went in, into every cell of my body. It wasn't just my body . . . themselves . . . themselves . . . it's all connected.
>
> When the patterns began, I said to myself, "Let me go through you." At that point, it opened, and I was very much someplace else, being, dancing with a star system. I asked myself, "Why am I doing this to myself?" And there was, "This is what you've always been searching for. This is what all of you has always been searching for."
>
> Colors were words saying to me, "Go in." I was looking for God outside. They said, "God is in every cell of your body." And I was feeling it, totally open to it, and I kept opening to it more. . . . The colors kept telling me things that I not only heard, but also felt in my cells. I say *felt* but it was like no other *felt,* more like a knowing that was happening in my cells—that God is in every thing and that we are all connected, that God dances in every cell of life, and that every cell of life dances in God. The euphoria goes on into eternity. And I am part of that eternity.

Elena, a psychotherapist who at the time was taking a lengthy sabbatical from her highly stressful career, reported after her first high dose:

> I could only hold on, remembering not to fall off into the distracting light show. Then, everything stopped! The darkness opened to light, and on the other side of space, all was utterly still. Then

the words "Just because it's possible" emerged out of nothingness and filled me. The great power sought to fill all possibilities. It was amoral but it was love, and it just was. There was no benevolent God, only this primordial power. All of my ideas and beliefs seemed absurdly ridiculous. I wondered, "Why come back?"

After her second high dose, she reported:

It came on fast and big, and an incredible pressure arose in my head, pushing me back. It blasted me into the realm in which pure living energy begins to take form. As it began to slow down, I saw the process of separated awareness, the creation of form and consciousness. Before the slowing down, it's not there. It's not unconscious, but it's not conscious. There is the endless outflow of creation, and then this vast process takes it back in. My little piece of energy goes in and out, too—not more or less than any other piece. You can't die. You can't go away. You can neither add nor subtract. There is a continual outflow that is immortality. The "I am" notion goes around and around.

I was not disoriented, but there was no orientation. I didn't know where or who I was, but there was nothing to know who or where I was. I didn't have to wonder what to do next. There are empty spaces, they were all filled up.

Sean, a physician who had not taken any psychedelics for nearly twenty years before beginning our study, received 0.3 mg/kg DMT every hour, four times, in preliminary work for the development phase of our tolerance study. After his third session, he noted:

I noticed five to six figures walking rapidly alongside me. They felt like helpers, fellow travelers. A humanoid male figure turned toward me, threw his right arm up towards the patchwork of bright colors, and asked, "How about this?" The kaleidoscopic patterns immediately became much brighter and moved more rapidly. A second and then a third asked and did the same thing. At that point, I decided to go further, deeper.

I immediately saw a bright yellow-white light directly in front of me. I chose to open to it. I was consumed by it and became a part of it. There were no distinctions, no figures or lines, shadows or outlines. There was no body or anything inside or outside. I was devoid of self, of thought, of time, of space, of a sense of separateness or ego, or of anything but the white light. There are no symbols in my language that can begin to describe that sense of pure being, oneness, and ecstasy. There was a great sense of stillness and ecstasy. I have no idea how long I was in this confluence of pure energy, or whatever or however I might describe it. Finally, I felt myself tumbling gently and sliding backward away from this Light, sliding down a ramp. I could see myself doing this, a naked, thin, luminescent, childlike being that glowed with a warm, yellow light. My head was enlarged, and my body was that of a four-year-old child. Waves of the light lapped at me as my body receded from it. I was almost dizzy with happiness as the slide down the ramp finally ended.

INVISIBLE WORLDS

Several of the volunteers' reports contain descriptions of more-or-less well-formed visual images made up of kaleidoscopic colors, bright light, and swirling energy. In many sessions, however, novel, strange, or bizarre images were noted. Images that fall into this category are those I consider invisible or unseen. Contact with alien beings falls into a variant of this category. In some ways, these journeys into invisible realms suggest a world different from that which we usually inhabit and perceive. Further, entity or being contact only adds to the equation by explaining who can be found there.

The *where* of this type of DMT session is not as easy to identify as it is in the personal, more psychologically oriented sessions. In this category of DMT experience, the subject receives intimations of not only internal awareness, but also the existence of different levels of external reality. These appear to be entirely different worlds or universes, planes of existence that the subject is now capable of perceiving with the aid of DMT.

At least half of our volunteers had these types of experiences in one or the other of their high-dose sessions. Several volunteers perceived a microscopic reality—that is, seeing DNA-like images: "spirals of what looked like DNA, red and green," "DNA twirling and spiraling . . . gelatin-like, like tubes, inside which were cellular activities . . . a microscopic view of them." Others beheld visual forms that also contained implicit meaning, but the images perceived were not typical of the reality that might be revealed by a microscopic lens: "[T]hree-dimensional circles and cones with shading . . . moving a lot . . . almost like an alphabet. A fantasy alphabet, like it was data, not random."

Heather, a midwife, saw this: ". . . a Mexican woman who threw a white blanket over the scene, and then pulled it back repeatedly. There were numbers, like numerology and language. The numbers became words. Where do words come from? I looked around and there were numbers all around. They were separate in their little boxes, and then the boxes would melt and the numbers would all merge together to make long numbers."

Eli, an architect-turned–software developer, saw the Logos, the cosmic reason giving order, purpose, and intelligence to the world, in "the blue-yellow core of meaning and semantics. . . . When I looked around, it seemed like the meaning or symbols were there, some kind of core of reality where all meaning, the raw bits of reality, are stored. I burst into its main chamber. It is a lot more than only ones and zeroes. It's a higher level, very potent bits."

Gabe, a physician, found himself "in a nursery . . . [with] cribs and different animals, vibrant. . . . I was in a stroller."

Aaron, a consciousness-enhancement technology entrepreneur,

described "hieroglyphics, which turned into a room. There were toys there. It was cute."

Tyrone, a psychiatry trainee, beheld ". . . an apartment from the future. The places to sit, do things, the counters, were molded out of the walls. It wasn't just functional, but there was life in the furniture. They were molded out of something alive, an animal, a living being. . . . I went past, beyond the apartments, and entered a space, a crack in the earth . . . a crack in space."

In one of his sessions, Aaron also perceived: ". . . a psychedelic, Day-Glo-colored space that approximated a room whose walls and floors had no clear separations or edges, pulsating and throbbing electrically."

Philip, a clinical psychologist, found himself ". . . above a strange landscape, like Earth but very unearthly. I was hovering miles above it. I had the very distinct sense of doing this, not just the visual perception. There were telescopes, or microwave dishes, or water towers—things with antennae on them. The sun was different, different colors and hues than our sun."

While it is perhaps a relatively small transition between the strange and unfamiliar *where* of the high-dose DMT session to the *who* of the following descriptions, this small transition represents a huge conceptual leap. Whereas the invisible images of the previous examples do not belong to the material of this everyday world, they nevertheless seem to be minding their own business, existing on their own, and they can be observed passively. Even when they are moving, swirling, and glowing, their movement appears to take place within things that are inanimate or at least not animate according to our normal conception.

In the following descriptions, however, subjects meet with beings, entities, or creatures that possess awareness, willfulness, and intelligence—sometimes much greater than our own. Most startling is their awareness of us. Sometimes they seem to be expecting us, and other times we seem to have surprised them by appearing in their world. In both cases they know we now are in their space. At times their reception is welcoming, but sometimes they greet us with anger and hostility. In some instances, subjects arrive in their "world" by traversing great distances through the vacuum of deep space—or they may be with these beings in the proverbial blink of an eye, instantly, with no sense of having traveled at all. In such instances, these beings seem to appear as opposed to the subjects arriving in their space. In time spent with them, the beings may impart knowledge and healing or pain and suffering. They may give portents or predictions. Either they want to help or they request help.

Karl, a blacksmith and metalworker, beheld ". . . lots of elves, prankish, ornery, maybe four of them along a highway. They commanded the scene; it was their terrain. They were about my height and held up placards showing me these incredibly beautiful, complex, swirling geometric scenes. . . . There was no issue of control; they were totally in control. They wanted me to look."

Aaron transitioned from viewing a beautiful mandala-like image to a situation in which:

> . . . an insectlike thing got right into my face, hovering over me as the DMT was going in. This thing sucked me out of my head into outer space . . . a black sky with millions of stars. I was in a very large waiting room, observed by the insect-thing and others like it. We were aware of each other. Then they lost interest. I was taken into space and looked at!
>
> They have an agenda. It's like walking into a different neighborhood. You're not really sure what the culture is. The sense of possibility is so strange.

Lucas, an author, experienced the typical buildup of pressure as the effects of the high dose of DMT began, and when he "burst out," he saw

> . . . a space station below me, and to my right. Presences were guiding me to a platform. I was also aware of many entities inside the

space station—automatons, androidlike creatures that looked like a cross between crash-test dummies and Empire troops for *Star Wars,* except that they were living beings, not robots. They had checkerboard patterns on parts of their bodies, especially their upper arms. They were doing some kind of routine technological work, and paid little attention to me.

Chris, a computer salesman and actor, felt on his second 0.3 mg/kg dose of DMT in the tolerance study: ". . . a set of many hands feeling my eyes and face. They were recognizing and identifying me." On his third dose: ". . . there were three beings, three physical forms. There were rays coming out of and then back into their bodies. They were reptilian and humanoid, trying to make me understand not with words, but with gestures. They wanted me to look into their bodies. I saw inside them and understood reproduction, what it's like before birth, the passage into the body."

Jeremiah, retired from the military, was a newly graduated psychotherapist. In his first high-dose session, he found himself ". . . in a nursery—a high-tech nursery with a single Gumby-like figure,* three feet tall attending me. I felt like an infant—not a human infant, but an infant relative to the intelligences represented by Gumby. It was aware of me, but not particularly concerned. Then I heard two or three male voices talking. I heard one of them say, 'He's arrived.'"

During another high-dose session, Jeremiah observed: ". . . one big machine in the center of a big room, with round conduits, almost writhing—not like a snake, more in a technical manner. The conduits were not open at the end. The machine felt as if it were reprogramming me. There was a human, as far as I could tell, standing at some type of console. I observed some of the results on that machine, maybe from my brain." In his last session, he described ". . . four distinct beings.

---

*Gumby was a green clay-and-wire figure that starred in an American television show in the 1950s and 1960s.

They had done something and were observing the results. They are vastly advanced scientifically and technologically."

Later, Jeremiah reflected on his experiences:

The DMT state shows you something real. It's totally unexpected, quite constant and objective. One could interpret your looking at my pupils as being observed, and the tubes in my body as the tubes I'm seeing. But that is a metaphor and this is not at all a metaphor. It's an independent, constant reality. There is the real possibility of adjacent dimensions. It may not be so simple as that there are alien planets with their own societies. This is too proximal. It's not like some kind of drug. It's more like the experience of a new technology. You can choose to attend to this or not. It will continue to progress without you paying attention. You return not to where you left off, but to where things have gone since you left. It's not a hallucination, but an observation.

Dmitri, a Web designer and Heather's partner, found himself in:

. . . a landing bay, or recovery area. They had a space ready for me. They weren't as surprised as I was. It was incredibly nonpsychedelic. I was able to pay attention to detail. . . . I am so disappointed I didn't talk with them. I was confused and in awe. I knew they were preparing me for something. Somehow, we had a mission. They had things to show me. But they were waiting for me to acquaint myself with the environment and movement and language of this space. They were so friendly. I had a bond with one of them. It was about to say something to me, but we couldn't quite connect. It was almost a sexual bond . . . not sex like intercourse, but a total body communication. Their work definitely had something to do with my presence.

Ben, a former military security officer, reported:

There were four to five of them, and they were on me fast. As crazy as this sounds, they looked like saguaro cactuses, flexible, fluid, geometric, green. Not solid. They weren't benevolent, but they weren't nonbenevolent. They probed, really probed. They seemed to know time was limited. They wanted to know what I, this being who had shown up, was doing. I didn't answer. They knew. Once they decided I was okay, they went about their business. I felt like something was inserted into my left forearm, right here, about three inches below this tattoo on my wrist. It was long. There were no reassurances with the probe. Simply business.

Sean, whose mystical experience we described earlier, also had an encounter during one of his four 0.3 mg/kg sessions:

I noticed a middle-aged female with a pointed nose and light greenish skin, sitting off to my right, watching this changing city [whose image had appeared to him in the preceding few moments]. She had her hand on a dial that seemed to control the panorama we were watching. She turned slightly toward me and asked, "What else would you like?" I answered telepathically, "Well, what else have you got? I have no idea what you can do." Then she stood up, walked up to me, touched my right forehead and warmed it up. She then used a sharp object to open up a panel in my right temple, releasing a tremendous amount of pressure. This made me feel much better, even though I realized I had felt fine in the first place.

On his first high dose Rex, a journeyman carpenter and singer-songwriter, described:

. . . insect-creatures all around me, trying to break through. I was fighting letting go of who I am or was. The more I fought, the more demonic they became, probing into my psyche and my being. I finally starting letting go, because I was certain I was dying. As I accepted my death and dissolution into God's love, the insectoids began feeding on my heart, devouring the feelings of love and surrender. They were interested in emotion. As I was holding on to my last thought—that God is love—they asked, "Even here? Even here?" I said, "Yes. Of course." They were still there, but I was making love to them at the same time they were eating me. They feasted as they made love to me. I don't know if they were female or male or something else, but it was extremely alien, though not necessarily unpleasant. The thought came to me with certainty that they were manipulating my DNA, changing its structure. Then it started fading. They didn't want me to go. I didn't feel stoned or intoxicated. I was able to observe quite clearly. I had my capacities. It was just happening.

During another session, Rex again struggled with his reaction to the beings' initially sinister presence:

One of them began reassuring me. Then the space opened up around me. There were creatures and machinery. It looked like it was in a field of black space, going on forever. They were sharing this with me, letting me see all this. There was a female who, when I felt I was dying, appeared and reassured me. She accompanied me during the viewing of the machinery and the creatures. When I was with her, I had a deep feeling of relaxation and tranquillity. . . . She had an elongated head. The creatures were pouring communication into me, but it was just so intense, I couldn't bear it. There were rays of yellow light coming out of the face of the reassuring one. She was trying to communicate with me, and was very concerned for me as to the effects I was experiencing due to her attempts to communicate. Something green appeared in front of me, rotating, doing things. She was showing me, it seemed, how to use this thing, which resembled a computer terminal. I believe she wanted me to try to communicate with her through that device, but I couldn't figure it out.

Rex's final session continued with the theme of insectoids in a huge space, which he described as:

> . . . an infinite hive. There were insectlike intelligences everywhere, in a hypertechnological space. I felt wet stuff hitting me all over my body. They were dripping stuff on me. They wanted me to join them, to stay with them. I was tempted. I was looking down a corridor that was stretching out forever. I lost awareness for a moment, then I found myself in that hive. There was another one helping me—different from the previous helper. It was very intelligent. It wasn't at all humanoid. It wasn't a bee, but it seemed like one. It was showing me around the hive. It was extremely friendly and I felt a warm, sensual energy radiating throughout the hive. It said to me [that] this was where our future lay.

Sara was a housewife, mother, and freelance science writer. Her first high-dose session flung her "backwards through my DNA into a psychedelic buzz saw of colors" that she was afraid would consume her. She "reverted to being simply one energy form with no body, back in the staging area for life, where souls wait to incarnate." Despite some anxiety she experienced during this first high dose, Sara returned for the tolerance study, receiving four 0.3 mg/kg doses in the morning, one every thirty minutes. Early on, she saw:

> . . . clowns performing. They were like toys or animated clowns. Suddenly, a pulsating entity appeared out of the patterns of color. It sounds weird to describe it as Tinkerbell-like, but that is how it looked. It was trying to coax me to go with it. I was reluctant because I didn't know about finding my way back. By the time I had decided to follow it, the drug was wearing off and I wasn't high enough to follow the entity.
>
> It followed me back until I sensed it had reached its boundary. I felt like it was saying good-bye.

After some coaching to help her get past the distracting colors, Sara's third and fourth sessions were more focused. During her third, she said she

. . . quickly blasted through to the other side, in a void of darkness. Suddenly, beings appeared, cloaked, like silhouettes. They were glad to see me. They indicated they had contact with me as an individual before, and were pleased we had discovered this [DMT] technology. They wanted to learn more about our physical bodies, telling me that humans exist at many levels. It seemed as if they, not the nurse, were collecting blood and heart data, and appreciated my doing it for them. We had something in common. They told me to "embrace peace."

With her last dose:

They were ready for me. They told me there were many things they could share with us when we learn how to make extended contact. Their interest in emotions and feelings prompted me to say, "We have something we can give you: spirituality and love." I felt a tremendous energy, a brilliant pink light with white edges, building on my left side. They were on my right, so I reached out my hands across the universe and prepared to be a bridge. I let this energy pass through me to them. They were grateful, but I was a little disappointed that my final session was spent giving, when I wanted my own spiritual enlightenment. I always knew we weren't alone in the universe, but I thought the only way to encounter them is with flying saucers in outer space. It never occurred to me to actually encounter them in our own inner space. I thought the only things we could encounter inside were things in our own personal sphere of archetypes and mythology. I expected spirit guides and angels, not alien life-forms. Oh, and I saw equipment or something . . . sticks with teardrops coming out of them. It looked like machinery.

Not all encounters with beings were ultimately benevolent and gratifying. For example, Ken, a full-time student with a great fondness for the emotional warmth of MDMA (Ecstasy), did not have much experience with the more powerful classical psychedelics. His first high dose of DMT, thankfully with no rectal temperature monitor in place, resulted in finding himself in this situation: "There were two crocodiles on my chest, crushing me, anally raping me. I didn't know if I would survive. At first, I thought I was dreaming, having a nightmare. Then I realized it was really happening. It was awful. It's the most scared I've ever been in my life. I wanted to ask to hold your hands, but I was pinned so firmly I couldn't move and I couldn't speak."

Kevin, married to Sara, was a mathematician, whose first high-dose session was marked not only by a potentially dangerous rise in his blood pressure, but also by an especially frightening encounter:

I felt a tingling in my body, a strange, lifting sensation. I saw colors coming at me in the darkness. Then I saw a light, a matrix of cells that looked like skin under a microscope. All of a sudden, off to the upper right, I saw a figure. She looked like an African war goddess. She was black, carrying a spear, a shield, and appeared to have a mask on. I surprised her. She took a defensive and aggressive posture, saying, "YOU DARE TO COME HERE?!" I mentally replied, "I guess so."

I felt a tremendous rush in my chest. My heart was hammering. I felt waves coursing through my body. I thought, "They've killed me." Then my subconscious or someone said to me, "You're dying. Don't die." Far away I heard what sounded like an alarm [which was the blood pressure machine reacting to his high blood pressure with an alarm]. I thought something had gone very wrong. I thought of Sara and our little son, and I fought. I'm not going to die. I felt as if I'd dived off a ten-meter platform, hit the water, and was at the bottom of the pool. I swam for the surface.

SIMILARITIES TO ABDUCTION EXPERIENCES

These "beyond the veil" experiences share much with alien-abduction literature as it has been summarized by the late Harvard psychiatrist John Mack in his book *Abduction*.[1] In a "typical" abduction experience, a bright light, humming sounds, strange body vibrations, and inner tension or paralysis mark the beginning of the occurrence. Then one or more beings, more or less humanoid, appear, sometimes seeming to emerge from the background. Some abductees find themselves in a parallel world that has ordinary or familiar features, such as a room or a park. Others find themselves in an examining, treatment, or laboratory setting. In all cases, the individuals are absolutely under the control of the beings in a situation that they consistently describe as more real than real.

Beings are busily moving around, attending to tasks the subjects do not understand. Some abductees feel some type of neuropsychological reprogramming or a transfer of information involving unusual visual symbols, rather than words or sounds. The beings may gaze very closely at abductees. On other occasions, the abductees report probes being inserted into their bodies. They may feel their psyche has been transformed. The beings appear to be greatly interested in our physicality and emotionality. They seem to need something that only human love can provide. Commonly, the initial contact is cold and indifferent. One entity in particular is more or less in charge, and the abductee seems to have a special relationship with this being. Some abductees report being greeted by aliens upon emerging into their reality, a type of "welcome back!" reaction.

There are striking commonalities between the reports of Mack's subjects and those of our DMT volunteers. It is tempting to speculate that there is a relationship between the two sets of observations. Perhaps elevations in endogenous DMT levels occurred in those individuals who claim that they experienced an alien abduction. Supporting this theory is the fact that many of Mack's volunteers were under tremendous stress before their abduction experiences, and we know that in nonhumans, DMT levels in the brain rise in response to stress.

Yet none of our subjects had any visible evidence of having made contact with "real" beings—even the volunteer who claimed that aliens implanted a rod into his forearm. In this case, it may be worthwhile to consider a spectrum of encounter phenomena along an axis that has at its two extremes *physicality* and *noncorporeality*. At one pole, purely consciousness-to-consciousness contact is made, and objective physical data resulting from an encounter are not necessary to establish the veracity of contact.

MODELS FOR UNDERSTANDING THE DMT EXPERIENCE

The vast range of DMT effects seen in our volunteers makes it difficult to formulate any single explanatory model. Putting aside for the moment the question of how any drug or plant modifies consciousness, we may conceptualize the effects of DMT along a trajectory of explanations, from the very likely to the very speculative. With respect to the psychotherapeutic effects seen in the *personal* category of DMT sessions, it is relatively easy to postulate effects on some of the mental processes involved in psychotherapy of any kind: enhancements, reductions, or novel effects on projection, suggestibility, transference, repression, denial, and the like. DMT also may modify imagination, creativity, and symbolization of conflicts in order to allow an individual more flexibility in dealing with painful feelings and memories.

In terms of *transpersonal* experiences, there are several levels of explanations from which to choose. There exists a growing field of *neurotheology* that posits that particular brain centers mediate such states. While these studies have determined the anatomical location of such changes, they have not identified their proximate cause. Any involvement of DMT would add an important element to this equation.

Psychological counterparts to these brain changes, particularly those within a clinical psychological framework, have not been particularly well articulated. The fields of cognitive psychology, which borrows heavily from computer science, and transpersonal psychology, which borrows heavily from religious studies, have made the best attempts at framing these experiences in the language of psychology. Yet the otherworldly, invisible experiences at both the microscopic and macroscopic levels—particularly those in which there is contact with beings—push us onto rather thin conceptual ice, but we must make the effort to understand them.

My primary reaction to such reports by my initial nineteen DMT informants and then to reports from our own research volunteers was "This is your brain on DMT." In other words, I assumed we were dealing only with brain chemistry changes. It is difficult, however, to conceive of one chemical's effects on so many different psychological functions over an extended period of time—especially because it elicits a seemingly seamless synthesis of such complex and novel content. This hypothesis failed to appeal to either my or the volunteers' scientific intuition—that is, intuition that emerges out of a scientific worldview.

Similarly, psychological explanations alone did not seem likely to account for these experiences, although devotees of Freudian and Jungian deconstruction of symbols, images, feelings, and thoughts could most likely build coherent explanations. Nevertheless, volunteers (and, ultimately, I) rejected an insistence on the symbolic, dreamlike foundation of the subjects' experiences. Clearly and unequivocally, the volunteers were able to distinguish between experiences on DMT and those of a dream. What's more, it was extraordinarily difficult, if not impossible, for this rather psychologically and psychotherapeutically sophisticated group of volunteers to believe that unconscious mental contents and processes could be at the root of these types of sessions. Further, more philosophically, such an approach led to an interpretation of these experiences as something other than what they seemed to be. To paraphrase Jeremiah, "This is not a metaphor." The only explanatory model that held itself out as the most intuitively satisfying, yet the most theoretically treacherous, involved assigning a parallel level of reality to these experiences. In other words, I engaged in a thought experiment forced upon me by the insistence of the volunteers and the consistency of their reports: I had to accept their reports as descriptions of things that were "real." I allowed myself, at least theoretically, to accept that under the influence of DMT, these things do happen—in reality, although not in a reality we usually inhabit.

What were the results of this thought experiment? One result is that it helped lessen my own uncertainty about navigating this uncharted territory. A more open-minded, less interpretive approach also led to greater comfort on the part of volunteers, and, subsequently, they more readily disclosed some of their unusual experiences. Yet this experiment also strained my scientific worldview and went far beyond any scientific training I had brought to bear on this research. If such an assumption was true, and even if it was not, it is worth considering where, within contemporary science, we might find support for such a theory—not that contemporary science is the only model. Shamanic traditions, from which grew our own religious traditions, assume multiple levels of co-occurring reality that we can enter and perceive while in an altered state of consciousness.

For the moment, let us hypothesize an effect of DMT on the receiving characteristics of consciousness occurring through changes in the physical-chemical-energetic properties of the brain. This is comparable to the effects of X-rays, telescopes, or microscopes on our everyday perceptual apparatus. The things we see with the aid of a microscope, for example, are utterly alien, but because they are perceived in a state within which most of us exist most of the time, we can validate them consensually.

In the case of a microscope, however, we are dealing with an extension of our senses via hardware. In the DMT scenario, the wetware of the brain is modified, leading to the opening of other realms. These data are harder to validate because, at this point, they are very difficult to share in the same way as traditional data. Within our model of science, however, it appears that the nascent fields of parallel universes, dark matter, and other highly abstract scientific pursuits are those in which we might find ways to explain some of what our DMT volunteers described. These fields are highly theoretical and, for the most part, exist only within the minds of the scientists working on their explication. We ought not lose sight of the analogous nature of these two sets of data, both relating to thought experiments.

FUTURE STUDIES

Several relatively simple studies could follow from this first phase of our human DMT research. One project could measure levels of endogenous DMT in people who have naturally occurring experiences with DMT-like features. These levels could then be compared to those from people in ordinary, waking consciousness. States of interest would include mystical ones, near-death experiences, alien abduction, psychotic episodes, and dream sleep (perhaps REM phase). Another series of studies might involve administering DMT to people who have had any of these experiences, and comparing the effects that occur under the influence of DMT to those that occur naturally. For example, such a study might discover whether administering DMT to someone claiming to be an abductee would elicit all or part of an alien abduction experience.

It is most important that we gain more familiarity with the DMT state, particularly over a longer time period, in order to establish a consensually validated topography. Ayahuasca sessions last four to six hours, and we can learn much about DMT worlds through careful examination and collation of reports involving this DMT-containing preparation. In addition, a longer-term infusion of DMT, perhaps over several hours, would provide less-chaotic access to these dimensions and generate valuable information on the effects of pure DMT itself, rather than DMT combined with beta-carbolines, as in ayahuasca.

DISCUSSION OF THE RESULTS OF DMT STUDY

No matter how we explain the phenomena of the DMT experience using the tools of Newtonian or quantum mechanisms, the very existence of the DMT experience changes an individual's worldview by highlighting how we habitually limit our discourse to what is usually perceived. The fact that a substance such as DMT—residing within our own bodies and regulated by a physical gene—can propel us into seemingly freestanding inhabited worlds requires further examination. In some ways, the discovery, acknowledgment, and discussion of these states is comparable to the discovery, acknowledgment, and discussion of the unconscious. DMT and similar drugs provide reliable access to realms that are almost always imperceptible but under the influence of the drug are experienced as real or more real than the normal waking state.

Dreams, and religious and near-death experiences are altered states of consciousness that have had tremendous impact upon humans, both individually and collectively. Dreams, however, can be capricious and chaotic, and religious and near-death states occur to us only rarely, if at all. DMT-induced altered states of consciousness are easily accessible, and during them, we maintain relatively intact powers of observation, whereas after them, much of the experience is retained. Perhaps we may tap this awesomely vast reservoir of experiences using DMT. If it turns out that endogenous DMT is associated with naturally occurring, highly valued states, we can more readily accept these DMT-induced states as "natural" or "biological"—perhaps even our birthright.

DMT AS THE ENDOMATRIX

The endogenicity of DMT, however, is not the only property that we must ponder. We must also consider its active transport into the brain across the normally impenetrable blood–brain barrier. DMT may be a necessary constituent of the brain's nutritional requirements. What does this suggest about this substance's role in the normal waking state? One possible answer is that DMT mediates everyday waking consciousness. In addition to its intensity and strangeness, the DMT state is perceptible—that is, most of the time, while under the influence of the drug, there is something of which we are aware. In other words, in both the DMT and normal waking states, the consciousness-awareness element functions normally. Time generally seems to exist, as do the basic building blocks of visual, auditory, emotional, and other categories of mental experience. If we consider that we are now, all of us, for this moment experiencing a DMT trip (remember, there is no tolerance to DMT—its effects can be experienced continuously), how are we to relate to where we are now? Will we act and feel about things any differently? What about questions of life, self, and other? What of questions of God, free will, and good and evil?*

Closer to home, in relation to the particular theme of this book, the presence of DMT may suggest a previously unappreciated fluidity, permeability, or plasticity of the membrane separating us and other worlds. This barrier, then, may exist more inside of us than outside of us—in inner rather than outer space. Therefore, travel across great distances in outer space may not be the only way to reach worlds that are different from our own, seemingly remote in time and space. Moreover, it may be unnecessary to restrict this search using methods based upon a view of reality limited to what is physical and measurable. It is perhaps this one-sided vantage point that has removed us from potentially

---

*Note that I have focused my research on DMT because of its endogenicity. Though 5-methoxy-DMT is also endogenous and powerfully psychedelic, the relative ease of performing a DMT study led me to work with it rather than with this closely related compound. The lack of any previous published human studies with 5-methoxy-DMT would have required years of additional animal toxicology testing. In addition, as with DMT, the previously discussed salvinorin A (in *Salvia divinorum*) and ketamine also produce states of consciousness that seem to allow perception of strikingly real, nonordinary realities. If and when endogenous compounds with the properties of salvinorin or ketamine are isolated from the human body, we will need to appropriately modify a model of our consensus reality derived solely from DMT. We will then have to incorporate into this model the unique qualities of these other compounds and the effects of their interaction with DMT.

unlimited nonphysical realities. We can challenge this limitation intellectually, scientifically, spiritually, and, most important, practically. Establishing—with a sober, altruistic intent—reliable and generally available means of contact with these different levels of existence may help us alleviate some of the pressing issues we are facing on this planet in this time–space continuum. It even may be that the information and resources we gather in these noncorporeal realms are more important to our survival—and ultimately our evolution—than that which we obtain via strictly physical means.

✧

DMT is a psychedelic substance found with great consistency within many living creatures, from psychoactive plants to the human body. Though we can describe its chemistry and pharmacology using the traditional tools and language of science, the subjective experiences of DMT are more difficult to place into a conceptual framework. Furthermore, its endogenicity and special but unknown role in normal brain function suggest that DMT exerts an impact on both extraordinary states of awareness during our lives and our fundamental perception of these lives.

4

Ayahuasca
The Sacred Vine of the Amazon
Luis Eduardo Luna, Ph.D.

For thirty-five years I have been concentrating a great deal of my attention on ayahuasca, a plant preparation originally developed by the indigenous people of the Upper Amazon and made from the stem of a jungle vine (*Banisteriopsis caapi*). In most areas, it contains at least one more additive, the leaves of a DMT-containing plant: In Colombia and Ecuador, this additive is usually *Diplopterys cabrerana,* a vine from the same family as *B. caapi* (Malpighiaceae). In Peru, Bolivia, and Brazil it is *Psychotria viridis,* a shrub from the Rubiaceae (coffee) family. Of these plants, *P. viridis* is probably best known in the West, because much of contemporary knowledge of ayahuasca derives from either the Peruvian mestizo tradition or the Brazilian religious organizations that use the preparation as a sacrament. (Both use *Psychotria viridis* as the visionary additive.) *Banisteriopsis caapi* contains harmine and tetrahydroharmine as its primary active alkaloids, with smaller amounts of harmaline and other compounds, whose major function is to allow the orally ingested DMT to attain psychoactive levels in the brain. Ayahuasca, the name given both to the vine and to the final preparation, has been the subject of an increasing number of popular and scientific publications, documentaries, conferences, and seminars.

I first learned about ayahuasca in 1971, when I met Terence

McKenna traveling with Erica Nietfeld in my native town of Florencia, the capital of Caquetá, in the Colombian Amazon. I was twenty-four and almost finished with my studies in Spanish and Latin American philology and literature at Madrid University after two and a half years of philosophy and theology studies with the Piarist Fathers, a religious order. I was visiting my family after an absence of seven years from Colombia. Terence was twenty-five. I spoke enough English to communicate with him, and he told me of his and his brother Dennis's experiences with *yagé* (ayahuasca) and the mushroom *Psilocybe cubensis* some months earlier at La Chorrera, a small settlement with an impressive waterfall by the Putumayo River, some two hundred fifty kilometers southeast of where we were.

They had reached it after a long journey up the river from Puerto Leguízamo. I was amazed by Terence's story and the breadth of his knowledge. Terence and Erica planned to leave for Bogotá, the capital of Colombia, the next day, on their way to the Peruvian Amazon in pursuit of yagé. Excited, I went home and told my father about my encounter. He had never taken the brew, but knew that the Coreguaje and other indigenous groups of the area used it. He said: "Tell your friends they do not need to go to Peru to look for yagé. They will find it right here." He also told me that it was used for divination by don Apolinar Yacanamijoy, an Ingano Indian I knew since I was a child, because he used to go with his family to my grandmother's *granero,* a small general store.

My father told me that I could invite them to stay in Villa Gloria, a wooden house and land we owned some twenty kilometers from Florencia. The three of us moved in, and Erica spent several hours a day typing the manuscript of what came to be *The Invisible Landscape.*[1] They were traveling with a short library of interesting books. Terence and I read during the day or made short excursions into the surrounding pasture, looking for pictographs that were rumored to exist in the area and for mushrooms, none of which we found. After sunset, and with only candles and flashlights to help us through the dark, we talked about strange ideas associated with the use of hallucinogenic plants, including time travel, mind reading, and contact with other dimensions.

A few times during the following two months, we boarded an old truck that brought to Florencia—at least an hour's journey—passengers from several small villages populated by recent colonists. The best restaurant in town in those days belonged to Ernst, a one-eyed German Rosicrucian who knew don Apolinar and who used to live with the Tukano Indians of the Colombian Vaupés River. There he learned about yagé (which they called *caapi*) and about *borrachero,* the vernacular name given to several species of the genus *Brugmansia,* all of which contain powerful atropine alkaloids.

Ernst introduced us to Carlos, whose real name was Karman, a Hungarian ex–soccer player who had deserted his Italian team in Venezuela when he fell in love with a Venezuelan woman who subsequently left him after spending all his money. Stranded in South America, he went to the Amazon, where he spent some time with various indigenous groups. He made ends meet by repairing typewriters. Ernst sold us a small bottle of yagé, which he had received from don Apolinar. The four of us took it that night in Villa Gloria. Karman reported seeing beautiful, naked women, and then he kept silent. Neither Terence nor Erica saw anything, but both vomited profusely and had diarrhea. I had visions of a city with tall, organic towers with birds flying around them and populated by long white humanoids. I also saw what I thought was a DNA molecule.

Don Apolinar was an Ingano who lived in Yurayaku, then a tiny settlement. Inganos are a Quechua-speaking indigenous group that live in southeastern Colombia. He had moved with his family from the Mocoa area, in the Putumayo, to Caquetá. Many years later I learned that he was regarded as a great shaman by natives of that area. From time to time, he used to go to a certain small pension in Florencia, and I went there occasionally to inquire about him. I finally met him at the end of my stay in Colombia.

He told me, "If you are interested in yagé, you would have to keep a six-month diet. At the end yagé will come to see what you want."

"How is yagé?" I asked.

"*Simpático,*" he said.

After I finished my studies in Madrid, I moved to Norway, where I taught Spanish and Latin American literature at Oslo University for the next seven years. At the same time, I continued my own education, taking courses in various disciplines that I thought would help me to integrate and illuminate my experience with yagé. In the summer of 1973, I flew to Berkeley and spent two months with Terence and Erica, strolling up and down Telegraph Avenue and buying secondhand books during the day. In the evenings there were always interesting visitors in the house, often writers, scientists of various disciplines, or seekers of various kinds. There were only a few publications about yagé available at that time, and the best known of these was *The Yagé Letters,*[2] a book composed by William Burroughs (1914–1997) and consisting of travel notes and letters to Allen Ginsberg (1926–1997) written during his seven-month expedition in search of yagé. The book also contains Ginsberg's own accounts of his experiences with ayahuasca in the Peruvian Amazon in 1960. According to Ralph Metzner,[3] the shamanic lore of ayahuasca entered Western culture most strongly and initially through *The Yage Letters,* which has been republished recently with an excellent introduction by Oliver Harris.

In 1965, Peter Matthiessen, in his novel *At Play in the Fields of the Lord,*[4] told the story of a Cheyenne who takes ayahuasca, flies his airplane until its fuel is exhausted, and parachutes into the midst of an Indian community, where he becomes one of its members. The book, which shows the conflicts involving missionaries, the army protecting the interest of colonists, and an Indian community that is finally obliterated, appeared on the big screen with the same title in 1991 under the direction of Héctor Babenco. In 1971, a landmark in Amazonian studies appeared, *Amazonian Cosmos: The Sexual and Religious Symbolism of the Tukano Indians.*[5] It was written by Gerardo Reichel-Dolmatoff, an Austrian-Colombian ethnologist and archaeologist, who realized the crucial importance of caapi in the cultural life of this tribe. The next year brought Peter Furst's anthology *Flesh of the Gods,*[6] which demonstrated the existence of serious scholarship focusing on the use of sacred plants in various cultures. In 1973, there appeared *Hallucinogens and Shamanism,*[7] an anthology edited by Michael Harner, with several articles dealing with ayahuasca in the indigenous context.

In January 1979, I moved to Helsinki, where I became Spanish lecturer at the Swedish School of Economics. It was then that I decided it was time to revisit my home continent. In the summer of that year, I made a journey from Buenos Aires to Valparaiso, in Chile, up to Antofagasta, then on to La Paz, Cuzco, Lima, and Bogotá before arriving in Florencia to visit my parents for a few days before returning to Finland. Naturally, yagé was on my mind. I invited my brother Alvaro to come with me to Yurayaku, where don Apolinar lived. Seven years earlier, my brother visited him briefly, walking to his home through a muddy *trocha,* a narrow passage through the forest, for some twelve hours from the small town of San José de la Fragua. Now, however, it was possible to take the bus all the way to the new settlement that had been built about half an hour walk away from his home, which was located at the other side of the Fragüita River.

Don Apolinar had aged considerably since the last time I saw him; he must have been about eighty years old or older. He was tired and bitter, because the colonists had destroyed his fields of medicinal plants, including his plantations of several kinds of yagé. He was reluctant to give my brother and me yagé that night, which was my only opportunity to acquire it, for I had to return to Europe shortly. We were disappointed, but we had little to offer don Apolinar for the great favor we were asking, so we went for a walk with don Roberto, his son, through the pastures surrounding Yurayaku. The land was grazed by humped Indian Cebu cows and was dotted with *Psilocybe cubensis* mushrooms, which grew on the cows' dung. I asked Roberto whether he or the others ever ate them.

"We do not, because it does not go well with yagé, but the gringos eat them as soon as they spot them," he said.

I proposed to my brother that we have a mushroom experience. Don Roberto blessed four large ones solemnly, and my brother and I had two each.

A distinctive landmark in that area was a huge rock, and from the effects of the mushrooms I thought that if Indians had been living in the area in the past, the rock must have been a sacred site. It was completely covered by moss, but as my brother and I started to peel off some of the growth, we found traces of petroglyphs.

"These were made by the old ones," said don Apolinar, who also told us that when he first arrived there years ago, a huge rubber tree was growing on top of the rock. After he had cut its roots and set it on fire, reducing it to ashes, he discovered the petroglyphs.

I again implored don Apolinar to give us yagé. "I have been waiting for this for the last seven years," I said.

Finally, he said: "But we do not have batteries for our torches and no candles."

"We will go to buy some," I quickly replied.

A heavy rain had been falling for the last few hours. Still under the effects of the mushrooms, my brother and I made a run to one of the shops and purchased some batteries, candles, and a bottle of *aguardiente,* a distilled sugarcane drink spiced with anise of which don Apolinar was fond. It was beginning to get dark, and once again, we had to cross the perilous hanging wooden bridge across the Fragüita River to reach don Apolinar's house. While crossing the bridge, I looked down and saw what seemed to be a huge serpent coming down the river toward us. At first I thought it was a hallucination, for I was still feeling the effects of the mushrooms, but then, as it came closer, I saw that my brother behind me on the bridge was also looking in amazement at the serpent, which was probably caught in the rain and trying to get to shore.

It was dark by now. Don Apolinar drank the bottle of aguardiente in a few gulps. He was now wearing his crown of feathers, a jaguar-tooth collar, and a Catholic medal around his neck. Don Roberto was also there, wearing a smaller crown. He gave us a small cup of the bitter drink, prepared as a cold infusion of the pounded stem of *B. caapi* and the leaves of *chagropanga* (*Diplopterys cabrerana*). We were told to lie down on cow skins on the floor. I waited for the effects to come. At some point, I was distracted by the stars above and forgot where I was—then I suddenly realized that I was inside don Apolinar's house, looking at the sky through the roof. I shuddered in fear and amazement. The image of the serpent in the river came to my mind and I started to crawl like a snake and thought about the frogs croaking out in the rain. A burst of vomit came too fast to control, and my brother helped me out to the veranda, where I promptly threw up. The night was filled with stars and fireflies that formed a continuous, pulsating, magical background. I returned to the house in awe.

"Don Apolinar," I said. "You know so much!"

"It is not me," he said. "It is yagé."

The next morning I felt wonderful and took pictures of don Apolinar and his family. Natividad, don Roberto's wife, had also taken yagé the night before. I asked her what she saw. "*Culebras* [snakes]," she said. My brother and I returned to Florencia, and I flew back to Bogotá and then on to Helsinki a couple of days later, even more convinced that I had been sorely lacking in my knowledge of the indigenous population of my own region.

Back home in Helsinki, I learned of the work of Rafael Karsten, a Swedish-Finnish ethnologist who, in the early 1930s, had exactly the job I had: a Spanish lectureship at the Swedish School of Economics. Karsten (1879–1956) made several expeditions to South America between 1911 and 1929, and in the 1920s and 1930s he published several ethnographic books, one of them a massive volume describing his travels among the Shuar (Jívaro), including information about their material culture, social life, religion, and art. Karsten witnessed several collective *natém* (ayahuasca) rituals among the Shuar as well as more private shamanic ceremonies. In 1920, he published the first detailed description of the religious ideas connected with natém's use. When Karsten asked the Shuar why they drink natém, he received the following answer: "It is in order that the people may not die away." He then adds the following commentary:

> By this kind of divination they try to find out what dangers are threatening the family, whether enemies are planning an attack against them, whether evil sorcerers are operating against them, whether they will be successful in their own undertakings, and so forth. The magical drink . . . purifies the stomach from harmful substances and the magic arrows of wizards. . . . At the same time both men and women are, by drinking natéma, made strong and clever for their different occupations and duties, the men for hunting, fishing, war, etc., the latter for agriculture, for the education of the children, for the care of the domestic animals, and for other domestic work incumbent on them.[8]

I also learned about the work of the American anthropologist Irving Goldman (1911–2002), who documented his 1939–1940 fieldwork on *mihí* (a *B. caapi* drink) rituals among the Cubeo of Colombia. Goldman points out that this culture values inebriation as something sacred. Mihí is intimately connected to ancestor cults and is used in drinking parties together with tobacco juice, manioc beer, and coca chewing, the backbone of the Cubeo social life, as well as in "moaning festivals," which produce as their final outcome transformation of anger and grief into joy. Neither Karsten nor Goldman took ayahuasca. Reichel-Dolmatoff, however, did. In *The Shaman and the Jaguar,*[9] he recounts in amazing detail a Barasana ceremony in which he participated, tape recording his experiences. The next morning, he recounts:

> I was drawing in my notebook, trying to recapture some of the images I had seen. A man who was looking over my shoulder when

I was making a series of dotted lines, vertical but slightly undulating, asked a question about it, and I answered that I had seen this design last night.

"Look!" he called to the others. Several people came and gathered around me, staring at my drawing.

"What does this image mean?" I asked.

The men laughed. "It's the Milky Way," they said; "You saw the Milky Way! You were flying up with us to the Milky Way!"

Perhaps the first anthropologist to have reported his own experience with ayahuasca was Michel Harner, who partook of a session among the Conibo in 1960 (see chapter 9). His experience set Harner in the direction of creating an institution dedicated to the revitalization of traditional shamanism and its introduction to the Western world using the drum as a tool to access other realms.

VEGETALISMO

My experience with don Apolinar was always on my mind. I conceived a project in which I would make a film about three generations: don Apolinar and his wife, who walked barefoot, their toes spread like fingers; don Roberto, don Apolinar's son, and his wife Natividad, who wore sandals; and don Apolinar's grandchildren, proud of their tennis shoes. I began preparations, together with Gregory Moore, an American living in Helsinki, who told me he had experience as a cameraman. We borrowed equipment and gathered enough money to buy tapes and one and a half hours of 16 mm film. One month before the planned departure to visit don Apolinar, my father wrote me that the don had died, but I was determined to make a short documentary on yagé. Greg and I went to Los Angeles to see Jorge Preloran, a well-known Argentinian filmmaker who had made remarkable anthropological films using very simple equipment.

"What equipment do you have?" he asked.

"A 16 mm Bolex and a Sony recorder. No connection between them."

"Great," he said. "I made more than forty films with equipment like that."

Preloran advised me to choose a person as a subject for the film. He also suggested that every evening I record, with the same volume, the subject's ideas about himself and the world. The next day, I was to transcribe what was recorded the night before and study the manuscript carefully, looking for a narrative thread. Then I was to shoot the pictures that would go with the narrative. I went to see Terence McKenna, who had moved to Sebastopol, near San Francisco, with his wife, Kat Harrison. He told me that recently he visited Iquitos, then a city of about three hundred thousand on the shores of the Amazon River in Peru. He said there was an *ayahuasquero* tradition there worth looking into, so I decided to go. He gave me the names of three ayahuasqueros he had heard of. Gregory went to Iquitos a couple of days ahead of me, and following Terence's directions, he met the ayahuasquero don Emilio Andrade Gómez. When looking for a place to stay, Gregory had been offered the very same room where Bruce Lamb had written *Wizard of the Upper Amazon*,[10] the story of Manuel Córdoba Ríos, a famous ayahuasquero in Iquitos who claimed that he had been kidnapped by Amahuaca Indians, who taught him about ayahuasca and other medicinal plants, which enabled him to become a shaman. This was one of the first English-language books that contributed to the spread of information about ayahuasca.

From the moment I saw don Emilio, I knew I had found the person I was looking for: he was humble and eloquent, had a great sense of humor, and knew the forest where he had lived all his life. He was then sixty-three years old and lived with his wife and his youngest son twelve kilometers from Iquitos along a road that was still under construction at that time and would eventually join Iquitos and Nauta in the south, on the shores of the Marañón River. He called himself a *vegetalista,* a term used to denote a specialist in the use of certain powerful *vegetales* (plants), of which there are several kinds. Don Emilio was an ayahuasquero, but I learned that there were also *tabaqueros, toeros, camalongueros,* and *perfumeros,* who used tobacco (*toé; Brugmansia* sp.), *camalonga* (*Strychnos* sp.), and the perfume derived from various powerful plants, respectively. Don Emilio had taken ayahuasca for the first time when he was fourteen years old in order to "get stronger," but ayahuasca "loved him," and in his visions and dreams it taught him *icaros,* or magical songs, until he finally became an ayahuasquero.

I followed Preloran's advice word for word. Every night I spent several hours with don Emilio, recording his words. The next day I transcribed what I had recorded the night before—and I soon realized that I had in my hands much more than a film. To me, it was about the discovery of *vegetalismo,* a Peruvian shamanic tradition of imprecise origin that I later learned had been partially documented by Castillo, Dobkin de Rios, Ayala and Lewis, Chiappe, and Lamb[11] and was one of the variants of nontribal ayahuasca use found in the Amazonian regions of Colombia, Ecuador, Peru, and eastern Brazil. According to don Emilio, ayahuasca was *un doctor,* a plant teacher, one among many others, some of which were cooked together when preparing the brew or were used independently in various ways. All these plants have a spirit who, under certain circumstances, gives information to the person who ingests them. Before ingestion there is required a particular diet that includes not only food restrictions but also sexual segregation. The spirits of the plants taught *icaros,* songs used for curing, for protection, and for other tasks such as increasing or diminishing the strength of visions during a session.

I collected plants, which I later sent to Timothy Plowman, at the Chicago Field Museum of Natural History, for identification; participated in ayahuasca sessions with don Emilio and other mestizo practitioners; recorded songs; and gathered information about this cultural tradition that was apparently born during the so-called rubber boom period (1880–1914). During that time, indigenous populations were forcefully displaced, and a mestizo syncretic river culture emerged that blended Amazonian and Andean cultural elements and Western ideas. For example, instead of power animals and helping spirits typical of traditional shamanism, mestizo practitioners relied on the supernatural help of angels with swords, soldiers armed with guns, and even warplanes fitted with modern weaponry. Don Emilio told me that under the effects of ayahuasca, he was able to diagnose illness with the help of his *doctores*, spirits from nature and also those that came from distant countries. Sometimes, he said he had been taken to strange places where he saw beings using all sorts of advanced machines.

I recorded about thirty hours of interviews with don Emilio and other ayahuasqueros. The transcriptions yielded a manuscript that was not only the base of the narrative for the 1982 film *Don Emilio and His Little Doctors,* but also the beginning of my doctoral dissertation under the direction of Åke Hultkrantz, a specialist in shamanism and the head of the Institute of Comparative Religion at Stockholm University. Stockholm was relatively close to Helsinki, and I could buy an inexpensive ticket on board one of the large boats that connected the two cities, a sixteen-hour journey.

In the summer of 1982, I went back to Iquitos, where I took ayahuasca and interviewed several other practitioners. Don Emilio introduced me to don José Coral, who he said was a good ayahuasquero and could be my teacher. I was particularly intrigued by the learning process. I arranged for don Emilio's son Jorge, who was twenty-one years old and who lived with him, and Alirio, a neighbor who was twenty-two, to move with me into the house of don José Coral, near Peña Negra, about twenty-five kilometers from Iquitos, where José lived with his wife. He had a few animals and cultivated mostly maize and manioc. The idea was to keep the prescribed diet, which in this area consists of plantains, rice or manioc without salt, and at times a little fish, and also includes sexual abstinence and the taking of ayahuasca. I would record the process on film. Don José had two patients in his home when we arrived, Señora Rosa, who had a bad rheumatic ailment in her knees, and Señora Dominga, who had a terrible cancerous infection near her mouth. I was able to follow the healing procedures, learning at the same time the local ideas about health and illness. Don José used a combination of medicinal plants, massage, dream interpretation, and of course ayahuasca sessions in which he sang icaros, songs taught him by the spirits that came "from the end of the world."

A few days after starting the diet, Alirio could not stand eating without salt and broke the regimen. Jorge followed it for eighteen days. I found myself to be the only one interested in keeping the diet—and I could not make a film about myself. The process was very interesting, however. Ingesting little food and following the dietary prescriptions kept me in an altered state of consciousness nearly all the time; for me, the difference between being awake and dreaming was not very clear. I often had what Stephen LaBerge later called *lucid dreaming*—that is, dreaming while being conscious of doing so, a phenomenon he was able to verify scientifically by means of signaling agreed-upon eye movements during rapid eye movement (REM) sleep from the dreamer's mind to the outside world. "You see, you are learning," was don José's comment on this.

For one month I stayed with don José and his patients. Señora Rosa recovered fully. "*Contenta me voy*" (I go home happy), was her final comment when she left. Señora Dominga died some weeks after I headed back to Iquitos. "She was brought to me too late," don José said to me. In Iquitos I stayed in the home of Gunther Schaper, an older German engineer who had lived for over fifty years in the Peruvian Amazon. In the 1930s he had sent several kilograms of *Banisteriopsis caapi* to Merck Laboratories in Germany as a possible treatment for Parkinson's disease. Mr. Schaper lived only two hundred meters from the Plaza de Armas, the main square. His house was surrounded by a small botanical garden, the greenest block in the center of town. He had several rooms that he rented to botanists, anthropologists, and explorers; it was the best place to meet the most fascinating people visiting Iquitos. There, I wrote my first two papers about mestizo ayahuasca shamanism. These were proofread by Nicole Maxwell, an American woman who had spent many years in the Amazon collecting plants, and who was the author of *Witch-doctor's Apprentice*,[12] an interesting book I had acquired some months earlier in Stockholm.

I sent the manuscripts to Richard Evans Schultes (1915–2001), head of the Botanical Museum of Harvard University and the world authority on the botany of hallucinogenic plants. Several months later, he wrote me a letter in Spanish telling me that he had sent my papers to Laurent Rivier, editor of the *Journal of Ethnopharmacology* and an ayahuasca researcher, for publication. Schultes wrote: "I think that in the year 1941, I met in Puerto Asís a relative of yours, an old man whose surname was Luna, who helped me greatly when I was a novice explorer of the Putumayo region. Was not Pedro Luna a relative of yours? And what a surprise to find in Helsinki and in a Scandinavian language a citizen of our 'Caquetá!'"

My father told me that Pedro Luna had been my great-uncle.

PHARMACOLOGY OF AYAHUASCA

In 1984, I was invited to a symposium on shamanism in Vancouver, British Columbia, Canada, and used the occasion to visit Dennis McKenna, who was making a comparative study of the activity of ayahuasca and *Virola* snuffs for his doctoral dissertation in the department of botany at the University of British Columbia. The resin from several species of *Virola,* usually large trees, was used by indigenous groups of the Upper Amazon to make DMT-containing snuffs to use ceremonially. Snuffs made of yet another genus, *Anadenanthera,* also containing tryptamines, were used in South America and the Caribbean. In the northern part of South America, indigenous tribes used *A. peregrina,* and in the south, tribes used *A. colubrina,* together covering a huge area.[13] If we add the many species of psilocybin mushrooms used in Mesoamerica, we find in the Americas a remarkable concentration of tryptamines, like nowhere else in the world.

Dennis McKenna was excited to confirm experimentally that harmine is indeed a monoamine oxidase inhibitor (MAOI), as proposed by the prominent toxicologist Bo Holmstedt (1918–2002) of the Karolinska Institute in Stockholm, which explains the oral activity of DMT in the ayahuasca brew. DMT taken by itself is inactive orally, because it is destroyed in the gut and liver by monoamine oxidase (MAO) enzymes. When taken together with an MAOI, however, it is protected and is thus able to cross the blood–brain barrier and act on serotonin receptor sites. This is an amazing discovery by Amazonian Indians.

Years later, I met the American pharmacologist Jace Callaway in Finland, who completed his doctoral dissertation for Kuopio University on pinoline, which, as its name indicates, is a compound produced in the pineal gland. Callaway pointed to yet another mechanism underlying the ayahuasca experience: tetrahydroharmine, the second major alkaloid in *Banisteriopsis caapi,* closely resembles pinoline, and is a moderately potent presynaptic serotonin reuptake inhibitor that contributes to higher levels of serotonin in the synapses of serotonergetic brain cells. Subjectively, this would translate into higher alertness while the person is experiencing the effects of DMT. We could say, metaphorically, that under the influence of ayahuasca, an individual is both fully awake (due to the higher levels of synaptic serotonin) and dreaming, as Callaway presented in his hypothesis that DMT may be involved in the experience of dreams, particularly during REM sleep.[14] As Rick Strassman has indicated,[15] DMT is present in all mammals, including human beings, and it has been detected in blood, urine, and cerebrospinal fluid. Callaway coined the term *endohuasca* to indicate that the human organism synthesizes compounds identical or similar to those found in the ayahuasca brew.

Ayahuasca brews vary, depending upon the mode of preparation and the specific specimens used. McKenna et al. calculated that the 100 ml dose of ayahuasca used among mestizo ayahuasqueros contains 467 mg of harmine, 160 mg of tetrahydroharmine, 41 mg of harmaline, and 60 mg of DMT.[16]

THE FIRST AYAHUASCA SYMPOSIUM

Dennis McKenna and I became close friends and collaborators. Back in Vancouver, we wrote a proposal for a biomedical study of ayahuasca which found no funding at that time, but which, years later, was the basis of the first study of this kind, carried out in Brazil. I also thought of organizing an interdisciplinary symposium on ayahuasca within the 45th Americanist Conference, a biannual meeting of social scientists that took place alternately in Europe and the Americas and which was to take place in Bogotá in July 1985, at the Universidad de los Andes.

It turned out to be a fruitful conference, with participants from several countries and a number of disciplines—including botany, pharmacology, archaeology, ethnography, and ethnomusicology, all papers that were published in a special issue of *América Indígena* in Mexico. Among the lecturers was Guillermo Arévalo, a young Shipibo shaman I had met the year before in Pucallpa, Peru. I asked him to write a twenty-page paper to be presented at the conference, which was the first he'd ever attended. He told me he followed the prescribed ayahuasca diet while he wrote the paper, a landmark in the study of Shipibo shamanism.

Another interesting guest was Clodomir Monteiro, a pioneer in the study of Brazilian religious organizations that use ayahuasca as a sacrament. He had invited me to Rio Branco, capital of the state of Acre, some months earlier. I learned that in the 1930s, in the vicinity of the city, Raimundo Irineo Serra (1892–1971), a black man who had moved to the Amazon from Maranhão, in the Brazilian northeast, created a new religion after receiving ayahuasca from a Peruvian vegetalista. In his visions, so the legend goes, the Queen of the Forest, a manifestation of the Virgin Mary, had appeared and asked him to create a new religious organization using ayahuasca—under the name Santo Daime—as a sacrament.

Daniel Pereira de Matos (1904–1958) took Santo Daime several times with Irineu Serra and several times by himself. During one of these experiences, he is said to have received a blue book from an angel, and in 1945, he created a second organization, known as Barquinha (little boat). After the death of Irineu Serra, a group led by Sebastião Mota (1920–1990) separated from the parent organization and created Centro Ecléctico da Fluente Luz Universal Raimundo Irineu Serra (CEFLURIS), another religious organization. Finally, José Gabriel da Costa (1922–1971) created a third organization in 1961, the União do Vegetal (UDV), in Porto Velho, the capital of the state of Rondonia, also in the Amazon. These churches are syncretic Christian religious organizations that use ayahuasca as a sacrament and incorporate Afro-Brazilian religious elements along with European esoteric and Amazonian concepts. Monteiro, the Brazilian anthropologist, organized a screening of my film on don Emilio, which was presented as a documentary on the origins of the Santo Daime religion and was attended by members of all three religious organizations. According to Monteiro, this was the first time they were all present under the same roof.

Guided by Monteiro, I visited Alto Santo, the original center created by Raimundo Irineu Serra and led until the present day by his widow, Senhora Peregrina. I also visited Colonia 5000, the original CEFLURIS center, on the outskirts of Rio Branco. A small group of men, including an Italian and an Argentinean, were cleaning and pounding the *Banisteriopsis* vine, while some women were harvesting the *Psychotria* leaves from a cultivated field. We took Santo Daime that night at the edge of the forest under a nearly full moon. Accompanied by guitars, the group sang *hinos,* songs received from the astral world by the founders and other members of the community. Their brew was stronger than those usually prepared by Peruvian ayahuasqueros. I had the overwhelming sensation that the forest out there was intelligent and populated by invisible beings. At some point, I felt my body dissolving into waves. Concerned, I did not dare abandon myself completely to the experience, and I made internal efforts to counteract it by focusing on my immediate environment. The deepest ayahuasca experiences involve ego dissolution, which requires that an individual be totally confident of the setting. I did not know my new friends well enough to let go as deeply as I might have otherwise. Finally, Monteiro took me to see Manoel Hipólito Araújo, the leader of the main Barquinha center, whom I interviewed, though I did not participate in any of the ceremonies.

COSMOGRAPHY OF MESTIZO SHAMANISM

After the Bogotá conference, Dennis McKenna and I met in Pucallpa, the second largest city in the Peruvian Amazon, on the shores of the Ucayali River. He had met don Fidel, an ayahuasquero, some years earlier while collecting plants with his brother Terence for Botanical Dimensions, an ethnobotanical garden they created in Hawaii. Dennis went to Pucallpa several days ahead of me. When I arrived at the dusty airport, a taxi driver was whispering my name to all disembarking passengers. I identified myself and went at once to a poor area of the city where Dennis was awaiting me.

I crossed a sparse garden and entered the wooden house where an ayahuasca session was starting. "Just in time," Dennis said. He introduced me to don Fidel, who almost immediately handed me a small gourd with the brew. I knew I was going to take ayahuasca in Pucallpa, but didn't expect it to happen so soon. It was the beginning of an intense period in which we collected plants with the assistance of Francisco Montes Shuña, a knowledgeable young man Dennis had met in 1983 in the Huallaga River area. Dennis told me Francisco had a cousin who also knew about plants.

"A little strange," he said.

"I am interested," I replied, as I was interviewing ayahuasqueros and desired any information I could find about the plant teachers.

Pablo Amaringo Shuña lived with his mother, two adopted children, and other members of his family in a humble wooden house with little furniture and no electricity or running water in a swampy area in one of the poorest districts of Pucallpa. He knew a great deal about plant teachers and medicinal plants and told me that for seven years he had been a vegetalista, but had deserted his practice after a spiritual crisis. He said that the spirits "had abandoned him" and he had been forced to leave his practice after a conflict with an ayahuasquera. He also showed us some beautiful gouache paintings on cheap paper depicting scenes from the life of river people as well as jungle landscapes. I was impressed by the accuracy of the elements in the paintings. I realized he had an excellent eidetic memory and wondered whether he could recall the visions he had when he was a vegetalista. He said he could, and some days later he showed Dennis and me his first two visions, giving each of us one of them.

Back in Helsinki, I studied the one he had given me, made a photocopy of it, and mailed it to Pablo, asking him about the meaning of various elements, including angels, warriors with exotic clothes, kings sitting on thrones, a city that was both ancient and futuristic, and a flying saucer. A few weeks later I received back from Pablo a long and detailed description, including the names of the beings depicted. I realized the importance of this kind of information, because through Pablo's paintings it was possible to see a concrete representation of the visions of a mestizo ayahuasquero. It was the beginning of several years of intense collaboration during which he produced approximately one hundred paintings, forty-nine of which were published in 1991 in *Ayahuasca Visions: The Religious Iconography of a Peruvian Shaman.*[17] Besides placing Amaringo in the context of mestizo river shamanism, I identified plants and animals depicted in his work and found ideological and iconographic parallels between the paintings' motifs and the images in Amazonian and Andean cosmology.

What was striking about Pablo Amaringo was first of all the scope and variety of his visions. It was difficult to believe that this humble Amazonian man had visions of distant cities with amazing architecture, exotically dressed alien beings of all kinds, and strange flying machines and that he knew that we live in a multidimensional universe populated by intelligent beings whom we can contact. Was Amaringo an exception? Perhaps not. I showed prints of his paintings to many local people who used ayahuasca. Everyone recognized ayahuasca immediately as the source of these images. Moreover, once the book was published, fellow anthropologists took it to various indigenous Amazonian communities, causing a certain commotion. Perhaps there is something common to the ayahuasca experience that transcends cultural diversity to a certain extent, even though specific metaphors from its effects may vary.

In 1986, I received a John Simon Guggenheim fellowship to study the ethnobotany of the Colombian and Peruvian Amazon, thanks to recommendations from Richard Evans Schultes, Peter Furst, and other researchers. For the first time, I had the luxury of concentrating on this endeavor fully for a year. Up until then, I had only my summer holidays available. I spent several months in the United States, visiting various specialists. For several weeks, Schultes hosted me in his home, where I could examine his amazing private library. At some point he gave me what he called a "red carpet," a card crediting me as a research associate of the Botanical Museum of Harvard University. He also advised me to go to the Sibundoy Valley, in the Colombian Upper Putumayo, to get acquainted with the ethnobotanical knowledge of the Kamsá and Ingano, the two indigenous groups that inhabited this beautiful valley high in the Andes.

In 1941, Schultes himself had done extensive fieldwork in the region, which is especially famous for the large number of species of *Brugmansia,* locally known as *borracheros,* growing there. Some of these species contain great concentrations of atropine and scopolamine and are highly regarded by local shamans, who cultivate them in their gardens. Mel Bristol, one of Schultes's graduate students, wrote his doctoral dissertation on Sibundoy ethnobotany in 1965. He realized that yagé was used in this area to study the properties of other plants, which was one of the ways through which *curanderos,* local healers, were able to expand their pharmacopeia. I spent a month with don Salvador Chindoy and his son Miguel Chindoy, Kamsá shamans with whom Schultes had worked, and collected plants with the help of Pedro Juajibioy, also a Kamsá, who, with Schultes's help, had studied botany in the United States.

Two beautiful sayings of the Kamsá have remained with me. The first I received from a young apprentice who was staying with don Miguel at that time. In an interview he referred to the garden of medicinal plants that the Kamsá and Ingano shaman have around their homes as *el jardín de la ciencia* (the garden of science), another way of expressing the idea of Peruvian vegetalistas that certain plants are plant teachers or doctors. The second goes like this: When we are in the womb of our mothers, we are connected to the placenta, which is for us the universe. When we are born, the umbilical cord is cut. Yagé is a new umbilical cord connecting us to the universe.

A drawback for me while I was with the Kamsá is their use of alcohol. They drink *chicha,* a maize beer, heavily, and several times they tried to get me drunk. They also drink aguardiente, sugarcane liquor, in the yagé sessions, something that did not match my own habits or the views of don Emilio, who said that when you are learning with ayahuasca, you should not drink "even a drop of alcohol."

After a month in the Sibundoy Valley, I decided to go back to Peru to look for a teacher. My Shipibo friend Guillermo Arévalo advised me to go to Santa Rosa de Pirococha, a small indigenous settlement on the shores of the Ucayali River, where I would meet don Basilio Gordon, a reputed shaman who he said would help me. I took a ferry from Pucallpa and arrived carrying a few presents: tobacco and some clothes for don Basilio, beads for the women, and candies for the children. Someone advised me also to take several kilograms of sugar. I was well received by don Basilio, who let me stay with his family. The next morning, one of his daughters came to my mosquito netting–covered bed with a steaming cup. "Here is your tea," she said. I tasted it. It was hot water with sugar. Some hours later she came with another cup. "Here is your lemonade." It was cold water with sugar. Two days later they had run out of sugar. Don Basilio told me that we were all going to Orellana to get some things. I realized his whole family expected me to buy them presents! I took all the money I had with me, put aside the amount I needed to pay for the boat back to Pucallpa after my stay in

Santa Rosa, and gave don Basilio the rest to buy whatever they wanted. "This is all I have," I said. They bought some clothes and twenty-five kilograms of sugar, to which they were all heavily addicted, judging by the condition of their teeth.

I stayed with don Basilio for a month, during which I took ayahuasca thirteen times. My visions were mostly of a sort of underground, dark world. There was very little food available, just manioc and, from time to time, a little fish. I was able to watch don Basilio's work. He took ayahuasca nearly every night, and kept singing from nine o'clock in the evening to one or two in the morning, sometimes accompanied by an apprentice and a few patients. I did not see him using any other medicinal plants. "You need the plant only if you do not know its song," he told me.

After a difficult month during which I was tormented by mosquitoes and hunger, I was ready to leave. Don Basilio told me he was giving me an *arcana,* a protection, before I went back to the city. He sang a song over me, and I asked him, "What kind of protection are you giving me?"

From the floor of his house he took a skirt that was covered with geometric patterns, for which the Shipibo are well known. "I am giving you this," he said.

This was a confirmation of the work of the German ethnologist Angelika Gebhart, who realized that the colorful and intricate patterns found in the textiles, ceramics, and body painting of the Shipibo are to a certain extent representations of the songs of the spirits that shamans hear as they travel in the upper realm under the influence of ayahuasca. The shaman sings with the spirits, and then women are somehow able to transform the songs into beautiful patterns. The Shipibo believe their bodies are covered with normally invisible geometrical patterns. Illness is a disruption of the patterns. The songs of the shaman restore the patterns either directly or through a hummingbird spirit that creates music with his wings. The connection between ayahuasca visions and the artistic manifestations of Upper Amazon indigenous groups had already been pointed out by Reichel-Dolmatoff among the Tukano of the Vaupés

River region in Colombia and Brazil, and by Jean Langdon among the Siona of southeastern Colombia. These anthropologists also showed that a significant proportion of their narrative refers to journeys to other realms guided by shamans, and their encounters with the yagé people.

I had to wait for a boat back to Pucallpa. The family of a mestizo colonist gave me a plate of rice crowned by a fried egg, one of the best meals I have ever had in my life. The wait lasted for one and a half days. Finally, after quick good-byes to my friends, I was on board one of those Amazonian river ferries that has layers of hammocks hanging from its sides. There was nothing to do but chat, read, or look at the magnificent Ucayali River.

I had probably slept for several hours when I was awakened by one of the sailors: The captain wanted to see me. He pointed to the sky—at about 45 degrees above the horizon I saw a bright light that was about one third the size of the full moon, which over the course of about a half hour rose slowly in the sky until it became invisible. In the meantime, the captain told me stories of other such apparitions, for he spent many nights looking at the sky while at the wheel of his boat. Once he saw a huge saucer hovering some hundred meters in front of the craft, forcing him to stop the boat in terror before it ascended to the sky. I did not have a tape recorder with me then. About a year later and with my video camera, I looked for the boat at the Pucallpa harbor. I found it and went down to the machine room, where several people were working to clean the engine. I was told that the captain was now working on another boat somewhere else. Disappointed, I was about to leave when it occurred to me to ask the men whether they had seen any flying saucers. Nearly all of them said they had. I later realized that tales of flying objects in various disguises are quite common among the river people of the Peruvian Amazon.

Pablo Amaringo's ayahuasca visions include many depictions of UFOs. "They are not machines," he said. "They are spirits, and come from other dimensions" (see http://deoxy.org/ayalien.htm). As Valle has pointed out,[18] the UFOs are physical manifestations that cannot be understood apart from their psychic and symbolic reality. The UFO motif is a subject that should not be neglected by cognitive anthropologists, depth psychologists, and those interested in the mythologies of modern man. To my knowledge, there has been no study of this motif by anthropologists. I myself have avoided mentioning UFOs in my writings, because consideration of their accounts is not well received in academic circles. Yet they should be taken into consideration. I realized, for example, that the so-called *supay-lancha,* a big serpent boat believed by river people to appear sometimes at night, is one of the manifestations of the snake canoe of Amazonian myths. Flying saucers may be one more manifestation of the so-called *huairamama* (from the Quechua *huaira,* meaning "air," and *mama,* meaning "mother"), a flying serpent that alien beings of various kinds may use to travel.

STUDYING THE BRAZILIAN
AYAHUASCA PHENOMENON

In May 1991, Dennis McKenna and I were invited to be guest lecturers at the I Congresso em Saúde (First Conference on Health) in Saõ Paulo, organized by the Center of Medical Studies of the UDV, one of the three religious organizations that use ayahuasca as a sacrament and the one with the greatest number of members—about seven thousand spread across all Brazilian states. Approximately 5 to 7 percent of the members of the UDV are health care professionals, including medical doctors, psychiatrists, psychologists, homeopathic physicians, and chiropractors. During the conference, Dennis and I presented to them the possibility of carrying out a biomedical study of ayahuasca, which we had been considering since 1985. The idea was accepted enthusiastically and the study was started in July 1993.

I was not able to join the group, but Jace Callaway, the pinoline specialist I met in Finland, McKenna, Charles Grob, and Glacus de Souza Brito (a member of the UDV) conducted the research at one of the oldest centers of the organization, in Manaus, in the state of Amazonas, with subsequent laboratory investigations in Brazilian, American, and Finnish universities. The study was funded by Botanical Dimensions, the Heffter Institute, and the Multidisciplinary Association for Psychedelic Studies (MAPS). They performed psychological evaluations of fifteen members of the UDV, each of whom had been a member for more than ten years, and had been drinking ayahuasca once every two weeks, comparing the results to those of fifteen control subjects from a similar socioeconomic background who did not drink ayahuasca.

The published studies[19] showed that members of the UDV had exceptionally healthy psychological profiles. They had significantly greater confidence versus fear of uncertainty, trends toward greater gregariousness versus shyness, and greater optimism versus anticipatory worry. They also showed greater stoic rigidity versus exploratory excitability, greater regimentation versus disorderliness, and a trend toward greater reflection versus impulsivity. None of the UDV subjects showed evidence of any neurological or psychiatric deficits. Five of them had diagnoses of former alcohol abuse disorders, two had past major depressive disorders, and three had past phobic anxiety disorders.

The team took blood samples and also studied the pharmacokinetics of the alkaloids in the brew. An interesting finding was that ayahuasca drinkers have a higher density of serotonin transporter receptors in blood platelets. Back in Finland, Jace Callaway conducted self-experimentation with ayahuasca, and, using Single Photon Emission Computerized Tomography (SPECT) scanning facilities at Kuopio University, found a higher density of serotonin transporter receptors in his frontal cortex, which returned to normal levels after he stopped drinking the brew. It is not clear what this means, but it is interesting that a deficit of serotonin-uptake sites in this area has been found to correlate with aggression disorders in violent alcoholics. If tetrahydroharmine is able to reverse this deficit specifically, it may have applications in the treatment of this syndrome. Ayahuasca has been used in the treatment of alcoholism and drug abuse, especially in cocaine and heroine addiction, at Takiwasi, an institution created in Tarapoto, Peru, by the French physician Jacques Mabit, who arrived in the Peruvian Amazon in 1986 to work for Doctors without Borders (Médicins Sans Frontiéres). There he familiarized himself with the ayahuasca mestizo tradition and incorporated it into his own practice. Dr. Mabit has been working there together with his Peruvian wife, Rosa Giove, who is a psychologist.

My relationship to the Brazilian ayahuasca phenomenon deepened as I arrived in Florianópolis, in southern Brazil, to take the position of visiting professor in the department of anthropology at Federal Santa Catarina University. Professor Jean Langdon, one of the pioneers in ayahuasca ethnological research due to her work among the Siona of Colombia, encouraged me to apply for this position. I asked permission from the UDV to conduct research among its members, and was able to visit many of its centers all over Brazil, conducting interviews and participating in rituals. The UDV is an initiate religious organization with a highly hierarchical organization and four levels of initiation. Only men can achieve the fourth level, that of a *mestre* (master). Rising through the ranks depends upon, in part, the memorization of a series of *histórias* (stories), which are gradually revealed orally to the neophyte, and upon conducting a public and private life according to the precepts of the organization.

The main reason for taking the brew is, in the context of UDV, the individual's spiritual development. Regular members take vegetal (ayahuasca) every two weeks. Members higher up in the hierarchy take it more often and have special sessions reserved just for them. I was only invited to general sessions. The rituals are very simple and are conducted by a mestre. All members take the brew simultaneously and spend the rest of the session sitting in comfortable chairs. The temple is well lit and has a minimum of decorative elements. The main texts of the organization are read when people are already feeling the effects of the brew. From time to time, the mestre sings a *chamada,* one of the songs taught by the founder, Mestre Gabriel, or revealed to one of the members of the organization. The songs have to be approved by one of the highest committees in the organization. The mestre also addresses the community, commenting on various aspects of the doctrine. Members can ask questions or ask permission to address other participants. Prerecorded music is also played during parts of the session. Although members of the UDV emphasize the originality of Mestre Gabriel's teachings, these may be seen as arising within the context of a heretofore poorly documented Brazilian vegetalista tradition. I once met an ayahuasquero, Senhor Domingo, in Boca do Acre, a town some kilometers from Rio Branco, who sang variations of some of the songs received by Mestre Gabriel "from the astral plane."

Perhaps the most striking element of the UDV's use of ayahuasca is what they call the "mystery of the word." The organization's members cultivate a careful use of language, because they believe that words spoken under the influence of the brew are particularly powerful. Even mestres with a modest degree of formal education can be very eloquent when conducting sessions under the effects of ayahuasca. If we employ the frequently used metaphor of right–left hemisphere, we could say that the UDV is predominantly left hemispheric, seeking the orderly application of speech. Many of its members are highly educated, including university professors, lawyers, and journalists. It is to a great extent because of the influence of the UDV that the religious use of ayahuasca was approved in Brazil in 1987. The organization has some centers outside Brazil, including the United States, where, in 2005, a lawsuit seeking the exercise of its rituals was decided in the UDV's favor by the U.S. Supreme Court.

In June 1995, I went back to Rio Branco, in the state of Acre in the Brazilian Amazon, where I experienced for the first time the rituals of the Barquinha, the religious organization created by Daniel Pereira de Matos. In several ways, these are radically different from those of the UDV. The churches of the Barquinha are profusely adorned with effigies of Jesus, Mary, and various saints. The faithful participate in long rituals in which the whole community prays and sings *hinos* in the church. After midnight on special days, they have *festas* (celebrations) during which they dance for many hours, accompanied by the rhythm of musical instruments (drums, guitars, and electric piano). Some members incorporate spirits of the Afro-Brazilian pantheon: *pretos velhos* (spirits of black slaves), *caboclos* (spirits of Indians), *eres* (spirits of children), and *encantados* (spirits of princes and princesses incarnated in plants or animals). The first time I joined the members dancing around a *coreto,* a central bandstand where the musicians were playing, it was like entering an invisible stream that carried me along with the other celebrants. This is the Brazilian religious organization with the greatest number of church rituals. I calculated that during 1995, one of the three Barquinha churches had 173 rituals in the church and nineteen celebrations—a total of 192 ceremonies in which members took Santo Daime. In spite of this intense, ritual life, members of the church have regular jobs.

One of the consequences of repetitive use of ayahuasca is the need for less sleep. Jace Callaway speculates that the visionary state is perhaps equivalent to REM sleep; hence, the individual who take ayahuasca feels refreshed even if he or she sleeps only four or five hours every day. Among the members of the church, I did not see any signs of health deterioration due to the use of ayahuasca. Some of them are third-generation members of the church who have taken ayahuasca literally since they were in the wombs of their mothers—women take ayahuasca throughout pregnancy, give birth under the effects of the brew, and breast-feed their children while they are active members of the religious organization.

For several years, I dedicated my free time to conduct fieldwork among members of the Barquinha: I participated in many rituals and observed special healing and counseling sessions in which several mediums incorporate the spirits of black slaves to give advice about various matters to people seeking guidance in solving their physical or emotional problems.[20] The mediums in Barquinha claim that they are conscious and maintain their identity, while, simultaneously, they feel the presence of other beings who talk through them. More than once, I consulted with the pretos velhos, and I was always surprised at the wise words of these otherwise ordinary people. Once, I went to the forest to harvest *Banisteriopsis* vine, which may grow all the way up to the forest canopy; it is sometimes necessary to climb quite high to cut its farthest sections. The church members told me the story of one their fellows who suffered a panic attack when harvesting the vine twenty meters above the ground. He finally incorporated a preto velho, who helped him climb down safely. This made me think of the possible evolutionary advantages of altered states of consciousness.

Barquinha people prepare the strongest ayahuasca I have encountered in all the years I have been studying the brew. They add more *Psychotria* to the preparation than the other religious organizations and Peruvian mestizo shamans. Their dedication to their religion is total, encompassing both their spiritual and social life.

RESEARCH CENTER

In 1997, twenty-six years after my first ayahuasca experience, at the request of some friends, I invited them to take the brew under my guidance. Gradually, I gained confidence and started to conduct sessions from time to time, creating, ultimately, a simple ritual that incorporated some of the techniques I had witnessed during my years of exposure to various traditions as well as my own ways of conducting sessions. In 1998, I went back to Helsinki but did not cut my ties with Brazil. I acquired a piece of land in Florianópolis and built a house, the site of Wasiwaska—Research Centre for the Study of Psychointegrator Plants, Visionary Art and Consciousness, a nonprofit organization dedicated first and foremost to ayahuasca research. The term *psychointegrator* has been adopted from Michael Winkelman,[21] who proposed it as an alternative to *hallucinogen, psychedelic,* and *psychotomimetic* to represent the central effects of these important spiritual, therapeutic, and mystical agents as well as their primary effects at physiological, experiential, psychological, and social levels.

Several studies have been conducted at Wasiwaska. Two of them, led by Ede Frecska, evaluated effects of ayahuasca on binocular rivalry, a class of visual illusion in which an ambiguous but unchanging sensory input leads to sudden perceptual switches. Rivalry phenomena occur when dissimilar images stimulate corresponding retinal areas of both eyes. During rivalry, the image present in one eye disappears from awareness (i.e., it is suppressed), while only the other eye's image is perceived (i.e., it is dominant). Ingestion of ayahuasca resulted in a decrease of rivalry alternation rates and an increase in the length of one percept. In addition, there was evidence of perceptual fusion.[22] The latter may indicate the presence of inter-hemispheric fusion as an underlying neurological process of the psychedelic experience.

A second study explored the effects of ayahuasca on binocular rivalry with dichoptic stimulus alternation (DSA). Stimuli are applied to the eyes in a rapidly alternating, instead of constant, manner. It was concluded that ayahuasca induces changes of gamma oscillations in the visual pathways.[23] Gamma (20–70 Hz) brain wave oscillations are prominent in the active brain. They represent a widely studied band of EEG frequencies co-occurring with information acquisition and are associated with various behavioral functions ranging from sensory binding to memory. Neurons that oscillate together (within one millisecond precision) work together regardless of how far apart they are from each other in the brain.

Gamma oscillation can be conceptualized as the clock speed of the group of synchronized neurons that are processing the same task—for example, binding several sensory inputs (visual, auditory, etc.) into one subjective percept or performing memory tasks. Gamma synchronization may explain some experiences of altered states of consciousness. For example, synesthesia, such as "seeing" sound, can come from synchronized activity of some visual and auditory neurons. It may also reflect the "binding" of the elements in normal consciousness.

EEG studies of ayahuasca were carried out in 2000 by David Stuckey, under the direction of Professor Frank Echenhofer of the California Institute of Integral Studies, San Francisco. The study was carried out using only two experienced subjects. The most important finding was that in both subjects, global EEG coherence increased in the gamma frequency band for ayahuasca. Coherence is a measure of the similarities of the EEG at two different sites and can be considered as a measure of communication between two regions of the brain. Widely distributed cortical hypercoherence seems reasonable given the intense, synesthetic phenomena that often take place during the ayahuasca experience.[24] During intense meditative experiences by Zen monks,[25] there are reported high levels of gamma activity and coherence in the brain, especially in the frontal lobes, an area of the brain (the "new brain") that seems to be crucial in the process of awakening to a higher level of consciousness.[26]

In 2005, Frank Echenhofer and Katée Wynia conducted additional research in Wasiwaska during a seminar with twelve subjects from nine countries. Although brain wave analysis is not yet completed, preliminary results show alpha and theta decrease, while confirming gamma coherence increase as well as an increase in beta coherence. These changes can be viewed as suggesting an increase in cortical activation, alertness, arousal with enhanced information processing, and enhanced neural and cognitive complexity.[27]

✧

All these years of studying ayahuasca have been very rewarding for me, not only in terms of personal experiences but also as the result of collaboration with scientists in various disciplines as well as with artists and other creative people. My current work as a facilitator has garnered me contact with extraordinary individuals from many parts of the world. No doubt, ayahuasca has great potential for the study of consciousness as well as for therapeutic use. As Penrose has stated, "[A] scientific world-view which does not profoundly come to terms with the problem of conscious minds can have no serious pretensions of completeness. Consciousness is part of our universe, so any physical theory which makes no proper place for it falls fundamentally short of providing a genuine description of the world."[28]

I believe ayahuasca—as well as other psychointegrator plants and substances—can be an extraordinary tool for the study of conscious-ness. Ayahuasca and other plant teachers, as pointed out by Tupper,[29] may enhance "existential intelligence," which Howard Gardner, propo-nent of the Theory of Multiple Intelligence, characterizes as involving "a heightened capacity of appreciation and attention to the cosmological enigmas that define the human condition—an exceptional awareness of the metaphysical, ontological, and epistemological mysteries that have been a perennial concern for people of all cultures."

At the same time, it is necessary to exercise caution, for the number of contemporary ayahuasqueros from many countries is growing, and not all of them have enough personal training to deal with the wide spectrum of effects ayahuasca may produce. Special attention must be paid to set and setting, with *set* referring to the intentions, expecta-tions, and presuppositions of those participating in the ayahuasca ses-sion and *setting* referring to the concrete circumstances in which the action takes place, including the set of those in whose presence the aya-huasca is taken. If used in the proper setting, the negative side effects of ayahuasca seem to be minimal. Its strong emetic and cathartic effects as well as the often dramatic psychological effects it produces cause respect for its use, thus reducing potential for abuse. The spontaneous reaction of many people to ayahuasca is the acknowledgment that they are dealing with something sacred.

It is most important to take care in choosing the people with whom the brew is taken. When dealing with individual shamans or practitioners, it is important to discern the experience and intentions of the leader in question, for anyone who takes ayahuasca may enter into a vulnerable emotional space in which support is needed. Religious orga-nizations are usually trustworthy in these respects, thanks to the high ethics and the memberships' experience with ayahuasca. Yet these also have their limitations, as the framework they offer may be too rigid due to their doctrinal "truths" if they do not resonate with one's own convictions. The mystery of ayahuasca always remains, and it is beyond any particular set of ideas. In my own work, I emphasize exploration of one's own presuppositions and then the sharing of experiences, so that we may learn from each other.

In our current fragmented and ever-changing postmodern world, the rediscovery and restoration of traditional integrative techniques may become crucial, especially in view of the present ecological crisis caused by humans. There is no contradiction between the scientific and the shamanic understanding of human existence and the nature of reality. Instead, these approaches are complementary, and may allow a greater understanding of the multidimensional world in which we live.

5

The Varieties of the Ayahuasca Experience

Luis Eduardo Luna, Ph.D.

The use of ayahuasca has been documented among indigenous Amazonian groups, mestizo practitioners, and members of Brazilian religious organizations. There is also a growing body of scientific knowledge from various disciplines regarding ayahuasca as well as a number of reports in popular publications and on the Internet describing people's experiences with the brew in various contemporary settings. Here lies a great opportunity to learn about the potential of this powerful psychotropic combination, one of the greatest discoveries of indigenous Amazonians. We could also add to our exploratory list other South American discoveries: *curare,* the arrow poison made from several species of the genus *Strychnos,* which contain muscles relaxants without which open-heart surgery would not be possible; quinine, pivotal in the fight against malaria; and rubber, essential for the tires and tubes of the twentieth century's transportation revolution.

As they are with taking any other psychotropic plants or substances, set and setting are absolutely crucial to the effects of taking ayahuasca. When treating their patients, indigenous and mestizo practitioners usually demand a period of preparation that may include one to several days of dietary restrictions and sexual abstinence before and after a session, especially when illness is believed to be caused by an animate agent, spirit, or person. These requirements are much more flexible when these practitioners are dealing with non-Amazonians.

Among religious organizations, there is less or even no emphasis on diet, except for alcohol, which is generally not consumed at all. More important are the religious calendar (usually rather demanding), the particular doctrine of each organization, and the ritual procedures followed by the organization. Even within a religious organization, there are different kinds of sessions that affect participants differently. In the religious organization known as Barquinha, for example, some sessions may emphasize devotion, some may be focused more on healing, and some may emphasize the incorporation of spirits who give advice through mediums. The União do Vegetal (UDV) has regular sessions for all members and special sessions in which some members are initiated into specific, secret teachings. Especially important for religious organizations are the so-called *fetios* or *preparos,* during which the brew is prepared while members are under its effects. Unlike religious groups, independent practitioners often have their own rules, depending on the traditions in which they trained and their particular inclinations.

Traditional ayahuasca sessions are idiosyncratic to a certain extent, involving a variety of ritual procedures and the playing of different musical instruments. Among mestizo practitioners, there are often invocations to protective powers (which may include Jesus and Mary) at the onset of the ceremonies. Such invocations contribute to a feeling of trust, as participants are often apprehensive, regardless of their past experiences with ayahuasca. In the last decade, the advent of new ayahuasqueros who come from different countries and diverse cultural backgrounds has increased the variety of ayahuasca rituals. Some contemporary practitioners, for example, incorporate techniques and procedures from various therapeutic schools.

We will concentrate here on certain aspects of ritual ayahuasca use, rather than recreational use—a type of respectful practice that is neither strictly shamanic nor religious. Participants in this kind of ritual setting normally do not share a common cosmology, as is the case among indigenous groups, or a set of religious beliefs, such as that proposed by Brazilian syncretic religious organizations. In this model of ritual, the philosophical and existential presuppositions of each person vary, depending on each individual's background and inclinations. A comparable model is the work of Siona shamans as described by Langdon,[1] who, through songs, guide the community to specific locations of their spiritual geography, which consists of several domains characterized by specific sounds, rhythms, music, smells, and colors. They take yagé (ayahuasca) during three consecutive nights during which they visit, for instance, the High River of one of the domains of "the other side."

Under appropriate conditions, ayahuasca allows those who take it to enter into mysteriously deep states of consciousness in which a person may confront the great questions, especially those of our own temporality. Such questions deal with the great unknown—with the deepest mysteries of existence, and therefore with the sacred.

Certain procedures seem to be conducive to deeper experiences. By the time participants have their first session, they should be already acquainted, through lectures, films, or publications, with the botany, pharmacology, and different aspects of traditional ethnographic use of ayahuasca. Ideally, they have seen the living plants and know how the particular brew they are to take has been prepared. They should also be aware of the necessity to avoid substances such as antidepressants at least two weeks before the experience, as well as certain foods that may affect them adversely. All unnecessary medicines should be discontinued at least a week prior to the experience to avoid any possible adverse interaction with ayahuasca. The more thoroughly a person has prepared himself for the ayahuasca journey, the better the outcome of the experience.

All rituals presuppose the delimitation of ritual space and time. The space should be protective, beautiful, and as close to nature as possible, where participants can be sure that there will be no disturbances. An aesthetically pleasant environment supports deep inner exploration. The brew often takes a person to profound, even frightening recesses

of the human psyche. To emerge from such depths to a beautiful setting is comforting. The time of day is also important. Most sessions
begin at around eight or nine in the evening and extend into the early
hours of the next day. Astrologic variables may be taken into consideration. Based on substantial data related in public lectures, Stan Grof
and Richard Tarnas came to the conclusion that an analysis of natal
charts, personal transits, and world transits yields the best explanation
we have so far to account for the great variety of psychedelic experiences described by the same person at different times.

Group experiences often offer the best session results, perhaps
because a sort of synergistic process takes place. It is reassuring to know
that each of us is not alone in the potential struggle of accessing new
information about the self or the inner world. The metaphor of the
spirit canoe is sometimes used by ayahuasqueros: although participants
may have their individual experiences, there is also the feeling of soli-
darity during the journey.

Ayahuasca is full of surprises. Even in several sessions that occur
in succession within a few days, experiences may differ greatly. In fact,
there is great variability all along—from the preparation stage to the
ingestion stage. First, there is variability in the brew itself, depending on the specific plants used (admixture plants can be different and
include *Psychotria viridis* or *Diplopterys cabrerana* and other plants), the
age of the plants, the soil conditions in which the plants have grown,
the part of the plant used, and even the particular time of harvesting
(month, moon phase, and time of the day). The mode of preparation of
the brew is also important: the ratio of the plant ingredients, the hours
of boiling, and a number of other factors of which only experienced
ayahuasqueros may know—the intensity of the fire used; the way the
brew is bottled; even, as it is often claimed, the thoughts and intentions
of the people preparing the brew. Second, it is important to recognize
that every person is different physiologically, psychologically, and culturally. Some people are quick to metabolize the active compounds in
the brew; some metabolize them more slowly. Some people are more

sensitive to the brew. For some—probably most—it is best to have an empty stomach before taking the brew. For others, though, it is best to eat a little before or even after taking the brew to aid in the absorption of the active alkaloids.

Most people begin to feel the effects after forty-five minutes to an hour—but some people may feel them after only twenty minutes, and others may feel little until an hour and a half or even two hours have passed. In the Peruvian ayahuasca tradition, local ayahuasqueros often ask people to "keep the diet" three days before and three days after the session. This implies no salt or sugar, no sex of any kind, and no alcohol or cold drinks, along with some other dietary restrictions. How strict the diet is depends on the intention of the person taking ayahuasca: Is it for healing, for learning from the plants, or simply for curiosity? In traditional societies, when the aim is to become an ayahuasquero, the diet is much stricter, consisting of only plantains, manioc, rice, and small fish with little fat.

Ideally, an experienced leader—someone who is familiar with the varieties of states elicited by ayahuasca—should conduct the session. The role of the facilitator in an ayahuasca session is both crucial and delicate. Perhaps his or her most important role is to transmit confidence, inducing a spirit of courageous exploration, so that participants dare to go as deeply as possible into their experiences. They should trust that the facilitator is able to handle any situation that may arise. In the rituals of syncretic religious organizations, the entire setting is very supportive. Religious leaders usually have many years of experience leading rituals, and participants either sit or stand and the lights remain on. Sessions conducted the Amazonian way, in the dark, are much more demanding.

Theory cannot substitute for experience in leading these sessions, and can be acquired only through guided practice. Conducting an ayahuasca session is a matter of great responsibility. The facilitator, shaman, or religious leader, who normally also takes the brew, must be able to function under its influence and be available when needed—what

vegetalistas call *dominar la mareación* (to have control over the inebri-
ated state). In traditional and religious settings, the ritual leader always
takes the brew. This seems also to be the case among contemporary ayahuasqueros. It is essential, then, that the person facilitating the session
have the ability to function effectively under the effects of ayahuasca,
and that he or she be able to tackle whatever situation comes up during
a session. It is important to note that when leading a ritual, experiencing the effects of the brew is not equal to impairment; under the influence of the brew, an experienced person seems to be in touch with some
higher source of knowledge, a higher self, or a transpersonal power and
may perceive, think, speak, and act differently and more effectively, as
if an inner voice was speaking through him or her. Something similar
may be observed among some leaders of religious organizations who are
often very eloquent under the influence of ayahuasca, even if they have
only a modest educational background.

On the other hand, caution is also important. Ayahuasca is a powerful substance, and people who take it often have deep and meaningful experiences. Because participants in a session are usually grateful
to the person who facilitates the experience, there is a potential for
abuse—some may use the sacrament only as a means to obtain material gain or even sexual favors. It is advisable not to place too much
emphasis on the particular person who happens to facilitate the experience, thus avoiding altogether the creation of cult leaders and the traps
of power. Perhaps the greatest danger in this path of knowledge is ego
inflation. Humility seems to be essential to any leadership progress. In
traditional societies, ayahuasca is considered to be the real teacher; the
shaman simply helps the neophyte to deal with the plants. In our time,
the number of ayahuasca practitioners, indigenous and otherwise, is
growing, and each legitimizes his or her practice in various ways. Such
phenomena as projection and transference are quite common. Ethical
standards similar to those used in psychiatric and psychological practice should be in place. Unfortunately, the current legal situation does
not permit an open discussion of these issues.

It is usually beneficial to have as clear an intention as possible or to pose a specific question or questions before the session. Thoughts and wishes during an ayahuasca ritual seem to be highly operative in a mysterious way. The Shuar, of the Ecuadorian Amazon, believe that we take ayahuasca not "to *see* the future," but "to *create* the future." A strongly felt intention may set the course of the experience.

Most people approaching the ayahuasca experience are usually respectful, regardless of their cultural background; such is the reputation of the brew. Here are some statements recorded during fieldwork among educated Westerners from many countries and religious backgrounds when asked why they were taking ayahuasca:

- "To look at approaching my life in a different way."
- "I am experiencing some health issues and need guidance."
- "I am looking to explore my creative side at a deeper level."
- "I want to take ayahuasca for personal growth and psychological insight—that is, through deep inner explorations, I may learn more about myself, my capabilities, potential, and the best path or way to live."
- "I have some blockages, and I want to have courage to look at that."
- "I want to gain some clarity in those areas of my personality that are obscure for me."
- "I want to work through my destructive thought patterns."
- "I want to see visions that may help me in my healing process."
- "I want to recover my true essence, before [I experienced] any trauma."
- "I want ayahuasca to help me to become as good a therapist as possible."
- "I want to continue working with the spirits."
- "I want to reclaim my lost soul, to heal the shame I [have] carried most of my life."

After successive sessions the intentions may become more specific:

- "I want to go deeper. I just want to accept whatever comes."
- "I want to let go, not to be in control."
- "I want to learn where my anxiety comes from."
- "I want to explore more of what I was experiencing last night."

Many people take ayahuasca for personal healing; spiritual uplift; enlightenment; insight and inner peace; connection or union with the cosmic consciousness, nature, or planet Earth; or to find creative energy. Others take it "just to know."

There is great variety in ayahuasca experiences. A common theme is contact with alien entities that may take many shapes or the visitation to alien and, at times, highly technological worlds. Representations of such worlds are found in the work of Peruvian painter Pablo Amaringo, who paints the ayahuasca visions he had when practicing as an ayahuasquero.[2] Here is the transcript of an abduction experienced by a forty-five-year-old American male during an ayahuasca journey.

On April 4, 2007, I was abducted . . . I think. I say I think because when I think about the experience, I find it all so hard to believe. I have read about other people's abduction experiences and thought to myself, "[T]hese people must be looking for attention, or are nuts, it all sounds so fantastic." I am a mechanical engineer. My mind works like a calculator, in that to arrive at a solution there must be a formula; things need to add up logically. I really am at a loss with this experience because there are so many missing pieces of the formula. Up until this happened to me I really did not believe it possible. Now I am starting to understand how it may be possible. In my case my abduction did not take place in the physical world, as we normally know it. It took place on another level.

Several years ago, I had a NDE—near death experience—in

which a tunnel opened up and started to draw me in, like a vacuum hose sucking up a bug. Needless to say I held on and did not get sucked up, but I was intrigued! After that life-changing experience, I did some research into what enabled that suction tunnel to appear. In my research, I found that the pineal gland that resides in the brain may produce dimethyltryptamine, a powerful psychoactive compound that, when a person is dying, may be secreted directly into the brain. The dimethyltryptamine enables the mind to see things in ways it otherwise is unaware of. I found that shamans regularly drink a brew that they make from vines and other plants that are high in tryptamines called ayahuasca, during rituals to invoke spirit guides and journey to other places.

That experience and research brought me to an anthropologist and facilitator in the forests of Brazil and to drink the sacred brew ayahuasca, in the hopes that it would invoke that tunnel again, so I could explore what lies on the other side.

During an evening ceremony I was given a cup of what looked like between 160 and 175 milliliters of wretched-smelling dark syrup, which I drank. An hour later I found myself in a deep meditative state searching for the answers to my place in the universe. All of sudden, I was bathed in this white light from above, it felt like anti-gravity energy that lifted me up and out of my bed, and through the roof. This white energy beam was cylindrical and seemed like it had a diameter of 5 to 7 feet and reached up into the night sky. It seemed to separate me in two and lift an ethereal duplicate of my body. I tried to analyze the experience. As I was lifted up I could still see the other half of me still lying down in my bed. I felt that certain parts of my essence, a hologram of my body, and an impression of my mind and most of my consciousness was being pulled up. It felt good to be weightless and floating up, although I could still feel gravity. I was transported into a room within a ship, very clean, very sterile, well maintained, stainless steel and white, very muted white lighting, full spectrum. I was on a table, the kind of table you would see in the morgue because it was like a shallow tub and it had drains and a hose to wash it down. But it had cushioning, so I got the impression from the cushioning that I was not there just to be dissected, because there was some semblance of comfort that was provided. Nevertheless I was strapped down by the arms and legs, I don't think my chest was. Right away I felt that my consciousness was being sedated, but whatever it was that was sedating me was not enough. I immediately became conscious of my surroundings and tried to sit up and look around; at that point I became acutely aware of these beings—tall, skinny, kind of lanky, very thin-featured but with a praying mantis head, triangular and very bug like. I got the feeling they were very conscious and technologically advanced. The air conditioning in the space felt just right, I could hear the sound of a steady hum. The hum of a ship, structurally strong yet hollow-sounding, vibrating with energy.

Around me, around this table were instruments, tools of some kind, probes, strange manipulating instruments. They were hanging from the ceiling and some were attached to the walls. It wasn't a square room by any means, it seemed almost round and cylindrical and there were counters around the edge with a white muted light that seemed very full spectrum almost like shaded windows of some kind, but it seemed artificial, piped in. It was very relaxing and it had a soothing frequency to it. This hum seemed to manipulate and soothe me; it may not have been the sound of the ship, but possibly some kind of acoustic energy that permeated me in my mind. Somehow, with enough effort and concentration, I was able to overcome it. At some point they started adjusting the instruments and moving closer with them. I felt a little fearful but they assured me that it would be OK, and I responded with, "Look, I feel captive, and when a human feels captive, they have the innate feeling of the possibility of being raped or sexually violated. If it's a male, through his anus, or a female, through her vagina, and I think that for a woman, it's even worse, because if an unwanted seed is implanted in her, it could mean carrying an unwanted baby. Worse yet, a part-alien baby."

They seemed to just look at me in astonishment that I was trying to sit up and communicate with them. I further stated: "This is a give and take, if you need something, you are welcome to it, but as long as I'm undamaged and I leave this place intact and whole, just as I came or better, things will be OK. I don't want to break out of this state and wreck the place." After my statement, they seemed to be in a rush and quickly plunged these probes into my chest. I am not quite sure if they inserted devices or not. I get the feeling they were just looking and checking and taking some small biopsies and some blood and sperm and samples from my gut and bacteria that were in my body. Every time I felt uneasy, they somehow seemed to soothe my brain and told me to "relax" and that "it's going to be OK." As they were working on me, I forced myself back to semi-consciousness and looked around. It was very, very clean and sterile and well maintained. Everything just seemed shiny and spotless. After seeing how well maintained the room was, I felt comfortable there, yet apprehensive about what they were doing. At some point, a dog started barking back where my real body was (I thought it was interesting that I could still hear what my original body was experiencing), and I said, "I have to go." They said, "OK," and my chest was closed up and I said goodbye. I was quickly transported back to my bed and merged back with my self.

That ship took off and it seemed like another one immediately, very quickly assumed a position over the house and transported me up, somewhat violently and quickly. It was not a very comfortable ride up. I woke up on a dirty table; again it looked like a morgue table, but dirty and unsanitary. They had devices all around the table, and they were also a little dirty. They immediately started plunging instruments into my chest and clamping things around my organs, cylindrical metallic devices that they clamped around my aorta and my kidneys and my liver and my intestines and my spine. I'm not quite sure about my spine. I got the sense of something around my neck, like a collar. . . . Anyway, I forced myself into consciousness. They had a very sharp, piercing auditory energy, which was somewhat painful, that seemed to try to push me back into unconsciousness. I fought it and willed up a burst of energy that felt as if I had burst out of my body. I looked at them when I came out of my body. I looked around, and pulled up very quickly and hard on the restraints. Later, when I woke up, I had a bruise on my arm, and I don't remember bruising it in any way that week. That sound forced be back to semi-consciousness and they plunged the things into me. It was very scary and painful. I felt like I was totally out of control. They did seem to stay away from my anus. I remember somehow conveying to them "You know, if you do something bad to me, things are not going to be good for you; it's going to get violent in this ship, and you will be discovered. I will wreck this place and I don't care what kind of restraints you have. It's not going to be a good situation for you." (Or me for that matter.) I felt that it could end up being a fight to my physical death. I looked at them, they looked reptilian with elephant-like, tough grey skin, with very little hair, the few hairs they did have were thick (they may have not been hairs at all but feelers like cats whiskers or the hairs of a bug). They had large eyes like an elephant's eyes. Their consciousness felt very reptilian with almost instinctual kind of thinking and quick communications. They stood [3.5 to 4.5 feet]; they had little arms and a large round cylindrical body with webbed feet with little claws. The closest thing I can relate them to is "Cousin Itt." (Cousin Itt was an alienlike caricature in a television show from the 1960s called the Addams Family. Cousin Itt was about three feet tall and was covered from head to toe with long hair. Cousin Itt spoke in a high-pitched squeal of gibberish that only the Addams family members understood.) They seemed to be able to move rather quickly and had a good amount of strength. I remember thinking: obviously they have been around longer than we have because they've got this technology and this ship, but they really should clean it up and maintain it better. And try and work with us rather than forcefully taking from us.

At some point it seemed like another presence was coming near, and they zapped me back to my bed. As soon as I was back, I was gently lifted again, it seemed like their ship left and another ship assumed their position over the house. I was lifted up into the other ship very gently, fluidly, smoothly, nicely and placed in a very comfortable bed without restraints and a nice pillow. I looked around and saw beings. They were a little scary, about seven feet tall with candelabra octopus-heads with what seemed like vast brains spread out within this large head. Kind of compartmentalized. At some point I felt three brains but I am not sure. One part of the brain was communicating, another part was taking care of bodily physical functions and another part was thinking and communicating with the other beings. A very spread-out brain situation. They had very strange, almost octopus-like heads with tentacles coming out of their head. But they had arms too; I think large very strong arms. I felt that I did not want to end up in a physical confrontation with them. It felt like they were gently probing into my chest and repairing the sloppy work the previous aliens had done, and were cleaning me up. However, they did not try to remove the devices. They seemed very understanding of my discomfort with the devices that the other aliens put in me, but indicated that they would not be taking them out. I looked around the ship, and noticed different colors. It wasn't as white as the first ship, or as dark and depressing as the second. It was cheerful, but very sophisticated in its depth. These beings were friendly. I indicated that I wanted to come out of my semi-consciousness state and meet them at a fully conscious level. They said, "Not yet; you're almost there; soon," almost like an invitation, like it was going to happen soon, maybe on my next voyage.

I'd like to meet those beings again. We can learn a lot from them. They have been around a long time. I'm not quite sure if they were from another dimension, but they certainly know how to travel. I got the sense that they have traveled far and for a long time. I indicated that I was getting the feeling that it was time for me to go, so they gently transported me back and I felt at peace. Although I wasn't happy about the implants, I felt that there was a resolution coming.

DOSAGE

In indigenous ceremonies as well as in ceremonies conducted by mestizo practitioners, it is the shaman who decides the dose (often a standard small cup or bowl is used). It is a common complaint by Westerners who visit the Amazon region that vegetalistas often under-dose them, perhaps to avoid difficult situations with foreigners who do not speak Spanish. The potency of the brew may differ greatly from shaman to shaman. There is also variation in the brew used by Brazilian syncretic religious organizations. If the set and setting are appropriate, it is best to take a strong dose—between 80 and 100 ml—of a well-prepared brew. The facilitator should, of course, be familiar with the potency of the brew in order to advise participants. In general, it is best not to be too conservative. An under-dose may bring all the undesirable effects of nausea and diarrhea and none of the transcendental ones. Ayahuasca is not toxic—the lethal dose is around 6 liters, an amount impossible to drink without vomiting.

Once participants are familiar with the strength of the brew, they should decide for themselves how much to take in subsequent sessions, increasing or decreasing the dose depending on their previous experience. After two or three sessions, participants usually know the optimal amount they can take. The facilitator should always be alert, however, because sometimes participants are too eager to have a strong experience and underestimate the potency of the brew. Participants must try to keep the brew in the stomach for at least one hour in order for the active components to have time to be absorbed fully. Body weight is a factor to be considered, although often it does not seem crucial, because people have different sensitivities to the brew. After about one and a half hours, participants may take a small booster. Slow metabolizers must be aware that they require a longer time to feel the effects; they should therefore wait longer before taking a booster. In rare cases a participant does not feel any effects even after repeated ingestion attempts, probably due to his or her metabolic processes. In addition, some people resist the experience altogether and are able to minimize it. Normally, though, a sufficient dose of ayahuasca is enough to produce powerful effects in most people.

DARKNESS AND STILLNESS

Among indigenous groups, there are roughly two models of ayahuasca ceremonies: collective ones, which take place in large, communal houses or *malocas,* where the space is illuminated by torches and there are dances to the sound of flutes, rattles, and other musical instruments; and private ones, which are shamanic in nature and are conducted in the dark. The mestizo riverine tradition follows the latter model, though in the Brazilian syncretic rituals, the temples are always illuminated. Darkness, however, strengthens the experience and minimizes distraction so that participants can turn toward their inner world. In contemporary indigenous and mestizo shamanic settings, near total darkness is a requirement.

Stillness also enhances the journey within. In traditional Amazonian settings, participants sit with their backs straight, but it is also possible to lie down, keeping the spine straight. Stillness is essential, especially during the hours in which the brew is most potent. Any movement—even movement of the eyes—and any word pronounced in the ritual space may sidetrack participants from their journey. Focus on the forehead, between the eyebrows, helps greatly in navigation. Geometrical patterns often appear in front of the inner eye. By using intention, it is possible to enter these patterns and see a three-dimensional or even four-dimensional space of unfathomable beauty. A participant should breath deeply and slowly and find a state of inner peace, especially when encountering difficult situations during the journey.

MUSIC

When used wisely, music can be an extraordinary navigational tool. Among the Cubeo, Makuna, Barasana, and other Tukanoan indigenous groups of the Vaupes region in Colombia, session participants tie rattles around their ankles and play panpipes or trumpets. Shuar shamans in the Ecuadorian Amazon may play a *tumánk* (a Jew's harp) or a *kitiár*, a two-string violin. In the mestizo tradition, the shaman sings throughout the session, often accompanied by a rattle made of leaves of a plant (*Pariana spp.*), with some breaks from time to time. Peruvian mestizo ayahuas-queros call these power songs *icaros*, and they say they receive them from the spirits of the plants during their initiation period. The number, variety, beauty, and at times complexity of the icaros are a sign of power or efficacy in the work of indigenous and mestizo shamans. Participants in the sessions often report that icaros have an influence in their visions or have healing properties by themselves. Among the Shipibo-Conibo of the Ucayali River, in the Peruvian Amazon region, the songs sung during the session are visualized as *quenés*, the complex geometrical figures women use in their ceramics, textiles, and body painting.[3]

Music has a marked effect on ayahuasca experiences and plays a role in shaping the general mood of a ritual. During a session, contemporary non-Amazonian rituals may make use of a wide range of recorded music, from traditional icaros to world music, classical, folk, vocal, instrumental, electronic, and so forth, with each type of music being conducive to different emotional states. During the ayahuasca experience, participants often have a heightened perception of music and are very susceptible to its influence. It may be that participants experience particular music as greatly healing. Some may experience interesting synchronicities involving a specific musical track that correspond to important moments in their subjective experience. It is sometimes interesting to use music that is culturally relevant for a specific group—for example, songs that were popular during certain periods of their lives, folk songs, or even children's songs that may evoke childhood memories. A certain melody may touch an inner chord, eliciting a torrent of emotions. Sometimes, participants experience certain music as particularly horrible. It is useful to study these emotions, because they may evoke inner states, memories, or associations that are rich in content.

During ayahuasca sessions, participants are especially open to experiencing music that they might not pay attention to or might dismiss as too far from their personal taste under usual circumstances. Through music it is possible to travel in time as well as in space. In this respect, tribal ethnic music may be especially evocative; it may allow for experiencing the extraordinary cultural diversity still existing in the world.

At some point, usually after several hours, dance music may be introduced gradually as a means to evoke a mood of celebration. It can even be therapeutic in itself, after the hard work of earlier hours. People may experience enormous joy, a release of tension. Through the movement of dance, participants may be able to express inner processes. Further, although it may seem far from traditional, dancing is an integral part of the great communal ceremonies of the Shuar and Cubeo as reported by Rafael Karsten and Irving Goldman. Dance is also an integral part of some of the rituals of the Santo Daime and Barquinha syncretic religious organizations.

Regarding the use of music throughout the session, every ritual and group has its own dynamic that must be respected. The ritual leader should be sensitive to the particular mood of each session, so as to harmonize with it while at the same time gently leading it through the choice of music. Today, through computer programs such as iTunes, it is easy to select the tracks to be played in any session in a way that is far less noisy and distracting than working with multiple compact discs.

Finally, the presence of the ritual leader can be made manifest by means of a rattle, drum, or other instrument that serves as a sort of Ariadne's thread for grateful participants so that they can feel there is somebody present who is watching over them in case the journey becomes difficult.

It is important to remember, too, that periods of complete silence are often very special. In addition, participants may sing either one after the other or simultaneously, according to an agreed-upon ritual, or they may hum gently. As a grounding tool in difficult situations, it may help to use a rattle. Of course, the possibilities are endless.

AYAHUASCA'S PHYSICALITY

As with other psychointegrator agents, the strong physical effects of ayahausca are notable. Vomiting and diarrhea often occur, especially during the first sessions. Some people even spend hours retching or having dry heaves. Other feel such weakness that they are almost unable to get up to go to the toilet or even ask for help. Some people experience waves of hot and cold flashes. In the initial phase of the journey, blood pressure may go down. Rarely, a person faints altogether for a few seconds. On occasion, some people have tachycardia; a strong heart and a properly functioning liver are necessary for any who embark upon the ayahuasca experience. It is advisable that participants receive a medical checkup before repetitive sessions. It is important to note, however, that after several sessions, participants usually become accustomed to the brew and either do not throw up at all or do so without much fuss.

The facilitator must take all these possibilities into account, checking participants often to be sure that everything is going well. It is advisable to have some salt at hand to help restore blood pressure, as well as water, because after several episodes of vomiting and diarrhea, it is important to drink to prevent dehydration. People should also be warned that the effects of ayahuasca often come in waves; they should not leave the ritual space before they are sure the effects have completely passed and before they have consulted with the facilitator. It is also best to ask novice participants not to lock the door from inside when they go to the toilet in case they need help and are unable to unlock it themselves. Participants should be instructed to ease themselves down to the floor at any sign of losing consciousness to avoid hurting themselves. In addition, during the session, some people have cramps, shake, or feel pain in various parts of the body, usually those parts that need healing.

All these symptoms that may appear dreadful are in fact a blessing; they add depth to the experience. The emetic and cathartic properties of ayahuasca may be associated with an inner cleansing process by which participants can rid themselves of bad habits, negative emotions, traumas, and so on. Ayahuasca may indeed be a detoxifying agent. After a series of sessions, one woman found that her blood levels of mercury poisoning had decreased drastically. When the session is over, participants very often report that they feel purified. This adds to the next morning's feeling of inner peace and clarity.

FEAR

Ayahuasca produces a profound modification of consciousness. Sessions may be dramatic for beginners and at times even for people with a degree of experience, as we can never be sure what will arise. An individual may undergo changes in body perception—such as transformation into an animal—or may have an out-of-body experience. Similarly, the visions participants experience may have terrifying content—individuals may even relive traumatic experiences—which are augmented by the physical reactions produced by ayahuasca. Some participants speak in seemingly strange languages (*glossolalia*); others are convinced that they are going to die and may undergo some kind of symbolic death or encounter apparently malevolent entities or monsters that threaten to devour them or experience being dismembered or disintegrated into countless pieces. Some people think they are becoming mad and that their mind is going around and around in a loop that seems to have no beginning and no end. Others see extraordinary landscapes, strange cities that are simultaneously ancient and futuristic, or realms of beauty beyond description. They may meet benevolent entities of many kinds or experience great adventures in strange realms or see themselves at past stages in their lives. Some even claim to experience their past lives.

Before a session, participants should be prepared to travel not only to ineffable, beautiful worlds but also to enter the shadows, to see the dark side of themselves. Often the worst experiences are the best ones. By going to the edge, people are confronted with their innermost fears, and therefore have a chance to be aware of them and perhaps resolve them. As one of the leaders of a syncretic Brazilian religious organization commented: "Taking ayahuasca is like going down into the cellar with a torch." A session participant once said that taking ayahuasca is like digging into the archaeology of the mind.

If participants have been properly prepared, they usually are able to deal with their fear, and they can surrender to the experience. Resistance often makes things worse. It is best to face fears—even give them a name—for when fear becomes more concrete, it is easier to handle. The emetic and cathartic properties of ayahuasca may be interpreted and experienced as some sort of detoxification in which participants dispose of physical and psychological problems. Many people report experiencing a kind of cleansing or rebirth after difficult situations during a session. We may say that the deeper a person enters into the experience, the richer are its benefits.

Despite preparation, however, some people are not able to deal with the fear or body symptoms they experience. It is crucially important that they receive proper and gentle but not intrusive help. Every facilitator develops his or her own ways of doing this. One way that some facilitators deal with a participant's inordinate anxiety is to place a thumb lightly between the eyes of the participant and the middle finger of the other hand in the participant's solar plexus. The participant is then invited to breathe deeply and slowly, concentrating all attention on this breathing activity. During this breathing, the facilitator hums, maintaining the tone as long as possible. This simple procedure has a remarkably calming effect: gradually, participants may synchronize their breathing with that of the facilitator or even hum with the leader. The finger in the solar plexus serves to monitor the heartbeat, the depth and intensity of breathing, and any possible bowel movement. After a few minutes of this, most people regain their confidence: Their breathing slows and their heartbeat returns to normal. When participants sigh deeply a few times, it is a sign that they are recovering their peace. When an individual has regained calm, a facilitator may ask whether he or she can cease attendance.

Some people have difficulty asking for help—indeed, asking for help may be experienced as a kind of healing in itself—or they may be too weak or terrified to do so. Because of this, the facilitator must be attentive and check that everybody is well. If they are thoroughly prepared in terms of what they may experience, however, most participants go through it without much drama. In this respect, most sessions are uneventful.

VISIONS, SYNESTHESIA, AND OTHER PHENOMENA

Though in general terms the ayahuasca experience has been charted,[4] as has been noted, the outcome of each particular session is rather unpredictable, even when the same person takes the same dose in successive sessions and the setting remains the same. Interestingly, participants often experience reverse tolerance: Effects tend to be stronger when several sessions take place within a few days. This is especially the case when the traditional dietary restrictions of salt, sugar, and alcohol are observed.

With either opened or closed eyes, participants have reported seeing visions of beauty and complexity impossible to describe and uniformly sharp. At times, these may appear as more real than normal reality. These strong aesthetic feelings are enormously uplifting, liberating, and therapeutic. Synesthetic experiences are frequent, such as auditory hallucinations and tactile sensations and an array of other possible effects. For participants, it is advisable to be active within the experience, to remember intentions, and to try to navigate purposefully within the visions. If, for example, the intention is to try to recall an episode from childhood, in trying to remember their childhood bedroom, they may suddenly be transported to the past. On one occasion, an Argentinean psychologist was able to recall in detail that she had witnessed the death of a girlfriend when she was about seven years old. Her parents had denied the episode, calling it a dream, and had told her that her friend had gone to live in another country. She discovered that this repressed memory had an adverse effect on her life, and she considered this recollection an extraordinarily healing event. Sometimes, for instance, participants may "discover" that as a child they were sexually abused by a relative. Some who were unwanted or unplanned children may even experience being in the womb of their mothers.

Participants in ayahuasca sessions are often deeply touched emotionally. Many people report that an ayahuasca session has been among the most important experiences in their lives. People often claim that the ayahuasca experience has led them to see their lives with new eyes, perhaps, for example, recognizing previously unconscious behavioral patterns. Some people feel the urge to get in touch with their partners, parents, or other family members to tell them how much they care for them. Others find a new perspective on their place in the web of personal and professional relationships. For still others, the ayahuasca experience leads to the acknowledgment of a spiritual dimension, to the feeling of connection to the natural world and the totality of existence.

As in any other human enterprise, practice helps. Gradually, participants gain confidence in handling the particular state of consciousness elicited by ayahuasca. Some participants are especially gifted and obtain extraordinary results even in their first session. Others need more time. In most instances, a few sessions are quite effective, depending on the intention, and it may be years before the experience is repeated. There are others who pursue this type of path more assiduously and even decide to undergo serious training.

NAVIGATION

With some practice, conscious navigation in the ayahuasca state is perfectly possible. As in normal life, under the influence of ayahuasca, a variety of objects are presented to consciousness, and we may choose which ones to pay attention to. Some people are more visual than others. For some, the greatest effects are in auditory perception. For others, the most powerful responses occur in the realm of realizations and insights.

For visual people, it is possible—although not always—to zoom in to a particular area of the inner visual field and follow its development. Sometimes, the scene remains relatively stable. At other times, it changes dramatically. In some instances, the visual bombardment is such that it becomes a nuisance. When participating in successive sessions, similar patterns may appear again and again, but often in new colors. At times the whole scene appears in pure, shining gold—or, even with eyes open, the visual field may be filled with a black, metallic color. Certain motifs are very common—for instance, the sensation of transformation into a serpent; or feeling a serpent growing inside the body, at times coming out of the mouth; or the sensation of being devoured by a serpent. Among the Shipibo-Conibo of Peru, a great serpent is believed to be the mother of all visions, which she keeps in her skin. Very often, people experience these serpents as benevolent teachers or as primordial mothers, as is the belief among some indigenous groups of the Upper Amazon.

INTEGRATION

Integration is a crucial part of the ayahuasca ritual. In the morning following a session, it is important to feel free to write, draw, or meditate. The time following a session is particularly creative for many. Participants almost unfailingly feel well physically; they are liberated, creative, and optimistic, regardless of how hard the night's session may have been. Some participants may be deeply shaken by the experience of the night before. A period of organized sharing is extremely beneficial. For some, this sharing is an opportunity to somehow clarify their own experiences.

At the same time, listening to others speak about their sessions has a remarkably positive effect. It may happen that somebody in the group finds an answer to a question or a beneficial formulation of his or her own experience in the utterances of somebody else. For some people, just the act of talking about their experiences and deep feelings helps to release inner tension. Even the physical struggles of the night before are seen in a totally different light; they often produce more laughter than concern. In such a group, people may have the courage to speak about intimate matters, past or present wrongdoings, and future aspirations. This in turn can resonate with similar feelings or situations in other people. Some prefer to keep silent—the experience may be too ineffable to describe in words. Of course, there should be the freedom to speak or not about the events of the night before.

Recollection varies. Some privileged people are able to experience long, intricate journeys in which they meet entities and have dialogues they can recall and transmit in detail. More often, participants remember only glimpses or fragments of what happened during the night. In general, it is advisable to write down a session's experience as soon as possible or to consolidate experiences by relating them to somebody to keep them from fading away rapidly, like a dream. Yet some people feel that trying to put the experience into words makes it somewhat banal, that it is actually ineffable and beyond description. Some people remember only that something important took place, perhaps an encounter with some being or something else they cannot recall—but they might also feel that recollection it is not important, that they have somehow assimilated the experience subconsciously.

Organized sharing the morning after often reveals common themes that emerged during a particular session. For example, several participants may find that they were dealing with family situations during their session or larger questions such as the future of our civilization or of our planet. Sessions are therefore often collective as well as individual journeys.

It is surprising to note that many people, during these integrative circles, claim that they received concrete answers to their questions.

Many participants—even those new to the experience—spontaneously personify ayahuasca, saying: "The plant told me . . ." They may call the brew "mother ayahuasca" or "grandmother ayahuasca." Many people seem to develop a relationship with the spirit of ayahuasca—who is almost invariably feminine. Not every experience, however, is memorable—yet it is common to hear participants claim, "[T]he experience went beyond my expectations" or "[I]t went beyond my wildest dreams." This is perhaps one of the greatest rewards of the ayahuasca experience: recovering—if it was lost—the sense of the mysterious. Where does all this information come from? Is it inside us? Is it coming from outside sources? How is it possible that we have access to such novelty and such beauty, to such splendor as well as horror? It is typical to spend some time after participating in a session pondering or writing about what happened or engaging in philosophical discussions.

The feeling of being healed at some level is one of the most common themes raised in the integrative session. Many report invisible hands, beings, or energies working on the body, exploring it, going through old surgeries, reorganizing internal organs, taking out things, operating with alien technology, and, in general, healing. There are evident parallels to the work of the spirits, as described by Eliade, in various shamanistic traditions.[5] There are also so many various reports of physical healing that it would be difficult to explain them in pharmacological terms.

Ultimately, the most healing effect is the realization that we are united with everything. Participants therefore find a deeper meaning to life. Meaninglessness is one of the most prevalent conditions that modern humans experience, embedded as we are in a scientific paradigm that all too often views the world as pointless. After an ayahuasca session, people may see their lives as a whole and see patterns in their life—and therefore also see meaning. Becoming aware of dimensions beyond the ordinary that enrich this world is considered by many to be profoundly healing.

It is not surprising that such expanded views of reality make some people more sensitive toward ecological issues. Fieldwork among members of the syncretic Brazilian churches, for example, reveal that many of them decided after participation in rituals to change their professions so that they could work with natural products or environmental issues.

Another remarkable effect of ayahuasca in a proper setting is its capacity to awaken some kind of strong ethical imperative. Many people report becoming aware of their wrongdoings and having the desire to correct their lives. Quite often people claim that their first ayahuasca experience was the most significant event in their lives. Such intense experiences, however, do not induce a longing for repetition. The brew is usually treated as something sacred and is not taken casually or recreationally.

After a session, it is common to feel a state of inner peace and clarity, an "afterglow" that may last for days, weeks, or even months—especially if a participant gives attention to the inner world through meditation or activities conducive to reflection and through following recommendations regarding food intake, including reducing the consumption of salt, sugar, and fatty food. In fact, a considerable number of people participating in ayahuasca sessions claim they abandoned sugar altogether or maintained a healthier diet after their experience. It is remarkable that ayahuasca works simultaneously at so many levels involving the body, the mind, and the spirit.

Another common result of ayahuasca sessions is enhanced creativity. Some people start to paint again or write or make music. In fact, ayahuasca has a pivotal role in the artistic and musical manifestations of those indigenous groups that use the brew. Indigenous body painting, designs in the communal houses or other objects of material culture, songs, and narratives are often thought to have been inspired by the yagé people, the animate agents these people's ancestors contacted and that they may also encounter on their inner journeys.

Ayahuasca also may be particularly effective in the resolution of addictions. Many people within various churches that use ayahuasca claim they abandoned alcohol, tobacco, or heavy cannabis or cocaine use thanks to their experiences with the brew. The Center for the Rehabilitation of Drug Addicts and the Investigation of Traditional Medicine, located in Tarapoto, Peru, and under the direction of French medical doctor Jacques Mabit, specializes in the treatment of heavy drug use through ayahuasca and other medicinal plants, apparently with excellent results.

SOCIO-INTEGRATION

One of the most remarkable effects of ayahuasca use is socio-integration manifested in the deep feeling of appreciation participants usually show for each other—as if each of them was able to perceive the inner self or essence of those present at the session. A strong feeling of bonding, almost a tribal feeling of belonging, is quickly created among participants, especially if they have the opportunity to be together during successive sessions. It is not uncommon for a high degree of communication on many levels to continue after participants return to their countries of origin.

The use of ayahuasca and other psychointegrator plants probably contributes to social cohesion and may be one of the reasons for the maintenance of tribal identity in healthy societies such as the Shuar of Ecuador, the Barasana of Colombia, and the Shipibo of Peru, allowing them to better cope with the great changes brought about through contact with dominant cultures. Social cohesion is also visible among members of the syncretic Brazilian organizations that use ayahuasca as a sacrament, some of whom say their religion is a *religião do sentir*—a "religion of feeling." Finding ways to enhance a sense of community is of great importance in our alienated society—even more so if we take into account the imminent global ecological crisis that may engulf even today's privileged people in the not-so-distant future.

✧

Here we have, then, phenomena of which modern science has no good models or theories. Ayahuasca—like other psychointegrator agents—

offers many possibilities if it is used in a responsible way. For some, it is a cognitive tool, an instrument of exploration on the workings of the mind. For religious people, it provides a new way of feeling convictions and the revelation that whatever our interpretation of reality, the mystery always prevails. For the artist, it opens huge vistas of yet-unseen worlds. For the therapist, it can provide new ways of understanding both ourselves and those who seek help. For many people, it offers, independent from any religion or philosophical orientation, the possibility of a revision of our path in temporality.

6

Magic Mushrooms

Slawek Wojtowicz, M.D.

There are dozens of species of sacred (or magic) hallucinogenic mushrooms belonging primarily to the genuses *Psilocybe, Panaeolus,* and *Copelandia.* Their ingestion produces significant physical, visual, and perceptual changes by means of their psychoactive compounds, the tryptamine psychedelics psilocin and psilocybin. Nearly all of the magic mushrooms are small and brown or tan in color and can easily be mistaken for any number of nonpsychoactive, inedible, or poisonous mushrooms in the wild. This makes them somewhat difficult to identify in natural environments and thus potentially hazardous. The primary distinguishable feature of most psilocybin-containing mushrooms is that they bruise blue when handled.

HISTORY

Sacred mushrooms have been part of human culture as far back as the earliest recorded history. Many of these mushroom species grow in cattle dung. Ancient paintings of humans decorated with mushrooms dating to 5000 BCE have been found in caves on the Tassili Plateau of northern Algeria. Native Americans in Latin America have also used sacred mushrooms for thousands of years for both medicinal and religious purposes. Between 3000 BCE and 1000 BCE these cultures built temples to mushroom gods and created stone icons carved in the shape of mushrooms, with stems depicting human figures.

In the mid-sixteenth century, the Spanish priest Bernardino de Sahagún described in his Florentine Codex the use of hallucinogenic mushrooms by the Aztecs:

> The first thing to be eaten at the feast were small black mushrooms that they called *nanacatl,* which bring on drunkenness, hallucinations and even lechery; they ate these before the dawn . . . with honey; and when they began to feel the effects, they began to dance, some sang and others wept. . . . When the drunkenness of the mushrooms had passed, they spoke with one another of the visions they had seen.[1]

During the early twentieth century, some Western academics doubted the existence of psychoactive mushroom cults. Though Sahagún mentioned *teonanácatl*—sacred mushrooms—in his diaries, the American botanist William Safford argued that the priest had mistaken dried peyote buttons for mushrooms. In the early 1930s, Robert Weitlaner, an Australian amateur anthropologist, witnessed and described a Mazatec mushroom ceremony (*velada*) northeast of Oaxaca, Mexico. Little more was known until the early 1950s, when amateur mycologist Gordon Wasson and his wife, Valentina Pavlovna, became interested in the traditional use of mushrooms in Mexico. In 1953, Wasson traveled to Huautla de Jimenéz, where he observed an all-night ceremony under the guidance of a shaman named don Aurelio. The couple soon discovered, however, that even though Native American shamans were willing to let them observe their rituals, they would not share sacred mushrooms with foreigners. Wasson's lucky break came during two subsequent trips to Mexico, which allowed him to meet the Mazatec *curandera* Maria Sabina, who on June 19, 1955, permitted Wasson and his companions to participate fully in a velada. In 1956, one of Wasson's associates, Roger Heim, requested help from Sandoz Pharmaceuticals in extracting the active ingredients of the mushrooms.

Albert Hofmann, a research chemist at Sandoz, isolated psilocybin and psilocin and developed a synthesis technique.

Wasson continued to travel to Oaxaca over the next years, and published the first widely distributed article about psychoactive mushrooms and the Mazatec velada in the May 13, 1957, issue of *Life* magazine. Experimentation began with the mushrooms and the synthesized active substances, and "magic mushrooms" were soon part of the psychedelic movement.[2, 3, 4] Through the 1960s, mushrooms and their active ingredients were used in the West recreationally and therapeutically and as part of new spiritual traditions.

In 1968, possession of psilocybin and psilocin became illegal in the United States, and in 1970 they were added to the new Drug Abuse Prevention and Control Act, commonly known as the Controlled Substances Act, which came into force in 1971. Research into their medicinal uses continued until 1977. Though recreational use continued, scientific research in the United States and Europe was on hold through the 1980s and 1990s due to strict governmental controls. In recent years, psilocybin and its effect on the human brain and mind have once again become the subject of scientific study.

MECHANISM OF ACTION

The hallucinogenic effects of magic mushrooms are induced by several alkaloids, primarily psilocybin, psilocin, and baeocystin. Psilocybin is more stable than psilocin, but is broken down into psilocin, the most active component of the mushroom, after ingestion. These compounds are closely related to DMT. The chemical formula of psilocin is 4-hydroxy-N, N-dimethyl-tryptamine. Psilocin is also a close relative of the neurotransmitter serotonin, and its resemblance to serotonin is responsible for its psychoactive properties. Psilocin binds to a specialized type of serotonergic receptor know as the 5-HT2a, where it acts as a partial agonist, stimulating some neurons but not others. It is not clear how this pharmacological activity translates into the characteristic psychedelic experience. One hypothesis is that these compounds increase activity of the sensorimotor gating system of the brain, which normally suppresses the majority of sensory stimuli from conscious awareness. The conscious mind is therefore overwhelmed by sensory stimuli and cognitive processes that are normally hidden in the unconscious part of the mind.

SPECTRUM AND DURATION OF PSYCHOLOGICAL EFFECTS

Depending on how much and how recently a person has eaten, mushrooms generally take fifteen to sixty minutes (though sometimes as long as two hours) to take effect. These effects last for approximately four to six hours after oral administration. A high-dose experience with mushrooms appears to be quite similar to an experience with DMT but with less intensity, perhaps because of the slower onset of effect. Visual and auditory alterations and synesthesia (the combining of two sensory modalities, such as seeing sounds) are often reported. Also described is a feeling of euphoria and heightened awareness of the inner self, frequently leading to increased insight after the experience.

Within minutes after ingestion, mushrooms frequently cause a feeling of anticipation or anxiety. There may be a feeling of energy in the body, and the sense that things are different from usual. As the effects intensify, a wide variety of perceptual changes may occur: mental stimulation, quickly changing emotions, and in some cases paranoia and confusion. More-advanced users may experience expanded spiritual awareness or a sense of universal understanding. Closed-eye visuals are extremely common, though open-eye visuals are more likely to occur at higher doses.

High-dose effects are usually characterized by closed-eye visualizations that are significantly more elaborate. Users report religious revelations; spiritual awakening; near-death experiences; dissolution of the ego; talking to seemingly external, autonomous entities; extreme emotional responses such as fear and joy; repressed memories or latent psychological crises that come to the surface; an increase in artistic sense; or intense feelings of wonder. High-dose effects may also include extreme time dilation, with the subjective experience of seconds or minutes feeling like hours or days. One of the most interesting effects that may be experienced by some users is the feeling of awakening for the first time ever from a previous state of sleep. Paradoxically, it is this new awareness that feels normal and natural while any previous existence appears to have been unreal all along. The person experiencing this effect is convinced that, once gained, this awareness is impossible to lose, but, inexplicably, by the next day it is just a memory.

The physiological and psychological effects of mushrooms are influenced by the dose and the individual's sensitivity to psilocybin. For some people, an amount as small as 0.25 g of dry mushrooms can be sufficient for a full visionary experience, unpleasant stomach cramps or gas, and other effects usually present at higher doses. In others, the same amount might not cause any noticeable effects. More-profound effects are induced with doses that range from 0.75 g to 2.5 g of dry mushrooms. This range of doses might induce powerful distortions of time and space as well as spontaneous, detailed imagery. These effects are often more pronounced in those who have used mushrooms previously. Emotional sensitivity and an increased ability to focus on emotional problems can raise the probability of dwelling on a single feeling that may have a negative content—and thus can lead to a psychological crisis.

At a dose ranging from 2.5 g to 10 g, the user can expect all of the effects of the medium dose, but usually with greater intensity and with a significantly greater likelihood of uncomfortable side effects, which may include pronounced nausea that can result in vomiting and significant mental discomfort associated with feelings of fear. These side effects usually lessen as the experience becomes familiar to the user. For an unprepared person, however, high doses can lead to acute adverse effects and may produce extreme fear, panic, and even psychosis. These psychological effects may share several features with acute, particularly paranoid, schizophrenia.

SIDE EFFECTS AND ABUSE POTENTIAL

Psilocybin and psilocin have low toxicity. The traditional measure of toxicity of a drug is a therapeutic index: a ratio of the dose that is effective (effective dose, ED) in 50 percent of subjects (ED50) to the lethal dose (LD) that kills 50 percent of subjects (LD50). According to the Registry of Toxic Effects, the therapeutic index for psilocybin is 641 (higher numbers indicate a better safety profile). Therefore, it is relatively nontoxic in comparison to other substances. For example, the therapeutic index for aspirin is 199; for nicotine, it is 21.

The greatest danger in using hallucinogenic mushrooms is an accidental ingestion of other wild mushroom species that look similar to psilocybin-containing ones but are poisonous. Many wild mushrooms contain toxins that can lead to liver or kidney failure and death. In addition, the hallucinatory effects of magic mushrooms can put people at risk of accidents. Users may indulge in dangerous behaviors such as walking out in traffic or along railway lines and driving or operating heavy machinery while under psilocybin influence.

The physiological and psychological effects of mushrooms are influenced by both the dose and the individual's sensitivity. Physiological side effects are more likely to occur with higher doses and are usually self-limited, resolving within a few hours after ingestion. Effects most commonly reported are dilation of pupils, loss of coordination, dizziness, muscular relaxation, coldness of the limbs and abdomen, flushing of the skin, and a slight increase in body temperature. Various blood hormones and liver enzymes can also be elevated temporarily. Some less common side effects are nausea, vomiting, diarrhea, gas, stomachaches and cramps, shortness of breath, rapid heart rate, increased blood pressure, and headache. The medical literature reports one case of irregular heart rate (Wolff-Parkinson-White syndrome) and heart attack following ingestion of *Psilocybe semilanceata,* though these serious side effects occurred in a man with a genetic defect in the electrical wiring of his heart and likely were related to the high concentration of phenylethylamine in this particular sample of mushrooms.[5, 6, 7, 8]

Magic mushrooms and other psychedelics are powerful mental amplifiers and may trigger latent psychological and mental problems, particularly in individuals suffering from severe depression or anxiety or with a family history of schizophrenia or any other significant mental illness, specifically psychoses of the paranoid type.

Little is known about the long-term effects of magic mushroom use, though Mexican shamans have been using them for centuries. Psychological reactions to magic mushrooms are frequently affected by set and setting. *Set* refers to the subject's preexisting mind-set and *setting* refers to the surrounding environment in which the user experiences a psychedelic's effects. Recent negative experiences can induce serious distress and trauma following exposure to psychedelic substances.

Psychological side effects may include anxiety; unwanted, difficult, or frightening thoughts and visions; anguished introspection; and temporary changes in an individual's perception of life and reality. Panic and anxiety attacks can occur, but these usually disappear within twelve hours with support and reassurance. Some depression may occur in the days following the mushroom trip. Occasionally, frightening mental states produced by magic mushrooms can induce flashbacks days or even months afterward and may cause significant psychosocial distress. These flashbacks are similar to those experienced by people with post-traumatic stress disorder.[9, 10, 11]

Mixing mushrooms with intoxicants such as alcohol, marijuana, and street or prescription drugs, particularly MAO inhibitors (MAOIs), may significantly increase the potential for these and other adverse reactions. Combining MAOIs with serotonin-enhancing or psychostimulant drugs is unsafe, because a condition called serotonin syndrome may result or a hypertensive crisis may develop due to elevated levels of pressor monoamines in the body.

Magic mushrooms do not appear to produce physical dependence, though they do produce a short period of increased tolerance that lasts for one to two weeks after use. A literature review comparing twenty commonly used psychoactive substances found that oral psilocybin appeared to have the lowest risk of dependence and acute lethality, and intravenous heroin appeared to have the greatest.[12]

SCIENCE-FICTION VISIONS

Terence McKenna, one of the pioneers of the psychedelic movement in the West, claimed that magic mushrooms produce exo-pheromones—that is, volatile substances that attract intelligent species and induce them to eat the mushrooms in order to speed up their intellectual development. He also claimed that the mushrooms revealed to him that they were a gateway to the intergalactic communication network.[13, 14]

A significant proportion of people using magic mushrooms report spiritual and mystical experiences that are virtually indistinguishable from spontaneous mystical experiences, as confirmed by a recent study conducted at Johns Hopkins University.[15] Here is one description, provided by a friend of mine, of what may happen after ingestion of mushrooms during a journey guided by the shaman:

> I went deeper and deeper inside—I traveled through various realms, some of them beautiful, others magical, and others quite scary. It felt kind of like being in a computer game, where you have to figure out a way to go from level to level and there are hidden dangers, distractions, and traps awaiting you everywhere. Finally, I broke through to the top level—and to my amazement, I became simultaneously all the people (and other intelligent beings) who ever lived, are alive, and will ever live in the universe. I realized that there is only one Actor playing all the parts—it is God, and I am him. Thus, we all will be saved, there is no hell waiting for us after death (though we created one for ourselves on Earth), and God loves every single one

of us the way we are. I knew that our lives are merely a dream, a virtual-reality movie. We cannot really die or get hurt and we have potential to awaken to who we really are—when we will, this world will turn into heaven. I saw how perfect the story is and that everything is fine the way it is—there is no need to struggle to change things out in the world; instead each of us has to work on healing himself or herself. There is no need to suffer or to be unhappy ever again. This experience turned upside down my views of the world and religion and changed me profoundly—for better.

Other experiences frequently reported after ingestion of magic mushrooms include time travel (both within a personal time frame and across thousands of years into the past or the future), telepathy and merging with other individuals, and a wide variety of alien encounters and visits to alien worlds. Yet it is difficult to assess how often the science-fiction-like experiences are induced with the help of magic mushrooms, because no systematic research into these particular effects has been published. There are a few descriptions of magic mushroom experiences with science-fiction themes, as described on the Erowid website and reprinted here with permission.[16]

A True Hallucination by Mantid (ID: 2077)

... Within minutes of ingesting the mushrooms, I felt the first intimations of what was to come, huge waves of psychedelic energy manifesting as "wind" flowing through my body. I vomited violently, and retreated to the nearly pitch-black bedroom to lie down. My ... teeth started to vibrate horribly, in conjunction with the "wind" described above. A horrendous, joyous, and absolutely unbelievable set of events followed. . . . I thought I was dead. I knew I had done it to myself, but could not for the life of me remember what I had taken, why I was dead, or how it happened. I simply knew that I had done it, and I was somehow in a galactic prison or a purgatory perhaps. The visions were plentiful, yet solemn. At this point they were mostly in black and white. I could feel my ego being physically crushed, just like a can still full of liquid. As the pressure increased, the contents pushed "outward." Eventually, this culminated in some sort of squashed feeling which I can only relate to the poor 2-D creatures of the sci-fi classic *Flatland*. I spent some time in this suffering, progressively more terrifying state. Eventually, an entity came and delivered me unbidden personal attention. I was quite relieved to see another creature, for I suspected I was one myself (although not sure). At first I was captivated by its fluid motions and methodical actions. It was moving in rhythms, doing a dance of sorts.

Eventually, it occurred to me that the "dance" it was doing involved horrifying probes of my own form and that it was moving faster than I could comprehend while doing so. I was paralyzed. I wasn't sure if I had a body or not, but this thing was doing something to ME, which was still intact. As I concentrated more and more upon its "physical" form (which is a term I use as loosely as possible), it occurred to me that it looked somewhat familiar. Not [like] anything I had ever seen, but close. It was a giant praying mantis, although it had mental appendages and cartoon details about it. It also looked squatter than the terrestrial version of the insect, shorter and more robust. Its many arms worked up and down my existence, probing and testing every bit. It seemed to put no effort into comforting me, yet it did through some sort of telepathy, implying that it would be easier for both of us if I stopped struggling. Eventually, I did, and it left.

I lost almost all physical awareness, and felt my mind drifting through something resembling outer space. I saw stars, celestial bodies, etc., but was not sure if they were as such, or molecules. The difference seemed irrelevant at that point. I knew I had a brain, and a pair of lungs. I thought that was all. Imagining myself, I saw the brain connected to the lungs behind it, and realized that these two organs in this array must have influenced the design of that dreaded spaceship, *The Enterprise*. As I charted the cosmos, I became aware that through a bit of imagining, or some similar process, I could arrange them to my own satisfaction. I found that different arrangements produced different mental states, some I had known while others were wildly strange. Upon reflection, the impression that I had was that I was rearranging molecules which were fundamental in neuro-transmitting tasks. One arrangement of the "stars" felt similar to LSD, one to 2CB, and so forth. I was not aware of this at the time, however. I simply moved the stars according to whim, and felt pleased with the immediate physical results.

I'm not sure if it was intentional or not, but I eventually slipped into another "room." This was the typical round room deep psychedelics take me to. However, this time it was much larger than normal. Around the perimeter flowed the forms of creatures who looked more like cartoon drawings of dogs than anything else. They seemed Mayan, in as far as they all had dragging tongues and eyes which looked only backwards. They seemed to give me a grinning, sarcastic sneer as they drifted past me. Meanwhile, in the middle of the "sphere," I had other entities to deal with. I cannot come up with any words to describe most of them, although the frivolous doodles which cover the margins of my school lecture notes come closer than anything at approximating their forms. . . .

I finally relaxed, enjoying the inevitability of it all. Instantly, flowers looking like opium poppies surrounded me and the "machine-elves" of DMT fame came to visit. They assured me that I was safe, and really a nice guy to boot. In their high pitched collective voice, they sang a song revealing to me not only my own nature, but that of all creatures as well. They assured me that my DNA was not only similar to their own, but part of as well as "encompassing" their own "code." They stressed the simultaneousness of this seemingly contradictory statement. I started to laugh out loud, mostly at the absurdity of it all. My laughing became uncontrollable. It should be added that at this point I was so immersed that it did not matter if my eyes were open or closed.

Solstice Ritual *by Slawek Wojtowicz* © 2007

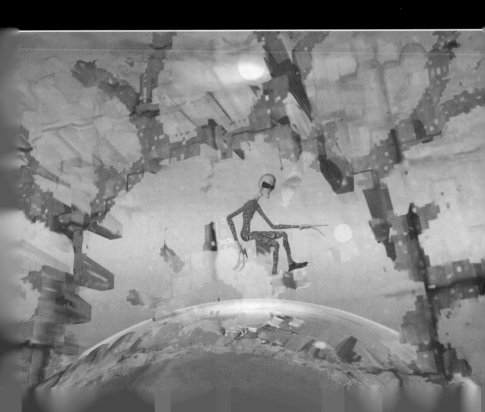

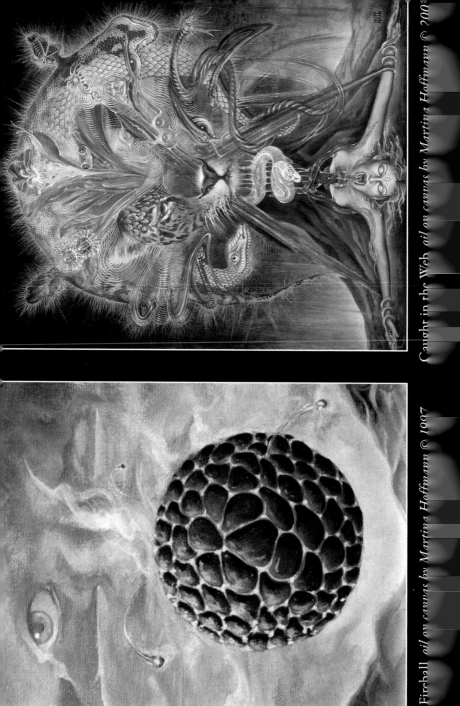

Caught in the Web *oil on canvas by Martina Hoffmann* © 2003

Fireball *oil on canvas by Martina Hoffmann* © 1997

Ayahuasca Dream *by Robert Venosa © 2007*

Searching for the Lost Soul *by Pablo Amaringo* © 1987

Cielo Ayahuasca by Pablo Amaringo © 1987

Mantids Rule! *by Slawek Wojtowicz* © 2007

However, this laughing was the first event in what seemed like months which reminded me of my personal form and body. And I laughed. . . . I could not stop! The laughing at one point "locked on" to a particular vocal frequency, and I could not get it to budge. Indeed, I was aware that I was releasing a mono-tonal hum. Even breathing did not seem to interfere with its clarity. I found it satisfying, and started to explore. By going with the sound, instead of trying to stop it, it grew louder and louder. Eventually, it culminated in what McKenna correctly describes as a metallic buzzing sound. Very much like the sound of a cicada, but with many other elements added. I did feel as a bug making the sound, and I had an intuitive understanding of metamorphosis. As this sound continued, I noticed it was affecting my visions. Before, the elves were rapidly and almost violently competing for my attention, each trying to show me a better toy than the last. But this incredible sound caused them to order themselves into intricate yet subtle patterns of the greatest coherency. By slightly altering the pitch of the growl, or modulating it, the patterns changed. After some time, I could actually sculpt three-dimensional objects. I did not attempt to make a chair, or a dog, or anything like that, but rather sculptures of pure light and revolving spheres, towers of emerald surrounded by throbbing orbs of sound and love. These were the toys I presented back to the machine-elves. This ability continued for what I would (with no way of ever knowing) say was roughly a half hour. This was the most satisfying, absurd, and enjoyable feeling I have ever had in my life.

Intergalactic Travel and Mutual Trips by Metatron (ID: 21742)

. . . This was the highlight of the trip. My girlfriend rolled over and we started looking into each other's eyes. The experience is incredibly intense and acts like a series of experiences that each seem to last a really long time but in actuality only last a very short time. Within her eyes, I see the oceans folding out with the moon sitting above them. Then I see them from outside of Earth and they become the entire Earth and we realize that we are each other's worlds. The order of what happened next isn't important but what happened was. I followed the lines of her face up through her forehead as they rose into this shining blue temple with an eye right above her hairline at the top of the temple. A blue, spinning cloud surrounded the eye. This faded away as I stared into her eyes again. She collapsed and started crying and explaining how she felt her body disintegrate and breathe out into me. I tried to accept her life into my own and felt her become my soul and fill me from the inside and overflow out my eyes in tears of joy. We stared into each other's eyes again, trying to pass our souls and lives to each other and the world disappeared. We slipped out into space and felt not as two people but as one traveling through the galaxy. We whisked through beaches and stars and spun in each other's arms in the heavens. We came back and there was sand or salt in her bed and it seemed totally believable that we had brought it back with us. This entire experience seemed to have lasted an eternity. . . .

Totally amazed, she and I just lay there for a few more minutes talking about the experience we just had. She had absolutely been there with me and experienced the same things. We had a mutual trip! I continued to look at her face and she said she could see her face in mine and I saw her face mold itself into mine and realized that we were the same person. The color in her right cheek turned into a rising sun painted on her cheek and I saw all my heritage of Native Americans in her face. I saw their painted cheeks and their pain and suffering of years flash across this beautiful face. . . .

Nonsmoking Elf Machines Will Cure Cancer by Biff Wheatly (ID: 7910)

. . . By the time I made it back into the bedroom and lay down, the tremors had begun to turn into actual shakes, and were starting to make me nervous. Almost as soon as my head hit the pillow, though, I heard a strange voice say something to the effect of,

"You can relax now—it's just your stomach. It'll be all right." Huh? I wondered to this strange voice, and then relaxed almost immediately when I focused my eyes to the darkness both in the room and in my head, and saw them. Everywhere were tiny, jeweled, spider or elf-like creatures: floating through the air, crawling on the walls, roaming the nether regions of my skull. I raised my hand in the dark and it was awash in these small, shimmering hyper-organisms.

It was at this point that my conversation with them began. By this time, the trembling having subsided, I noticed the knot in my stomach tightening, an uncomfortable feeling to be sure. I thought I might be getting sick from the mushrooms or something: the feeling of taking that last soggy, chunky gulp of tea now came back to me, and this intensified my sick feeling. Fortunately, they began to speak again. "Y'know that you're not feeling sick, not really anyway," they said. "The feeling you are feeling is the truth of your existence; we are showing you what is at stake here in this life, what you have done and are doing wrong, and what you must do to feel better. . . ."

(At this point, I noticed the colors of the entities more closely— they were red, blue, yellow, purple, and gold, as well as other colors which I cannot name here now; I also noticed that they spun clockwise and all together at one point, and then in beautifully syncopated patterns at another. . . . [T]he beings then clued me into what was going on inside of me: the pain and discomfort I was feeling and associating with the mushrooms or with digestion or something, was in fact the pain my spirit was feeling because of my smoking habits.

The beings explained quite simply to me that smoking cigarettes was a waste of my time, energy, and most importantly, my life, and by continuing in this behavior I was perpetuating cycles of fear, greed, and disease which reached both through and beyond time and space (at least as we commonly know them). . . .

"What to do, what to do?!?" I wondered as I lay in bed. "We will show you," they said back almost immediately. At this point, the entities changed appearance again, turning into bluish gold bits of light, less defined than before, and proceeding to "paint" whatever it was I looked at; I say "paint" because that's what it looked like— paint flowing onto various surfaces (although the most beautiful paint I'VE EVER SEEN!!!) as I passed over them with my gaze. I started to get the feeling that the ghostly painting going on in my room was surrounding me in some strange way; I didn't feel threatened, as I realized this pent-up feeling I was beginning to develop sitting there in the dark was simple ego-dissolution. The color-beings began to multiply and crowd around me almost as soon as I realized what I was feeling. "We will take over from here," or words to that effect, were pretty much the last thing I heard from these beings that night. Almost as soon as I'd heard this hyper-dimensional message, the painted surfaces began leaping off of themselves and congregating in the air, casting off a strange blue glow. As this fuzz ball of psychedelic energy materialized, I felt it start to cover me, as if it were a ghostly sheet covering my deceased body in the morgue or something; strangely, I felt no fear, dread, or even much discomfort as this thing, this shroud of or by or from these hyper-dimensional space aliens, covered me, wrapping me like a newborn child. . . . A NEWBORN!!! A non-smoking newborn. . . .

Another user reported experiences somewhat reminiscent of scenes in the movie *Altered States*.[17]

Alien Weirdness and Devolving into the Ape by davinox (ID: 39587)

. . . I then decided to go outside into my backyard, and there things get strange. It is 7:30, and the sky is glowing green. Everything seems alien. The grass was very strangely colored, and it was my own lawn. . . . The green alien sky and the sharp, strange, alien, pointy, detailed leaves on the trees and grass perplex me. I then look into the sky and notice strange orange birds, like baby dragons or dinosaurs, but ultimately strange and alien, drifting across the surreal sky. There were several of them, and they seemed just as real as everything else did at the time. . . .

I stare at my clock for what seems like minutes but I think was an hour, the shrooms pulling me hard in their alieness as I started to lose consciousness. It was very hard to analyze what was going on; I was dreamy, entranced and slipping away. Digits of the clock started to lose meaning, just red lines in an incomprehensible form. I don't think I could have read or used any form of human reasoning. In the trance, I only remember two things. The first was a feeling of floating around the room as a spirit-like face, morphing and flying around with incredible power. . . . The next thing I know, its 12:30 and I'm completely naked, slouched over and feeling strange. I wonder if the shrooms have worn off, wonder where I am, trying to put things together. I look up at my fractal poster and it's messed up, a sign that I'm still shrooming.

I get up, naked and dazed, foggy and thoughtless. I feel primitive, my only urge is to rub my chin and search for something to drink. I then get up and look at my room; it is completely trashed. All of my things were strewn about, a book torn, my chair taken apart (though not broken; it was made to be taken apart), the glass screen to my stereo completely ripped off, my stereo a little kicked in, my mini-shelf a little collapsed, a speaker completely out of place and turned upside-down, books and pamphlets and papers everywhere as if a tornado had touched down. I quickly discovered the reason for such squalor; I still felt the altered state surge through me, though I now had human control. I had devolved into an ape: not magically, not mystically, but my human body had started to express its primitive ape-like tendencies. Unaware of the technical details of biology, I began to theorize that my DNA was expressing an ancient part of its genetic makeup. I looked down and witnessed the result. My hands were remarkably primitive, my thumbs no longer opposable. My feet and legs were horrifically and magically primitive as well. It was difficult to say that it was a hallucination and easier to say that it was a transient expression of the ancient part of my DNA, because I could feel the changed parts of me; I could touch them. The joints of my big toes were hardened, as if strengthened to climb trees and grab things.

The hallucination (or, as I thought, transformation) was so strikingly real in so many ways. First, my dog was completely flipping out, trembling at me and becoming very submissive. He has never done this to me. Second, I am never a violent person, and not at all destructive. I have never, under any other drug, completely changed my actions in such a systematically classifiable way. I was very, very ape-like, and without the hallucination of looking like an ape. I had actually felt like my consciousness was creating my body, or influencing my body, to act in such a way. At one point I sunk into a depression, thinking my body would permanently remain primitive. I thought that I would be permanently disfigured, and that my family and girlfriend would all know about my shrooming and I would always have proof of it by my grotesque mutation. Slowly, as the late-night hours ticked away, I became more and more human, though for a while after, my jaw and skull felt much stronger than normal, and my hands still seemed a bit primitive. . . . The experience was powerful, uncomfortable, traumatic, distressing, mind-bending, and now, in retrospect, changed my brain chemistry. I now have much . . . stronger psychedelic experiences with cannabis. I also have learned how much the mind creates reality in that it perfectly created this ape-man version of me. It wasn't an actual physical alteration of DNA (like in the movie *Altered States*), but rather a mental alteration of my self-image. . . .

Revelations, Cosmic Unity, Entity Contact by Peter Pumpkin (ID: 42367)

. . . I am in a pool with some kind of alien in some other world, two other aliens are smiling whilst pouring a gold-reddish liquid over us both as we lay down unable to move. Strangely enough, for some inexplicable reason, I am not scared in the slightest by this! I smile back at the aliens, as the liquid is poured over me. It makes me feel warm and very happy. Something is then said, but I cannot understand because it is in some totally unknown language, and I am then whisked away to another world-dimension.

This part was very interesting to say the least! It's just a shame I have a lot of trouble recalling exactly what happened. I made contact with several entities that were made out of pure energy. All were female, and all were very playful and joyous. Some were clearly children. I remember dancing and flying around faraway planets and stars with some of them in some sort of cosmic dance. It was like a semi-lucid dream, only a million times more overpowering and spectacular. I cannot remember who I am at this point, nor do I care. For all I know, I could be dead, but I don't have any concept of death, nor do I have any concept of future or past. I purely exist in the present, in infinity.

I get the feeling I'm totally at one with the universe. It is total euphoria; I'm in some sort of state of spiritual nirvana. My physical body and the physical world not only doesn't exist, it's been totally forgotten. The only thing that matters now is pleasure and pure happiness. I am living purely for the moment, and this moment is eternity. After dancing around the universe with these child-like entities, I begin to communicate with what seems to be their Elder. I have no idea what she tells me, but it does make me begin to remember who I was again, and this throws me headlong into a new phase of my trip which was extremely intense . . .

I start to relive childhood events. I'm on a total mind trip . . . and it's really delving into the deepest corners of my mind. It's showing me mistakes I've made in mind-fucking detail, but also past loves, happy memories, friends, dead relatives. . . . All the memories and experiences that have affected my very character and being. They whiz past in seconds, like a giant, superfast slide-show, so fast I cannot make sense of some of them. I'm in total awe. I think about the friends and people that I'm surrounding myself in my life at the moment. I think about my aspirations and goals. I come to the conclusion that some things definitely need to change. . . . I felt as though I had been stupid to not see this before, though instead of dwelling on this fact I instead seemed to focus on the positivity of such a revelation. And for one fleeting moment, I felt complete in the feeling that I knew all the answers to my questions. . . .

The Peeling Back of the Surface World by Zebo (ID: 22708)

. . . Suddenly, I emptied out of my body and tumbled into the spiritual world. I saw stars and a light and felt myself drawn up towards a pulsating entity. . . . I shut my eyes again and once more tumbled away from reality. . . . Each thought peeled away another layer of reality and finally I felt as though I reached some core. It came to me in an epiphany. I was free from the restrains of reality and found myself in a sort of free-floating objective universe of math. I was being thrown around from idea to idea and spiraling down into the bottom of my psyche. Suddenly it all just kind of stopped and I was in darkness. Slowly I became aware of a light gently growing. It started as hardly visible but became enormous with time. All of a sudden I realized that I was going to be swallowed by this light, but I was not afraid; rather, I was looking forward to seeing what was on the other side. As I expected, it grew and grew until I was encompassed in the warm glow. In the light patterns developed and evolved until a city emerged from the radiance.

I stood on an alien street in some glowing symmetrical reality. I wondered where the people who lived here were. But as I thought of that, they too began emerging from the light. They were strange trans-dimensional beings that were basically indescribable. They spoke to me in a strange, telepathic language and told me the essence of being. They were beings of a deeper order than us. We are the culmination of molecular patterns that have evolved from matter (they didn't tell me this; it's just physics). We are carbon and other various elements that interact in such intricate patterns that we have developed a sense of individuality. They were beings of a subatomic level. They were not different than us, but they exist with us in another understanding of reality. . . .

Alien Possession by rawbear (ID: 16203)

. . . I became aware that I was no longer "me." Instead, I was an alien being from another world that had possessed my body. Making 360-degree circumspection, the entire planetary landscape had changed such that the huge evergreen trees screening the cliff face, the rocky beach, the glittering sea, the sun and clouds in the blue, blue sky, everything belonged to an alien world. "It" seemed experienced at this sort of thing but was fumbling a bit, looking for the "controls" to its new psychosomatic unit. Its self-image was something like the alien in the Schwarzenegger film, *Predator,* totally silent, all business, and on a mission. Then the realization struck that the alien world was actually Earth as seen through alien eyes. Something deep within though made an effort to remember my name, address, and telephone number in order not to lose itself completely. It was odd how there was no barrier or borderline between the alien and "myself." . . .

It is clear from these reports (provided anonymously by the visitors to the Erowid) that the experiences described by these psychonauts fall into the realm of science fiction. The question that remains: What really happened? Did these people indeed visit other planets and interact with alien entities or did they just imagine these adventures, perhaps after being exposed to science-fiction movies and literature?

The shaman's journey

Supernatural or Natural?
A Neuro-Ontological Interpretation
of Spiritual Experiences

Ede Frecska, M.D.

*A common thread seems to connect all shamans across the
planet. . . . That this commonality cuts across seemingly
irreconcilable ethnic and cultural lines attests to the mystery
and power lying at the source of myth, the human psyche.
. . . From Lapland to Patagonia, from the Paleolithic to
today, the archetypes activated during shamanic ordeals
and exaltations are astonishingly similar.*

JOAN HALIFAX,
SHAMAN: THE WOUNDED HEALER

It is my hope that a reader who is not appalled by the word *supernatural*
in this chapter's title would not mind speculating why the ideas of soul,
spirit, and rebirth echo across ages, and why these concepts appear and
reappear in widely different cultures. The belief in spiritual forces and
otherworldly realms appears universal in the human species. Rational
thinking deems such concepts superstitious and originating in illusion
or fear of death and representing anxiety over ego-dissolution. It consid-

ers them products of wishful thinking. Academic accounts see spiritual practice arising from the functioning of the human mind, with its supposed tendency to seek spiritual states or comfort in a hostile world.[1] Accordingly, in worshipping spiritual beings, humans are just paying homage to a rarified form of themselves.

We can see that certain beliefs and experiences crop up universally in spiritual practices around the world, maintained for millennia. The empirically established existence of resilient commonalities is remarkable. Regardless, the fact that spiritual teachings and mystical wisdom traditions share a remarkable cross-cultural similarity can be dismissed with a skeptical shrug and explained away as projections of intrapsychic structures common in every human being—and that a misinterpretation of universal experiences, such as dreams, may lead to the belief in existence of spiritual beings.[2]

There are some elaborate explanations that suggest parallels to a pathological condition. Similar to schizophrenia, which—as some speculate—is a price the human race pays for the gift of language,[3] the tendency to believe in supernatural beings is common in all humans because it is an offshoot of creative imagination. According to this view, something maladaptive resides in us universally and stays with us persistently, because it is closely tied to an adaptive trait—creativity. The most permissive, dispassionate scientific approach accepts universality as sufficient to establish phenomenological reality, but leaves the question open as to its ontological source.[4]

Skepticism is valued very highly in Western scientific thinking—as it ought to be to keep knowledge-building tightly disciplined. Why, then, can we not use skepticism in a self-referential way, from a self-critical point of view? First of all, we must be skeptical toward our own cultural background, which has many hidden presumptions governing even our supposedly objective way of answering questions. Setting boundaries is the essence of the scientific method when it isolates and separates systems in order to study them experimentally without confounding interferences from the outside.

Where, then, is the boundary of the scientific method itself? If science has limitations (this will be addressed further in the section about rationalizing and mysticism on page 182, under the heading Educatio Demistificationis—i.e., demystifying education), then it cannot be the bearer of the ultimate truth. Overvaluation of science, as in *scientism,* can take the form of cultural arrogance when it attempts to explain why people of different cultures do things the way they do, interpreting costumes and rituals while ignoring a culture's own reasons behind what it does. My agenda is not to follow cultural relativism blindly. However, I pay maximal respect to the interpretation of aboriginal cultures and will use those as a starting point.

COGNITIVE SCHEMAS

First, let us examine the soundness of Western confidence in scientism. We can summarize the basic concepts science holds about the human phenomenon as follows:

- **Man is the by-product of mere chance.** This follows from the combination of evolution theory and random genetic mutations. There is no divine plan, no Almighty Creator. From the chaotic movements of the material world, complex systems evolved as a result of chance and were chosen by natural selection.
- **We live in a universe alien to us and ignorant of our destiny.** The anthropic principle, either in its "soft" or "strong" form, is not able to come to the rescue of an individual person. The two forms of the anthropic principle diverge in their interpretation as to why the physical constants of our universe predispose it to be hospitable to human life, but agree that the cosmos is absolutely indifferent toward the fate of any one member of the species.
- **We have come from nothingness and will return to nothingness after death.** The meaning of this is the same as the decree

"dust to dust." Only the most basic components of our bodies will survive and continue on in the circle of life.

It is apparent to a mind trained in behavioral sciences that these basic concepts are strikingly similar to the Beck triad: The psychiatrist Aaron Beck noticed the cognitive distortion that depressed subjects perceived in self, the world, and the future, calling it the negative cognitive schema of depressive thinking. Derogatory views of the self, the world, and the future are core features of the depressed individual:

"I am a worthless person."

"The world is an inhospitable place."

"My past is a tragedy; my future is hopeless."

Beck suggested that depressed people draw illogical conclusions about situations, and these lead to a distortion of reality, which manifests in the magnification of negative experiences and the trivialization of neutral or positive ones. The cognitive triad is the source of the extremely low self-esteem of depressed subjects. Indeed, it can lead to *micromanic* (the opposite of grandiose) delusions, manifesting in the extreme form as psychosis. The parallel between the theses of scientism and the Beck triad is close and raises the following questions: Does the same outcome stand for scientific thinking as well? Is scientific thinking illogical or biased in its worldview in a way that is similar to that of a depressed patient? Of course, science is not illogical, but it may suffer from overexclusiveness. It must be biased in that direction in order to build a consistent knowledge system by keeping "soft," poorly validated concepts outside of its domain. Nevertheless, what lies outside of the semantic universe of "official science" today may be part of it tomorrow. There are more things in heaven and on Earth than are dreamed of in our current philosophy. . . .

Can the negative thinking of Western rationalism lead to a pathologically flawed underestimation of the human potential in a manner akin to a psychotic depressive delusion? A possible answer is hidden in the cognitive schemas of seven wisdom traditions that can be designated as unambiguously positive:

- **Christianity:** "The kingdom of heaven is within (or among) you" (from the words of Jesus).
- **Islam:** "Those who know themselves know their Lord."
- **Judaism:** "He is in all, and all is in Him."
- **Confucianism:** "Those who know their own nature, know heaven."
- **Taoism:** "In the depths of the soul, one sees the Divine, the One."
- **Buddhism:** "Look within, you are the Buddha."[5]

Apparently, the issue has to do with self-knowledge—yet it is not about the self-knowledge favored by Western individualism: "Be aware of your own coping skills!" Individualism, which has been nurtured in the West, is a cultural tradition of the last two hundred years. The wisdom traditions cited here, however, are at least fourteen hundred years old, and all of them were born in the East. There is one more, which formulates most concisely the essence of all of them:

- **Hinduism:** "Atman [individual consciousness] and Brahman [universal consciousness] are one."

In other words, if we descend into the depth of our psyche, we will arrive at something common in all of us and in everything. We discover this by consistently looking inward until *within* becomes *beyond*. Conversely, if we look far and deep into the universe and dare to go beyond, at some point we will face the observing self. There is no such thing as monotonous, infinite progression and regression with endless hierarchies, larger and larger supersystems on the way up and smaller and smaller elementary particles on the way down. Quantum physicists

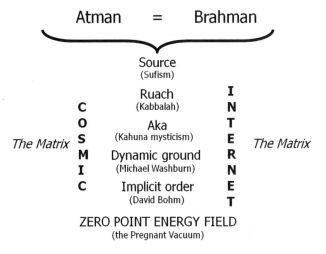

Figure 7.1. The most important revelation

have already stumbled onto the problem of conscious observer, and were temporarily able to find a way around it in the Copenhagen interpretation of quantum mechanics.

The great unification, the Theory of Everything, very likely requires better understanding of consciousness as the vehicle through which all things are known. As physicists struggle to tie together general relativity and quantum field theory in terms of quantum gravity, perhaps further insights will be obtained by understanding the nature of logic, cognition, and consciousness. The inside and outside paths will eventually converge in consciousness or in what is known as *source* in Sufism, *ruach* in the kabbalah, *aka* in kahuna mysticism, *dynamic ground* in transpersonal psychology, and *zero-point energy* or *topological field* among heterodox physicists (see figure 7.1). We may recognize it as the Matrix, the Cosmic Internet. At the deepest level of our psyche, at the bottom of our soul, we become one with the ultimate reality.*

---

*The message of the Gnostic Gospels—ancient Christian scripts at odds with the New Testament—is similar in that it conveys that to know ourselves, at the deepest level, is also to know God. In other words, by looking within ourselves to find the sources of love, hate, joy, and sorrow—at the bottom of our self—we would find God.

Any—even the last, most unfortunate—member of the human species carries the whole cosmos inside and has the potential to reach it, to tap in to it. This is exactly what we may realize as the most positive cognitive scheme, the most important discovery of all time.

This kind of teaching definitely soothes the soul. It would be interesting to find out whether the prevalence of clinical depression, anxiety disorders, and suicidal behavior is lower in cultures that nurture these teachings. Regardless of their positive impact on everyday life, doubts remain: Does spiritual wisdom represent wishful thinking? Does it have scientific meaning at all? Does it have a place in our worldview at the beginning of the twenty-first century? If the answers are negative, then why are no fewer than seven wisdom traditions (anyone knowledgeable in mystic teachings can add more) so unequivocal in their basic tenets? Why do mystics separated by two millennia and two continents achieve better accord on these issues than two scientists of the modern era on the nature of the universe or on the fact of global warming? It is notable that these teachers have never been guilty of theological quarreling or theocratic dictatorship, nor can their teaching be used for these purposes by others. As Alan Watts summarized: ". . . the plain fact [is] that there has otherwise been a single philosophical consensus of universal extent. It has been held by [men and women] who report the same insights and teach the same essential doctrine whether living today or six thousand years ago, whether from New Mexico in the Far West or from Japan in the Far East."[6]

Foolish, arbitrary thinking can hardly reach this degree of consensus. Not without sarcasm, Ken Wilber said: "Eighty-three hallucinating schizophrenics couldn't organize a trip to the bathroom, let alone Japanese Zen."[7] Wilber refers to the eighty-three followers of Zen master Hakuin as sages with mystical experiences and not schizophrenic subjects with perceptual distortions. The historically new rational thinking, the triumph of the era of Enlightenment, is an outlier of the wisdom tradition and definitely not of the enlightened one. If the sages are right about mystical enlightenment, their truth must also be correct in the framework of another knowledge system—Western science. The problem lies in finding a proper way of translation.

The purpose of this chapter is to answer the questions we've raised here as science at present will allow. By doing so, we may cross the ideas of different worldviews. I am fully aware of the pitfalls of both overinclusiveness and passionate thinking. Truly, the underlying methodological approach has minimal experimental support; it can rely only on neurophenomenology, model-making, searching for inconsistencies in rivaling views, and use of the power of converging evidence.

PHILOSOPHIA PERENNIS

The view held by a great majority of eminent theologians, mystic sages, and nonmaterialist philosophers at various times is known as *perennial philosophy*.[8] It is perennial because it holds profound, everlasting insights into life and nature, spanning cultures, and has been taught by the great thinkers of all time. Four crucial claims about reality and human nature lie at the heart of perennial wisdom:

1. There are two realms of reality. The physical or phenomenal world is not the only reality; another, nonphysical realm exists, and the two domains together constitute the ultimate reality.
2. All humans partake of both realms and mirror the nature of this two-sided reality.
3. Human beings possess a capacity, however unused and therefore atrophied, for perception of nonphysical reality.
4. Humans can recognize their divine spark (Atman) and the sacred ground (Brahman) that is its source. This perception is the final goal (mystical enlightenment), and its pursuit is the greatest good (holy life) of human existence. All the great messengers of the spirit and the masters of mysticism have declared with one voice that the supreme aim of humanity is reunion with its divine principle.[9]

Teachings of perennial philosophy suggest that the cosmos is not only interconnected and pulsating with life, but also multilayered. The physical universe is not the only domain; beyond its complex hierarchy, there is also the subtle realm of spirit, for which the most meaningful contemporary term is probably *consciousness.* The spiritual realm cannot be known through the physical senses and cannot be measured by scientific instruments. According to followers of perennial philosophy, the realm of spirit can be approached by contemplative methods such as meditation, rituals, and a sacred way of living.[10] Moreover, the perennial philosophy states that our true nature is spiritual. We are fundamentally creatures (as well as creators) of this realm. This is nothing less than a superpositive cognitive scheme, and in this chapter we attempt to bring it into a rational context in the hope of changing the contemporary scientific worldview into one that is less negative. For clinical practitioners and suffering patients, the message is that there is no tragedy in being human. The problem, rather, is that people who have been severed from spiritual roots see life as a disaster.

THE SPIRITUAL DIMENSION

As an anchoring point and clarification, here is a definition of *spirituality:* It is something that we may not perceive, but others can—and this kind of experience enriches those who undergo it. This is a relatively cautious approach; even people with an aversion to New Age, esoteric thinking may accept it. The Institute of Noetic Sciences found in a survey that about 75 percent of the population had at least one spiritual experience in life, but 75 percent of individuals employed in health care and those with strong academic backgrounds had no such experience. This revealed divergence calls for a second study to replicate these results, and must be a wake-up call for these professionals.

Human thinking has different forms—*rational thinking, emotional thinking,* and *spiritual thinking*—and each of them can be measured by IQ tests developed by David Wechsler, Daniel Goleman, and Robert

Emmons, respectively. An individual can score high on one or more or even all of them. In the film *Forrest Gump,* Tom Hanks plays a character who might definitely score low on the first test (rational thinking) but higher on the others. John Coffey of the *The Green Mile* probably has a high spiritual IQ, but expresses modest capacity in the other areas. In corporate and governmental America, some might make a rich career with a high Wechsler IQ (rational thinking) score, but these institutions make high emotional and spiritual intelligence disadvantageous for a career-seeking individual.

It is essential in the current codes of professional behavior to sort out emotional and spiritual feelings and to suppress them ("Don't mix business with friendship"). There is a recent trend in business management to promote emotional and spiritual intelligence to manipulate others, which is self-contradictory. Even in mental health care the basic tenet is to maintain boundaries: "Stay objective, stay away, and don't take your patients home!" Compassion toward patients is tolerated, perhaps, but is not considered professional. This can cause problems in health care, however, because millennia of history in the healing traditions indicate that to be effective, a truly authentic healer mobilizes her or his potentials in the emotional and spiritual spheres as well as in the logical sphere. To be an opportunist, then, we can be satisfied with our rational IQ, but to perform well and to everyone's satisfaction in the health care business, we must score high in all three areas.

THE EXTENDED BIOPSYCHOSOCIAL PARADIGM

Contemporary medicine defines human beings in a biopsychosocial framework. The concept of patients as biopsychosocial entities goes back to George Engel,[11] and comes from the observation that there are ailments that cannot be treated successfully by biological means alone. There are mental disturbances for which targeting the intrapsychic conflicts alone (e.g., as in classical psychoanalysis) is not enough—the therapist must address the subject's interpersonal relationships as well (perhaps in the form of family therapy). Involving higher levels of the biopsychosocial pyramid in health care may result in permanent improvement, and palliative, symptom-focused therapy can then be replaced by curative treatment.

The biopsychosocial paradigm is not complete, however. Something is missing from the top that would provide for a transformation into a mighty pyramid: the all-seeing eye (like that staring on the back of a dollar bill), the symbol of spirituality (see figure 7.2). There are anthropological observations, Oriental descriptions, and Western anecdotal reports about successful therapies incorporating spiritual elements. We must realize that the top of the pyramid is unsteady without a solid layer at the base. Likewise, the pyramid is just an impressive pile of rock without a radiant capstone at the top. On the one hand, a treatment should not be based solely on spiritual techniques; on the other hand, treatments with somatic focus are mostly palliative in Western medicine.

Here, we arrived at a modified, extended paradigm: the biopsychosociospiritual model. Therapy *sui generis* is reintegration *in toto* on biological, mental, social, and spiritual levels. Thus far, there is nothing mystical in adding the *spiritual* to the concept: moving from left to right (from bio to spiritual) along the gradations comprising the awkward term *biopsychopsociospiritual* means that the individual would identify step by step with higher realms of reality—with the psyche, with the community, and, at the end, with an entity above commu-

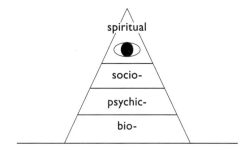

Figure 7.2. The extended Engelian paradigm

nity (i.e., environment, nature, universe, Mother Earth, or other entities depending on culturally determined worldviews). Meaning emerges from context; more purpose can be acquired from higher hierarchical perspectives. Consequently, spiritual orientation can provide a more meaningful life to individuals than does solely pursuing materialistic goals or following fundamentalistic views that bluntly ignore the value system of others.

The term *sacred* refers to a sense of respect for and humility toward the larger entities to which we are subordinated and that govern our lives. Based on the illusion that we are in command of our destiny, Western individualism has eroded this concept. The historical process of individualization involves slicing off, step by step from right to left, components of the biopsychosociospiritual unity. This process was begun millennia ago by gradual separation from nature and by the suppression of tribal ritual traditions. It continued during modernization by the destruction of rural communities and the rise of the nuclear family, and has culminated in postmodern, emotionless professionalism. The richness of the biopsychosociospiritual model of traditional societies has been boiled down to the bony *biorobot rationalis* skeleton of postmodern man.

Indeed, cross-cultural analyses reveal that increasing social and political complexity, particularly hierarchical integration, leads to a reduction in the use of spiritual techniques.[12] This negative—at times, antagonistic—relation to political integration reflects an inherent conflict between spirit and power: the psychosocial needs of hierarchical societies are not compatible with the individuals' direct relationship to a transcendental "other," especially not in an altered state of consciousness (ASC). Dobkin de Rios and Smith[13] suggest that spiritual techniques for altering consciousness are typically repressed in state-level societies because they constitute a potential threat to the religious interpretations of those who hold social and religious power.

In our complex, hierarchical society, addressing the biopsychosociospiritual totality is not tolerated on the level of direct personal experience, but is promoted in a symbolic form, as reflected by the familiar text of the prayer known as the "Our Father":

> Our Father, who art in heaven, hallowed be thy name.
>   Thy kingdom come, Thy will be done, on Earth as
>   it is in heaven.
> [Surrender to the spiritual force is formulated; the
>   virtue of humility is implied.]
> Give us this day our daily bread.
> [The basic, biological needs of the body are to be
>   taken care of, with moderation.]
> And forgive us our trespasses, as we forgive those who
>   trespass against us.
> [Here is the submission to social values and the
>   concern for others with expression of the
>   need for fairness.]
> And lead us not into temptation, but deliver us from
>   evil.
> [This is a request for the body's capitulation to the
>   psyche. It calls for temperance, for denial of
>   pursuing only hedonistic or material goals.]
> Amen.
> [Let it be.]

Could it be expressed more concisely? In this prayer, we find that anyone who wishes to do so can address all four elements of the biopsychosociospiritual paradigm within thirty seconds.

CHANGING VIEWS ON THE SHAMAN'S MISSION: PSYCHOINTEGRATION AND DIVINATION

In the course of recent studies in psychological anthropology, a consensus has emerged that the vast majority of ritual ceremonies are concerned primarily with healing in a general sense. They exert influence on physical well-being, heighten identity, enhance interpersonal cohesion, reintegrate community into the environment, and mitigate perceived conflicts with supernatural powers. In spite of the cultural diversity of therapeutic institutions and practices, the fundamental healing principles show a good deal of cross-cultural uniformity. Michael Winkelman emphasizes the traditional healer's role in the reintegrative process, and coins the term *psychointegration* as a description of the healing process.[14]

All traditional shamanic rituals pursue the same end: to destroy "profane" sensibility and create a sensory condition that is open to the supernatural. This is not only a matter of physiological techniques. Traditional ideology directs and imparts values to all these efforts intended to break the frame of profane sensibility. The result is an ASC: an ecstasy or trance, which is not the goal but rather the means of contacting spiritual realms in archaic healing ceremonies. Mircea Eliade defines the technique of ecstasy as the common denominator of all shamanic practices.[15] According to his view, the shaman is a skilled technician, a manipulator of the ASC of all participants, including that of him- or herself, an experienced navigator of spiritual realms as revealed in the shamanic journey.

Over the past decade it has become increasingly clear that though trance techniques are important, there are cultures in which there are exceptions. More universal is the shaman's function in the role of a communicator: the shaman is the traditional healer who encounters divine entities and spirits in order to fulfill his therapeutic obligation. This is psychointegration in the broadest sense. *Integration,* which is reintegration in the case of healing, means necessarily bringing information into the disintegrated system through a process known as *divination.*

We arrive, then, at a new definition of the shaman's mission: to act as messenger of divine information in the service of the community. Despite millennia of field testing, divination has no scientific validation. It may reach epistemological acceptance at best without ontological recognition.[16] Ignorance is more common from a scientific standpoint, due to lack of controlled observations—the result of academic indifference, it is extremely difficult to refer to well-organized fieldwork on the functional outcome of divination practices. Anecdotal reports are more common, but have only limited scientific value, though in some instances such reports can be persuasive.

Let us review three cases from widely separated locations in the world. A Tungus shaman in Siberia agrees to the request of tribal hunters to locate game during a poor hunting season. Using a drumming technique, he enters an ASC and provides information to help his hunters. The Western interpretation—if it accepts at all the validity of this kind of information—would be that the shaman calculates the behavior of the game according to weather and well-known environmental conditions. In other words, his is information based on cognitive processing of sensory data. The explanation of the shaman himself is different: Guidance has been provided by forest spirits.

On another continent, hunters of the Kalahari !Kung tribe leave the settlement to hunt for a period that may last anywhere from two days to two weeks. The tribe's timely preparation for the return of successful hunters is necessary for processing the game. The people left behind make the appropriate steps long before the hunters' reappearance. Their foreknowledge of the hunters' return could be explained rationally by attributing it to a messenger sent ahead or the use of tam-tam drums or smoke signals. The tribesmen report, however, that it is the spirit of ancestors who informs them when the hunters will return.

Next, we move to the Amazon basin. The Shuar shaman is facing a new disease in the community. An herbal remedy is sought by adding leaves of a candidate plant into the hallucinogenic beverage ayahuasca, a sacrament indigenous to the Upper Amazon region. The shaman drinks it and, upon return to ordinary consciousness, decides the usefulness of the plant in question. Is his decision based on accumulation of ethnobotanical knowledge of several generations in combination with trial and error? The headhunter Shuar are not likely to be merciful to an ineffective medicine man, and his techniques must be working. As Luis Eduardo Luna explained to me, according to ayahuasqueros, the spirit of a new plant reveals itself with the help of the spirits associated with the ayahuasca. Sometimes, they also tell which plant to use next.

We can point to the following contradiction: Healers from different cultures are unequivocal in their interpretation of the source of knowledge, whereas rational thinkers use diverging, unsystematic explanations. Which side should be slashed with Occam's razor? Also called the "principle of parsimony," Occam's razor is usually interpreted to mean something like "Do not multiply hypotheses unnecessarily" or "Do not posit pluralities unnecessarily when generating explanatory models." The principle of parsimony is used frequently by philosophers of science in an effort to establish criteria for choosing from theories with equal explanatory power.

At first glance it is the "primitives" who multiply causes unnecessarily by referring to the supernatural. Yet Occam's razor may be applied easily to the rational view, if those arguments are less parsimonious. What if there is no distinction between the supernatural and the natural world? Dividing nature into natural and supernatural, and delegating spirits to the supernatural, may turn out not to be parsimonious within the contemporary assumptions.

The split between the supernatural and the natural realm of the world doesn't exist in the view of tribal cultures and mystical traditions. Their experience of reality is different from Western understanding. According to the traditional concept, the world is made up of things seen and things hidden without boundary between them. The distinction exists only inside the mind of the unprepared, the uninitiated. For the "knower," natural and supernatural present themselves together as an unseparated whole, both woven into one seamless fabric of reality.

Then who gets the highest score of parsimony? West or East? More precisely, Northwest or Southeast, modern or traditional? (In the section *Educatio Demistificationis,* we will outline the methodology mystical traditions developed to support their view.)

We are not satisfied with the explanatory power of current reasoning. The approach presented here does not ignore the aboriginal view in developing a broader model. The view of divination presented here comes closer in interpretation to the *emic* view of native people—with the term *emic* referring to how cultural phenomena are understood by members of that specific culture, as opposed to *etic* viewpoints, which are based on rational explanations derived from Western science.[17] The basic questions can be formulated this way: To where does the shamanic healer travel, and what is the source of the psychointegrative information?

THE SHAMANIC JOURNEY

The centerpiece of shamanic practice is the shamanic journey. Also known as soul flight, it defines shamans and differentiates them from mediums, psychics, faith healers, and mystics. Only the shaman travels in an ASC, in a shamanic state of consciousness, according to Michael Harner.[18] The shaman is believed to leave the body and to travel at will throughout the expanses of the lower, middle, and upper worlds. Others may heal or minister in an altered state, but it is the shaman alone who primarily engages in soul flight. The shaman is a cosmic traveler because

> . . . his soul can safely abandon his body and roam at vast distances, can penetrate the underworld and rise to the sky. Through his own ecstatic experience he knows the roads of the extraterrestrial regions. He can go below and above because he has already been there. The danger of losing his way in these forbidden regions is still great; but sanctified by his initiation and furnished with his guardian spirit, a shaman is the only human being able to challenge the danger and venture into a mystical geography.[19]

The shaman's journey takes place in "nonordinary reality."[20] Along the way, the shaman may traverse strange landscapes and encounter numerous spirits. Such journeys are generally undertaken in order to learn, to heal, and to help in the service of the community. For instance, the shaman may journey to obtain knowledge or prophecy; to treat illnesses; to appease tribal gods; or to assist individuals in making the transition to the land of the dead. According to the shamanic traditions of five continents, spiritual beings are the source of the energy and information needed to fulfill these goals.

Shamans establish contact with guides or teachers in nonordinary reality from whom they solicit advice regarding individual or tribal problems. Healing (i.e., integrative) power is acquired through interaction with power animals, guardians, or other spiritual entities. In all these activities, during the information-seeking endeavor, the shaman remains in control of her or his faculties, maintains awareness for recalling experiences, and is able to interpret them to members of the community upon returning to ordinary reality. Hence, being able to remember what occurred during a shamanic journey is crucial, and distinguishes the shamanic state of consciousness as a unique ASC.

THE SHAMANIC STATE OF CONSCIOUSNESS

This type of ASC is dreamlike, but shares with the waking world a feeling of reality. In this state the shaman—like a skilled navigator—is keenly aware of the surrounding reality (both ordinary and nonordinary), and can give direction at will to her or his movements. An ASC is one that differs significantly from ordinary or basic consciousness. *Baseline consciousness* might be best defined by the presence of two important subjective characteristics: the sense of self at the center of perception and a sense that this self is identified with the body. States of consciousness in which we lose identification with our body or with our self are definitely ASCs. The former happens in the shamanic state of consciousness.

An ASC is marked psychologically by an individual's modified perceptual responses, processes of memory formation, cognitive skills, affective reactions, and personality structure relative to the basic or ordinary state of consciousness for that person. Integration in an ASC can occur because—based on set and setting (frame of mind and situation of the person, respectively)—an attenuation of the ordinary mode and its primary faculties permits the emergence of integrative symbolic and cognitive processes normally repressed by ordinary consciousness.[21] Orchestrated destructuralization, combined with patterning forces that redirect psychological functioning toward culturally desired patterns of experience, can lead to a stable, integrative ASC.[22]

Some examples of ASCs recognized by Western culture are hypnotic trance, deep sleep, dreaming (REM) sleep, meditation, use of hallucinogenic substances, and periods of peak athletic performance. Some of these states may be spontaneously achieved, instigated by, for example, psychological trauma, sleep disturbance, sensory deprivation or overload, neurochemical imbalance, epileptic fits, and fever. Yet they may also be induced by purposeful activities such as breathing exercises; extreme deprivations (fasting, social isolation); self-inflicted pain (flagellation); reductions or elevations in the level of sensory stimulation; rhythmic photic or sonic stimulation (drumming); and frenzied dancing, spinning, or chanting. Finally, they may be evoked by the use of psychoactive substances. Altered states of consciousness are frequently marked by vivid hallucinations and visions, the content of which is determined by the cultural background, set, and setting.

During its history, humankind has devoted astonishing energy and ingenuity to altering consciousness. In a survey of 488 societies in all parts of the world, Erika Bourguignon[23] found that 437 of the societies had one or more culturally patterned forms of ASC. This means that fully 90 percent of the world's cultures have one or more institutionalized ASC. In tribal societies and Eastern cultures these are regarded—almost without exception—as sacred or revered conditions. Mystical or sacred states of consciousness are called *samadhi* in yoga, *moksha* in Hinduism, *satori* in Zen, *fana* in Sufism, and *ruach hakodesh* in kabbalah. In the West they are known as *unio mystica* (Christian mysticism), a numinal state (Carl Jung), peak experience (Abraham Maslow), holotropic experience (Stanislav Grof), cosmic consciousness (Richard Bucke), and flow (Mihaly Csikszentmihalyi).

Western rational thinking marginalizes or even pathologizes ASCs:

it considers them not only altered but deviant states, cannot differentiate between their disintegrative and integrative forms, and cultivates only the basic state of ordinary consciousness. Hence, the West has been stuck in one state of mind, not capitalizing on the potential of integrative ASCs. To put it in ecological terms, Western civilization, with its institutionalized propensity to escape transcendence, is a monoculture, like a cornfield with low levels of biodiversity, in contrast to the flowery pasture of other traditions. Cultural relativism prohibits comparing and judging the validity of cultural values. Nevertheless, evolution prefers diversity. The West is largely suspicious of ASCs, lacks institutional means to experience the sacred directly, and is left without an understanding of the integrative properties of transcendent ASCs. Techniques for inducing ASCs—typical in tribal cultures—gave way to mere symbolic rituals; direct experience is replaced by faith; and living ritual tradition of the past is fossilized into dogma. The West would benefit from reexamining a deeper level of spirituality, paying respect to higher structures, living in accord with other *holons* (a term favored by Ken Wilber for denoting systems embedded in joint hierarchies), and working to regain personal access to transcendental realms. This infusion of more traditional spirituality into the West has been called the Archaic Revival.[24]

We have seen that the existence of institutionalized procedures for altering consciousness is a near-universal characteristic of human culture. The majority of societies regard ASCs as equal to or of higher value than ordinary consciousness. This raises an intriguing dilemma: if there is more than one accepted form of consciousness, then the reality to which ASCs of the integrative type provide access is multiple, and we cannot discard any one as irrelevant or delusional. Here, we arrive at the incommensurability of realities. It is untenable to make statements from one form of consciousness regarding the reality of another. Rationalists think about satori as a dreamlike state, while a Zen monk may say that it is the ordinary, rational people who live their lives in a dream world. Experiences of nonordinary reality are ineffable in ordinary consciousness. Judging or valuing one state of consciousness compared to another is logically prohibited. "Whereof one cannot speak, thereof one must be silent," said Ludwig Wittgenstein. A Zen Buddhist would agree with him on this accord. Yet we continue to break the silence.

EDUCATIO DEMISTIFICATIONIS

Competing epistemological theories of the last century agree on the nature of human knowledge as a constructive process that builds belief systems based on consensus. There is no such thing as mirroring objective reality, as it is "in itself"—independent from the observer. Emmanuel Kant pointed out the implausability of assuming Ding-an-Sich, a thing-in-itself.[25] Even scientific objectivity cannot achieve that ideal mirroring—even if there was such a thing as scientific objectivity. The evolution of theories is based on internal consistency, explanatory power, and external consistency with other substructures of the knowledge system. The experimental method is the "royal road" to reaching agreement, but this can hardly be applied to liberal arts, where an arduous process of long-lasting debates leads to the necessary consensus. Many people can become excellent experimental scientists, whereas the social sciences have only a few outstanding thinkers in each generation. Experimental science has a simple algorithm to be followed:

> Under such-and-such circumstances (like mine),
> Do this and this (like me),
> Observe what happens,
> And report it.

In other words: 1) set the experimental conditions, 2) define the method, 3) make observations, and 4) publish them.

It should not come as a surprise (but most of the time it does) that mystics follow a similar algorithm, the same methodological schema in their contemplative techniques of seeking knowledge. Authentic mystics ask that nothing be accepted on mere belief or verbal teaching.

Rather, they present a set of tasks within the laboratory of our mind. We experiment, observe results, and compare these results with the experience of others who perform similar experiments. Out of this consensually validated pool of knowledge emerge certain laws—the laws of the spirit.[26] This is a form of empiricism as well. The only difference is the lack of quantifiable measurement. It is not reality's problem, however, that it has immeasurable processes. Rather, it is the problem of scientism, which limits nature to the measurable.

Experimental science is based on quantified measures of external reality. According to its extreme form—scientism—whatever can't be measured in some way is deemed unreal, and thus its value is unknowable. Values, emotions, and intuition have no part in the scientific worldview; there is no room for thoughts and feelings, only measurements of what is "out there." The material side of life—not the internal or spiritual—is all-important. The inner world has been abandoned, and we have lost ties with totality. Scientists with high integrity are aware of the limits of their own method. As a line in the film *Dirty Harry* says, "A man's gotta know his limitations!"[27] The greatest scientific revolutionaries were mystical at heart: Kepler, Newton, and Einstein, to name just a few.

Consensus can be reached in a third manner: hammering concepts into the subject with the help of faith (the word *consensus* is used euphemistically in this case). This is not about attacking the general importance of faith, but is rather about the inflation of faith—exploiting it as the replacement of empirical experience. Dogmatic religions apply this method and thereby abuse faith. From this point of view, there is more similarity between a scientist and a mystic than a scientist and an orthodox religious believer. The claims of both groups of wise men are not based on mere beliefs or doctrines, but rather on direct experience. In the era of the holy Inquisition, scientists and mystics were in the same boat, while after the scientific revolution, mystics had to stay underground. We have so far attempted to demystify mysticism and to move it closer to the scientific method of knowledge building. Now, we will try to reconcile science and the realm of our inner universe.

LEVELS OF ORGANIZATION
RELEVANT TO CONSCIOUSNESS

The table that follows in figure 7.3 summarizes the levels of organization supposedly involved in generating the conscious experience. Because the topic of consciousness is mostly ignored by mainstream neuroscience, it is difficult to determine the opinion of prominent brain researchers concerning the subject. My department chairman once warned me: "If you want to make a career, you must avoid studying consciousness." Despite some positive trends in other disciplines, orthodox neuroscientists avoid the issue, and unorthodox ones use the politically correct term *awareness* when preparing their grant proposals. Nevertheless, with the exception of the levels at the very top and at the very bottom of the table, most neuroscientists would not disagree with the assumption that all these levels represented here are involved in the process.

Because no experimental data can be introduced to support it, this hypothesis is strengthened by pointing out inconsistencies within the current neuroscientific concepts. Again, this is not easy, because we rarely hear established neuroscientists expressing their views on con-

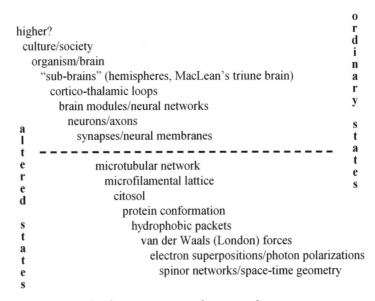

Figure 7.3. Levels of organizations relevant to the conscious experience

sciousness. If they do, they emphasize the neurological correlates of consciousness, as did Francis Crick,[28] who spelled out his radical reductionist vision: "You, your joys and your sorrows, your memories and your ambitions, your sense of personal identity and free will are in fact no more than the behavior of a vast assembly of nerve cells and their associated molecules. As Lewis Carroll's Alice might have phrased it, 'You're nothing but a pack of neurons.'"

Science writer John Horgan criticized such narrow views:

> In a sense, Crick is right. We are nothing but a pack of neurons. At the same time, neuroscience has so far proved to be oddly unsatisfactory. Explaining the mind in terms of neurons has not yielded much more insight or benefit than explaining the mind in terms of quarks and electrons. There are many alternative reductionisms. We are nothing but a pack of idiosyncratic genes. We are nothing but a pack of adaptations sculpted by natural selection. We are nothing but a pack of computational devices dedicated to different tasks. We are nothing but a pack of sexual neuroses. These proclamations, like Crick's, are all defensible, and they are all inadequate.[29]

To avoid the trap of radical reductionism, we must assume that all levels are at work with bidirectional, interrelated, causative processes. We should pay attention to the position of the dashed line in figure 7.3. We may call it the knowledge horizon, because it divides levels based upon their assumed causational role in generating the conscious experience. According to the theory of the neurological correlates of consciousness, the neuroaxonal system has a pivotal role both in the emergence of conscious experience and in the function of levels above it. In his book *The Blank Slate: The Modern Denial of Human Nature,* Steven Pinker writes, "[C]ulture is crucial, but culture could not exist without mental faculties that allow humans to create and learn culture to begin with."[30]

The effect of culture in shaping brain structure and neuroaxonal function is also permitted. This means that bottom-up and top-down interactions are at work above the dashed line, and every level has an active role. This is not the case for interactions below it: the assumption here is that subcellular levels are passive, serving higher levels by permitting, but not shaping, their function. Here the causation operates only from bottom-up, but the role of top-down effects is not believed to operate at this level in mainstream neuroscientific thinking. Above the horizontal line, there is a well-balanced cooperative hierarchy; below it, oligarchy is the rule. Of course, this is an arbitrary delineation with broken symmetry. For improved integrity, we may postulate that subcellular systems add to the experience something that is a characteristic of their level. They can also shape consciousness. Because the size of the subneural component is close to quantum physical measures, the suggested characteristic subcellular levels add to consciousness is their connection to quantum reality or "quantum weirdness," as some physicists like to say. The most outstanding case of quantum weirdness is *nonlocality*, more specifically *signal nonlocality*.

THE END OF LOCAL REALISM AND THE LIMITS OF QUANTUM THEORY

The most unusual feature of quantum reality is its independence of the space–time constraints of classical physics, which assume local realism and local causality. Local realism is a combination of two intuitive notions: 1) the locality principle, which states that physical effects have a finite propagation speed; and 2) the reality principle, which means that particle attributes have definite values independent of the act of observation. The Einstein-Podolsky-Rosen (EPR) paradox was first in formulating the following dilemma: The laws of quantum mechanics are not consistent with the assumptions of local realism. Based on the EPR paradox, Albert Einstein et al.[31] suggested that the theory of quantum mechanics was incomplete. John Bell's theorem[32] indicated that local realism requires invariants that are not present in quantum mechanics, and implied that quantum mechanics cannot satisfy local realism. Bell's experiments[33] provided overwhelming empirical evidence against local realism and demonstrated that under special circumstances, "spooky action at a distance" (using Albert Einstein's words) does in fact occur. Different interpretations of quantum mechanics reject different components of local realism.

In one interpretation, local realism is broken down due to the principle of nonlocality, which posits that distant objects can have direct, instantaneous influence on one another. The nonlocality principle derives from quantum entanglement: a set of particles that have interacted as parts of the same quantum system maintain their interaction after separation, regardless of space and time constrains. Quantum states of two or more entangled objects have to be described with reference to each other, even though the individual objects may be separated light-years in space and millennia in time. State correlation is preserved between observable physical properties of systems connected in quantum entanglement. *Entanglement* means that the involved systems are correlated; it doesn't imply that signals pass between them. To put it simply and anthropomorphically, entangled systems "sense" each other without space and time constraints.

If we add to quantum mechanics some seemingly plausible requirements such as locality, realism, and completeness, then contradiction emerges. In essence, quantum mechanics, with the wave function at its core, cannot be complete, unitary, real, local, nonlinear, and causal at the same time. Competing interpretations of quantum mechanics differ in choosing the conditions they are willing to sacrifice in order to save the rest, or choosing what one may modify with resultant change in the others. The living post–quantum theory is nonlinear, nonunitary, and spontaneously self-organizing, with a "two-way relation" between "it" and "bit."[34]

Though the theory of quantum mechanics has perfect internal consistency and strong predictive power, it has weak external consistency compared to other realms of current knowledge. Nevertheless, it maintains consistency with the theory of relativity. With the help of Heisenberg's uncertainty principle, the theory of relativity is not violated by nonlocal actions because some vital information is scrambled during the process. Some information can be obtained nonlocally, but no one can control the information in advance, in a easily replicable way: bidirectional information exchange with supraluminal (faster-than-light) speed does not occur. Therefore, lack of local realism does not lead to what could be referred to as "spooky communication at a distance."

Some interpreters of contemporary physics suggest that nonlocality is not an esoteric idea. On the contrary, it is a very realistic one. According to them, nonlocality is actually the basic principle of the universe, meaning that the whole universe is an interconnected, entangled totality. According to this view, consciousness is inherently nonlocal as well. This fundamental nonlocality of mind and universe collapses in the ordinary state of consciousness. Space and time are themselves manifestations of this breakdown, and with them the separated array of particles that dominate large areas of the universe. In this interpretation, individual consciousness arises from the interplay of mind—developing within the nonlocal aspect of the universe—and matter, which is the localized aspect of this same universe.

Where in the brain does this interplay occur? What part of the brain serves as an interface between nonlocal and local processes, between the mind and the material universe?

THE MATRIX

After the development of quantum mechanics, many physicists, and subsequently other scientists and nonscientist popularizers, were caught up in the excited belief that quantum theory might explain the mystery of consciousness. There exists a precise correspondence between physical reality and logic, for according to the laws of matrix logic,[35] these are two aspects of the same thing. The striking similarities between the general quantum and thought processes gave rise to the quantum hypothesis of the mind. Discovery of quantum computation added another impetus, and dozens of brain models were developed based on quantum computational principles. Among them, the most elaborate is the Penrose-Hameroff model,[36] though it may not necessarily be the entirely correct or ultimate one.* Nevertheless, the strength of our concept is not tied to the validity of one model, but to the argumentation outlined in the preceding paragraphs for avoiding the trap of radical reductionism.

Roger Penrose and Stuart Hameroff propose that consciousness emerges from biophysical processes acting at the subcellular level and involving cytoskeletal structures. In their model, consciousness is attributed to quantum computation in cytoskeletal proteins organized into a network of microtubules within the brain's neurons. The cytoskeleton is dynamic "scaffolding," a network of tubes and filaments providing both structural support and the means of transportation of subcellular materials in the cell. While the cytoskeleton has traditionally been associated with purely structural functions, recent evidence has revealed that it is involved in signaling and information processing as well.

The microtubules' periodic lattice structure (see figure 7.4 on page 190) seems ideally suited to molecular-scale computation and is possibly the source of the amazing feats of unicellular protozoa. These tiny, one-celled organisms swim, learn, navigate around objects, avoid predators, and find food and mates—all without the benefit of a nervous system. In multicellular organisms, microtubules are connected to each other structurally by protein links and functionally by gap junctions, self-assembling into a nanoscale network that is far more vast than the neuroaxonal system. The human brain has approximately 10^{11} neurons and 10^{18} microtubule units (tubulins). The dimensions of the neuronal cell-body are measured in micrometers; the diameter in nanometers. Microtubules interact with other cell structures, mechanically with the aid of proteins, chemically by ions and "second-messenger" signals, and electrically by voltage fields. In the brain, they organize synaptic connections and regulate synaptic activity responsible for memory and learning.

The microtubular network—with ten million times more elements

---

*A critical approach and an alternative model will be presented in chapter 8 of this book.

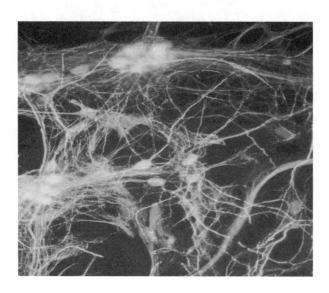

Figure 7.4.
The matrix of
the microtubular
system

than neurons and with a component size close to the quantum physical realm—is a reasonable candidate for quantum computation and nonlocal information processing. The recent paradigm is *signal nonlocality,* meaning that joint tasks that would require exchanging classical signals can take place without passing any information in an entangled system. Signal nonlocality is purely correlational; it doesn't involve information transfer exceeding the speed of light. Therefore, Einstein's principle is not violated. By the way, just as special relativity is a limiting case of general relativity, so is classical quantum mechanics with signal locality a limiting case of postquantum theory with signal nonlocality.[37] The latter is exactly what is implicit in the microtubule model of quantum consciousness and may help us understand what may happen in the mystical or shamanic state of consciousness.

THE QUANTUM ARRAY ANTENNA
OF THE BRAIN

Proposed is a biological model of information processing in which subcellular, cytoskeletal networks serve as a basis for quantum computation and represent a medium of quantum holography. Microtubules fulfill multiple tasks in the experiences of the human mind: they can influence learning at the macro level and shape consciousness at the micro level—and the cytoskeletal matrix may be immense enough to contain holographic information about the whole universe via nonlocal interactions. The discovery of contemporary physics that every form of matter is able to emit quanta of energy which are coherent and nonlocal and which carry usable information about the object demonstrates that quantum physics pertains to all matter of any size, not just elementary particles. The Planck constant can be applied to every size and scale, not only the nanoscale.[38] Furthermore, these energy emissions with nonlocal information sharing can be modeled by the same mathematical formalism used for laser photography, thus the term *quantum holography*. (Here, the word *quantum* does not necessarily imply particle physics.)

It is thought that quantum processes not only underlie all classical phenomena, but also that quantum laws can be applied to macroscale events. This means the quantum principle does not dissipate in the macroworld. The universe replicates, or, as Matti Pitkanen says, "emulates," itself on every level and within the brain's structure as well. In a quantum holographic model, the action of mind is not restricted to the brain, but instead extends to the whole cosmos: The mind breaks out of the skull.

Hank Wesselman, an eminent author of the neoshamanic movement (see more about him in chapter 9), arrived at a similar conclusion:

> Recent changes to quantum theory and current discoveries in neurobiology reveal that the brain organizes information holographically and functions like a massively parallel quantum computer, with the microtubules in the neurons of the brain being the likely quantum hologram receptors. It has been suggested that the quantum hologram is the wave portion of the wave-particle duality for macroscale objects. It has also been proposed that the quantum hologram may tie the phenomenal universe of quantum, micro, macro, and cosmic-sized phenomena together, and that the quantum hologram may

be the mechanism through which nature learns. This knowledge implies that the quantum hologram may be the basis for all perception, including psychic awareness. It also suggests that true psychic sight is not a sixth sense, but rather the first, because it may very well have been around since the Big Bang.[39]

Nonlocal information about the physical universe provides the missing link between objective science and subjective experience, including the mystical experience. Based on the principle of nonlocality and with the quantum array antennae of cytoskeletal networks, the brain is in resonance with the whole universe. If the brain truly contains the whole cosmos, like a hologram, then the perennial wisdom of "As above, so below," (or: "As within, so without"), "The kingdom of heaven is within you," and "Look within; you are the Buddha" obtains a fresh perspective, and there is hope for the integration of these ideas into Western rational thinking. The cytoskeletal matrix can be the mediator of the Jungian collective unconscious, and cytoskeletal quantum holography can explain a very common but obscure phenomenon known as *intuition*.

THE DIRECT–INTUITIVE–NONLOCAL MIND: A SECOND FOUNDATION OF KNOWLEDGE?

We must close our eyes and invoke a new manner of seeing . . . a wakefulness that is the birthright of us all, though few put it to use.

PLOTINUS

Ritual ceremonies and other spiritual practices based on the integrative forms of altered states of consciousness—an integrative ASC, contrasted with a disintegrative state such as psychosis or drunkenness, results in healing—seem to elude neuroscientific explanations based on classical cognition, which can be conceptualized as a perceptual–cognitive–symbolic way of information-processing characteristic of ordinary states of consciousness. This can be contrasted with another mode of information processing based on nonlocal connections, denoted here as direct–intuitive–nonlocal.

The perceptual–cognitive–symbolic mode is neuroaxonally based and relies on sensory perception, cognitive processing, and symbolic (verbal, logical, and visual language) mediation. This form of information-processing is an indirect way of achieving knowledge compared to the direct–intuitive–nonlocal method. In accordance with the indirect nature of its processing, this mode splits the world into subject and object, and then performs modeling. Its linguistic feature makes this mode culturally bound with knowledge transferable between individuals of the same culture. The perceptual–cognitive–symbolic method of information processing has been evolved evolutionally for the purpose of task solving, represents a "coping machine" at work, and reaches its peak in Western scientific thinking.

The introduction of a direct–intuitive–nonlocal channel is necessary for an ontological interpretation of the integrative ASC such as the shamanic state of consciousness. Supposedly, this mode of accessing knowledge is based on subcellular, cytoskeletal functions, provides direct experience bypassing sensory organs without splitting to subject and object, and is not bound by language or other symbols. Because the direct–intuitive–nonlocal channel lacks symbolic–linguistic mediation, it has universal characteristics and shows more transcultural similarity, although culture-specific interpretations exist. This may be why mystics, as compared to materialistic scientists, get better agreement comparing their "data."

David Lewis-William and David Pearce write in their book *Inside the Neolithic Mind*:[40] "In altered states of consciousness the nervous system itself becomes a 'sixth sense.'" We can agree with this and add that it is the cytoskeletal system that acts as a sixth sense. Regretfully, Lewis-Williams and Pearce navigate to the calm waters of academical concepts: ". . . [T]hat produces a variety of images including entoptic phenomena. The brain attempts to recognize, or decode, [these] forms as it does with impressions supplied by the nervous system in a normal state of consciousness." They are right, as are most of the authors who emphasize the "made-up" quality of the ASC. I am not arguing here for the ontological validation of every experience in an ASC, but instead for those few, very informative ones in integrative ASCs.

The direct–intuitive–nonlocal perception of the world also requires rigorous training for its highest development, as is common in all fields. It takes decades to train an indigenous shaman because the direct–intuitive–nonlocal route into the realm of nonordinary consciousness is seemingly capricious; its denizens are so unpredictable, and our perceptual–cognitive–symbolic mind is so unprepared, being incapable of distinguishing between what is personal and what is impersonal. What can be nourished can be atrophied as well, as has occurred in Western civilization, where the direct–intuitive–nonlocal channel has become "forgotten knowledge." Perhaps this was the source of ancient myths. Giving credit to mythical knowledge also means that the teachings of ancient myths and wisdom tradition should be considered as starting points for developing modern scientific theories and that they deserve to be tested as "working hypotheses" by the scientific method.

Gaining control is the means, the modus operandi, of the "coping machine" that is essential for the functioning of the perceptual–cognitive–symbolic mode. On the other hand, the need for control (control freakiness) is entirely incompatible with the direct–intuitive–nonlocal approach. Lao-tzu defines wisdom as "complete willingness to be the plaything of chance circumstances." Surrender opens the doors of a new way of perception. Every success of the coping machinery, such as fame, position, money, or another form of social acceptance, empowers the ego—unless the individual interprets his or her achievements as gifts from the "outside," "from above," and considers the self as a vessel, a mediator of majestic powers. Identifying too strongly with the agent of perceptual–cognitive–symbolic processing suppresses the direct–

intuitive–nonlocal way. As Matthew 19:24 relates: "It is easier for a camel to go through the eye of a needle, than for a rich man to enter into the kingdom of God." Wisdom traditions usually recommend a humble attitude for approaching the spiritual realm. Without humility, the full potency of this realm remains hidden beyond the veil.

Christianity's preoccupation with Original Sin is in essence the declaration of humans' inborn moral incompetence. Promotion of feelings of guilt is a powerful tool for controlling people and for supporting ruling hierarchies at the same time. Perhaps there is no need to use guilt as a method to smash the ego; elimination of ego-inflation might be enough for opening the doors of new perception, and what is left of the ego can be used in the service of the common good. In the realm of the mystical Beyond, the opposite of control freakiness is not loss of control, but rather the delegation of control to spiritual protectors. That may be sufficient for mitigating ego's overwhelming influence.

The perceptual–cognitive–symbolic foundation of knowledge is a result of the brain's interactions with the local aspects of the universe. The direct–intuitive–nonlocal perception of the world derives from the nonlocal features of the cosmos. In other words, the local universe of the classical, Newtonian worldview is the reality of our ordinary consciousness, based on the perceptual–cognitive–symbolic process. On the other hand, the mind's interfacing with the nonlocal universe (revealed by modern physics) generates the reality of nonordinary states.

We consider these issues in order to explicate the wisdom of perennial philosophy, which states that there are two realms of reality. The physical or phenomenal world is not the only reality; another nonphysical (i.e., nonclassical) realm exists. The Buddha rejected complexity of doctrine. His true understanding of the nature of reality was based on the direct experience (direct–intuitive–nonlocal) of that which cannot be put into writing (the principle of ineffability) and on the communion of the spirit (the latter, in our words: cytoskeletally mediated the universe with the help of quantum entanglement).

Besides stratification of reality, according to different states of consciousness, an intriguing corollary of these hypotheses is that intuition becomes a valid source of information. That is, intuition can now be liberated from being some vague offshoot of a multimodal, parallel-processing function of the perceptual–cognitive–symbolic mode. It belongs entirely to the nonlocal channel, which means that when we are talking about intuition and psychic processes—or indeed, any phenomenon belonging to the field of parapsychology—there is a quantum hologram with nonlocal correlations underlying the process. Nonlocality is to the physicist what interconnectedness is to the mystic, and the quantum hologram is the foundation through which to understand virtually all paranormal phenomena.

Accepting the direct–intuitive–nonlocal as the second foundation of knowledge, obscure phenomena such as channeling and divination can be viewed from a new perspective. Channeling is a unique way of gaining intuitive information that has been known for centuries.[41] It is a communication of information to or through a person from a supernatural agency. As such, it represents a form of a broader concept known as divination, which is an attempt to obtain information from supernatural sources. In many instances, the channeled information can stem from the channeler's own mind, but some experts in the field[42] are quite certain that not all channeled information can be traced to the channeler's individual mind. Channeling can be conceptualized by drawing a parallel between it and the tunneling effect.[43] Just as an elementary particle can show up in space, where its presence is impossible according to classical laws of physics, in channeling (and in divination as well), information surfaces where and when it is unexpected according to mainstream views.

In ordinary state of consciousness, the dominant input of the cognitive–symbolic processing is perceptual. In integrative ASC, a shift may occur with significantly more intuitive–nonlocal information passing through cognitive workup and taking the shape of symbolic expressions. If data of nonlocal origin enter the sensory cortex, those would be projected into the perceptual field in the form of visions and apparitions. The body, the somatic center of the "skin-encapsulated" ego, serves as an anchoring point for the perceptual–cognitive–symbolic processing. This reference center is missing in cases of out-of-body experiences (OBEs), when nonlocal data serve the main input of cognitive–symbolic processing with consequential projections into the perceptual field. For the subject, his or her perception during the experience is of colorful scenery and successive external events, whereas the journey actually happens in the quantum hologram of the subcellular matrix. Scholars judging OBEs as mental projections are right. However, the projectional element of the OBE is not entirely in denial with the validity of the information received.

The outlined dualism of human knowledge resembles Julian Jaynes's "bicameral mind,"[44] but we are not concerned as much about a left–right hemispheric distribution of work as about an up–down division between neural and cytoskeletal (nanoneurological) function. The detailed neuroaxonal and subneural processing serve as the basis of the two modes of wisdom known in esoteric traditions for millennia. As Rabbi Joel David Bakst puts it:

According to the teachings of esoteric Judaism, all knowledge, both spiritual and material wisdom, originally coexisted in a seamless unity within a higher dimension. Together these two modes of wisdom comprised a larger, all-encompassing Universal Torah (Torah meaning "Teachings"). A collapse, however, ensued in which the database of all knowledge split itself into "spiritual" and "material" planes of existence. Thus, we have the basis for the historical conflict between "religion" and "science." Yet, any given mystical or technological truth can only be one of two sides of the same puzzle. Thus, the material world is also a mode of spirituality, only externalized and concretized. Vice versa, the spiritual world is a mode of the material reality, only internalized and spiritualized. The ultimate truth is not revealed through the supra-natural alone nor is it only discovered through scientific development—it is more than both.[45]

As we discussed previously, technological truth (that is, the rational perceptual–cognitive–symbolic truth) reflects regularities of sequential events observed from the local aspect of the universe, and mystical knowledge (that is, the irrational direct–intuitive–nonlocal knowledge) results from experiencing correlations that originate from quantum entanglement within the nonlocal frame of reality.* The split must be eliminated, however. As Rabbi Bakst writes:

> Both forms of wisdom are destined to reunite with each other. Perforce, this is stimulating a worldwide paradigm shift in consciousness. This stage of global evolution is the Messianic Era that is central to the teachings of esoteric as well as traditional Judaism. Our role in the re-unification of these two modes of wisdom, according to this doctrine, is achieved by matching the right tool with the right job. In other words, we must use the new maps, models and metaphors of the "wisdom from below" in order to grasp the "wisdom from above." In turn, the transcendent wisdom of the Torah will cast its light of clarity and direction upon the enchanting and often over-powering tools of science and technology.[46]

This is exactly what this chapter has been trying to accomplish: providing a new neurobiological model and new metaphors. Those clumsy word amalgams such as *perceptual–cognitive–symbolic* and *direct–intuitive–nonlocal* are efforts to express the two forms of wisdom in a self-definitive manner. As Rabbi Bakst wrote in a personal communication,

---

*Measurement and replication are the cornerstones of scientific discovery. Both are inherently related to the principles of "local realism" (discussed in the section titled "The End of Local Realism and the Limits of Quantum Theory") and lose significance in the interconnectedness of the nonlocal realm. The uncertainty in the measurement of quantum correlations and their psychological effects helps to clarify why so many eminent scientists are reluctant to accept the existence of hardly replicable paranormal events and mystical phenomena. The study of the mystical experience needs its own standards, similar to those already established in meticulous contemplative techniques.

I would only like to [emphasize] that the two modes—the various amalgams we are compelled to conjure up or the ancient terms the Torah and the rabbis use to quantify them—are equally necessary and, in their roots eternal . . . but they are not equivalent. In other words, "localized" science relative to "non-localized" Supernal Wisdom is always as a body to a soul, a vessel to its light, a glove to its hand. Yet, when they are truly united, as they were before the collapse of the higher dimension, each reveals endless truths contained within each other! Now, that is a real marriage made in heaven!"

The dualism in information-processing carries consequences for artificial intelligence (AI): There are efforts to model the neural perceptual–cognitive–symbolic mode, but what about the subneural direct–intuitive–nonlocal one? Where is the nanotechnology for creating a quantum holograph of the universe, a "machine with soul," a computer capable of accessing the spiritual? We should be very disappointed by the ever-returning futuristic idea that numerous distinguished thinkers entertain of replacing neurons with silicon chips and "downloading" our consciousness into an artificial brain for the purpose of "mind cloning." This kind of mentality—so characteristic of current AI research—carries the bias of radical reductionism: it zooms in on modeling the neuroaxonal and forgets about emulation of other networks that contribute to the phenomenon of consciousness.

KEYS TO NONLOCAL REALMS

The use of psychedelic drugs, monotonous drumming, repeated refrains of chanting, extreme fatigue, strict fasting, frenzied dancing, and so forth during traditional rituals results in the breakdown of ordinary cognition. The outcome is neither chaotic behavior nor insanity. A shift occurs when the coping capacity of perceptual–cognitive–symbolic processing is exhausted in a stressful, unmanageable situation, when the "coping machine" cannot handle the situation (this might be the hidden agenda of the Zen *koans,* when the Zen master continuously frustrates the novice's cognition by paradoxes), or when its influence is turned off in meditation or eliminated by the use of a powerful psychedelic. Then the spiritual universe opens up in the quantum hologram of the direct–intuitive–nonlocal channel, with its particular content projected into the machinery of the neuroaxonal system, a process shaped by set and setting.

Rick Strassman has hypothesized that levels of dimethyltryptamine (DMT), the endogenous psychedelic compound in the brain, is released in near-death experiences or in religious ecstasy or by means of ritual techniques (spirit quest, shamanic initiation).[47] Psychedelic drugs in general, and DMT in particular, are some of the most powerful keys to hell or heaven. Proper doses dissolve ego boundaries. In conditions of total ego-loss, reason recedes as the mind's fundamental orienting function and the new compass must be faith—not inflated faith, which substitutes for empirical experience, but faith in service of the self. Reason is in service of the body-centered, skin-encapsulated individual ego, and the ego can barely guide someone under the influence of a powerful psychedelic or in some other ASC. In the mystical Beyond, in nonlocal realms, faith, guardian angels, or spirit guides can do a better job.

SPIRITED AWAY

Communication with spirits is a key feature of shamanic practice as well as serious mental illness. Where is the difference, then? Perhaps spirits may exist not only in the mind of a psychotic (seriously mentally ill) patient but also "outside" as projected mediators of nonlocal information emerging inside of a person with psychic skills. Spirits are not necessarily projections of unconscious conflicts or complexes (although they may certainly be). They have specific structure and carry information existing in the realm of the direct–intuitive–nonlocal approach. Bypassing the perceptual stage, that information can be brought directly into cognitive–symbolic processing and expressed linguistically in a culture-specific manner. Spiritual beings originating from nonlocal apperceptions have more informative value than do the ghosts of intrapsychic projections. That is one important difference between shamanic healers and schizophrenic patients. Shamanic healers enter an integrative form of an ASC purposefully in service of the community, while schizophrenic patients fall hopelessly into a disintegrative form of an ASC and are unable to bring out any socially useful information from that condition. The main tenet of this chapter is that the difference between psychosis and shamanic states of consciousness is lack of (in psychosis) and presence of (in a shamanic ASC) an integrative information-gaining process from the nonlocal domain.

"How could you, a mathematician, believe that extraterrestrials were sending you messages?" a visitor from Harvard asked the mathematician John Nash, one of the founders of game theory and Nobel Prize laureate in economics who suffered from schizophrenic disorder. "Because the ideas I had about supernatural beings came to me the same way my mathematical ideas did," was Nash's answer. "So I took them seriously." Thus begins Nash's story, a tale of a mathematical genius who slipped into madness and emerged after decades of ghost-like existence to win a Nobel Prize and inspire a major motion picture, *A Beautiful Mind*.[48] His statement is an excellent example of the occurrence of both integrative and disintegrative ASCs in the same person.

In his book *The Cosmic Serpent,* Jeremy Narby presents the hypothesis that shamans take consciousness down to the molecular level and gain access in their visions to information related to DNA, which they call "animate spirits."[49] In essence, Narby got it right. The DNA, packed in chromosomes, is closely related to the microtubular system. There are avant-garde, very nonmainstream theories about DNA being not an originator but rather a receiver of morphogenetic (structure forming) information "lying out there" (that is, in the nonlocal domain). It follows from the conceptual framework of this chapter that DNA receives information from the microtubular network, which is considered the antenna of nonlocal information. With the help of the genetic code, DNA translates that biologically relevant information into the language of protein synthesis in the same way the neuroaxonal system translates the direct–intuitive–nonlocal information into the concepts of cognitive–symbolic processing. In my opinion, Narby's shaman does not gain knowledge about the double helix from the DNA itself; rather, his neuroaxonal system accesses the same nonlocal source that the DNA molecule does!

TRUE HALLUCINATIONS

Shamanic states of consciousness constitute profound changes of perception that can include visual, auditory, olfactory (smell-related), gustatory (taste-related), and somatic (bodily) illusions or hallucinations as well as synesthesia, the blending of sensory modalities (for example, sounds that are perceived as images or colors that are perceived as smells). Nonlocal information can also blend with perceptions of the local aspects of an object or person. An illuminated healer can perceive an aura around the sick person and use its embedded information for therapeutic purposes. Auras in the presented model appear when synesthesia occurs between the two modalities of information processing (local and nonlocal). This kind of aura is different from visualized electromagnetic fields surrounding living or inanimate objects and cannot be photographed using Kirlian photography. Viewing auras entails the conversion of nonlocal information to visual percept with projection to the local realm of reality. Though no mental projection can be recorded instrumentally, this form conveys relevant information; therefore, some sort of reality must be attributed to it.

The outlined conceptualization of auras sets the stage for an interpretation of visionary experiences that is at odds with the current academic view. There is an unspoken assumption within scientific circles—based on the experiences of psychotic, schizophrenic individuals—that the brain simply fabricates hallucinations, whereas, with the images of normal perception, the brain perceives relevant data from the outside world. Both sides of this assumption have some aspect of truth, but both are hopelessly narrow in scope. The brain is not a passive receiver in the process of normal perception: cognitive psychologists have clarified its active role. Visionary hallucinations originating from integrative ASCs have informative value and therefore should be regarded as more than mere fabrications. Would it not be more consistent to state that our brain is both a receiver and a manufacturer of percepts regardless of whether those are normal or visionary? In conclusion: the brain handles the data the same whether coming from the local or the nonlocal domain of reality. The former is accepted as normal perception, the latter can be conceptualized as a hallucination (vision) of the integrative type.

MASTERS OF NONLOCALITY

Shamans are the masters, though not the only ones, of nonlocal realms. In the shamanic state they shift their consciousness from the neuroaxonal mode to the subneural one, enter the quantum hologram stored in the very intricate network of the subcellular systems of their body and journey there. They are in and out at the same time. I suppose that it is the nonlocal correlations that make the out-of-body experience possible. After navigating through nonlocal realms within the quantum hologram, shamans are able to bring information into the local aspect of the universe by mastering nonlocal connections. In essence, they manipulate nonlocal correlations and their conversion into local information, which may involve the transfer of direct–intuitive–nonlocal experience pertinent for healing to the level of cognitive symbolic processing. Yet they are humble, respecting the tenets of Albert Einstein and obeying the law of relativity. An authentic shaman does not exchange clear, quantifiable information in a replicable manner with supraluminal speed, but acquires new information with some uncertainty, expressing it in vague terms and symbols that can be understand only within the framework of shamanic belief system. As Matti Pitkanen phrased it in a personal communication:

> Sharing of mental images by quantum entanglement could be one mechanism that makes possible instantaneous sharing of information.

... It might be that limits in the speed of propagation of the information posed by the light velocity do not produce problems here, since the shaman becomes part of a system which can be arbitrarily large. Interpretation is, however, a problem, since it must be carried out in the conceptual framework provided by the cultural background.

Verifiable (i.e., replicable) information exchange requires transfer at luminal speed and occurs on the local level within classical, though relativistic, space–time boundaries. Signal nonlocality provides supraluminal but somewhat nebulous information. Therefore, even the most honest and respectable master of nonlocality is overshadowed by character features of a charlatan or trickster in the eye of the rational beholder.

REDUCTIO AD ABSURDUM

In the final part of this chapter, we look at a generalization regarding the law of neural pruning. The law states that during critical periods of ontogenesis and before important developmental milestones, there is a strictly programmed, finely patterned, marked reduction in progressively smaller elements of the information processing system of the brain (see box on page 205). Due to our programmed neuron death, we are born with significantly fewer nerve cells than we have during intrauterine life. In the neuro-Darwinian selection model of Gerald Edelman, this program is described as neurons competing with each other for survival. During the first two years of life, there is a reduction of *axon-arborization* (production of new nerve fibers), which is probably related to the development of critical periods of perception, communication, and socialization. In puberty, pruning of synapses establishes neuroaxonal conditions for abstract thinking, marking the onset of Jean Piaget's formal operations stage. Thus, more is not better for the brain. The pruning process in question is strictly programmed, however, and follows certain rules in particular environmental conditions. This is unlike the neural dieback resulting from the toxicity of alcohol in an alcoholic.

The Generalized Law of Pruning

During critical periods of personal growth and before important developmental steps, there is a strictly programmed, finely patterned, very marked reduction in progressively smaller elements of the information-processing system of the brain.

- Intrauterine life: programmed neuron death
  (neuro-Darwinian selection model of Edelman);
- First two years: reduction of axon-arborization
  (critical periods of perception, communication, socialization);
- In adolescence: synaptic pruning
  (Piaget's stage of formal operations, abstract thinking);

- -

- Dual consciousness, Jungian individuation may be related to
  pruning of the microtubular system (see Hameroff's model);
- Biological death—nirvana (after living properly): reduction
  (but not elimination) of the pattern of space–time left after
  the functioning brain (based on Penrose's "Orch OR" model).

Current neuroscientific thinking stops at this point (indicated by the dotted line in the box above). Yet do we ever complete this pruning procedure? Probably not. High stages of consciousness (non-dual consciousness in Ken Wilber's model) or the Jungian individuation may be related to pruning of the microtubular system, as is found in Hameroff's model. At our final exit, at the time of biological death, there is an ultimate step in the reduction (but not a total elimination) of the fabric of space–time left behind by the functioning brain. This idea is connected to Penrose's space–time geometry model of consciousness—based on spinor networks seen at the bottom level of figure 7.3 on page 184.

Can the last step in pruning be related to the survival of the soul? Here we have arrived at what Socrates, the father of European rationalism (and irrationalism), said: "The mind will find the final truth after leaving the body." Socrates believed that once the soul dissociates from the body after death, we are able to engage in pure thought without any deceit from the senses. Stuart Hameroff puts it this way: " . . . when the metabolism . . . is lost, the quantum information leaks out to the space–time geometry in the Universe at large. Being holographic and entangled, it doesn't dissipate. Hence consciousness (or dream-like subconsciousness) can persist."

✧

This chapter has tried to explain something not accepted by the mainstream in terms of something else not accepted by the mainstream. Certainly, this is not the best way to get the approval of the mainstream. Even more provocative, we may challenge the following concepts belonging to the foundation of current Western rational thinking:

- All information comes through the sensory organs, and we can know nothing that does not pass through the senses.
- All we are is within our body. Our consciousness is compartmentalized by the skull, and is a product of our brain's activity.
- There is one unilayered reality.

Only a person liberated from the overwhelming power of these dogmas can understand how the inside and outside paths will eventually converge in consciousness, how by consistently looking inward we can go beyond, and how *within* becomes *beyond*. We may find similar claims and statements in New Age literature. Yet I come from a neuroscience background and am thus approaching these issues from a scientific worldview. Nevertheless, if those who read this feel that their own basic tenets of viewing things have been threatened by this discussion, then perhaps this chapter has fulfilled its goal.

8

HOW CAN Shamans talk with plants and animals?

The Topological Roots of Plant Consciousness and Interspecies Communication

Ede Frecska, M.D.

Vegetalistas, like their counterparts, the Indian shamans of many indigenous groups of the Upper Amazon, claim to derive healing skills and powers from certain plant teachers, often psychoactive, believed to be their mother. Knowledge, particularly medicinal knowledge, comes from the plants themselves; the senior shaman only mediating the transmission of information . . .

LUNA AND AMARINGO,
*AYAHUASCA VISIONS: THE ICONOGRAPHY
OF A PERUVIAN SHAMAN*

In life sciences, plants are considered inferior organisms that passively adapt to different temperature, soil types, injuries, diseases, and physico-chemical and biological conditions. You may ask, "So what? Plants are vegetables, aren't they?" At odds with the canonized scientific and commonly held layperson's view, the traditional idea is of plants being more than helpless objects of elementary forces; they are interactive or—even more—proactive, conscious beings. The concept of *plant consciousness*—in the form of plant spirits—can be traced back to the Middle Ages, and from there to a much earlier time. Even nowadays, aboriginal peoples on five continents believe that plants have spirits or that certain trees are inhabited by their ancestors, and, as the epigraph to this chapter indicates, they claim that knowledge can be acquired from plant teachers.

The relationship between indigenous people and nature is based on shamanistic beliefs that shape adaptive behavioral patterns and provide the foundation for social structures in tribal communities. In the belief system of indigenous cultures, every plant and animal, all forests and meadows, lakes and rivers, mountains and caves have a consciousness of their own. Such notions were cast out entirely from the Western rational mind-set during the Scientific Revolution and the Enlightenment. For the skeptic, these beliefs are ridiculous superstitions and expressions of primitive, magical thinking. That everything in nature might have spirits and that some sort of sentience can be attributed to both living creatures and material objects have been widespread beliefs for millennia in aboriginal cultures. We cannot, then, consider such persistent, transcultural tenets to be useless, primitive misconceptions that have no adaptive value at all and that reflect nothing relevant in nature.

Is there any way to prove that animistic thinking is more than just pure fiction, that it might contain some truth? Definitely not yet. The only thing we can do in this chapter is to show a way toward rationalization by paying respect to what other people think and state about the world. Cultural relativism and linear Darwinism are not necessarily to be believed: the former has a tendency to give equal credit to every cultural accomplishment and the latter posits that the more we go back in time, the more we find primitive ways of thinking.

Here in this chapter we also try to avoid the typical mistakes that passionate New Age thinkers are prone to make. Recently, the concept of plant consciousness has received attention in New Age literature from plant healers, psychic mediums, and "green thumb" gardeners—those who claim to sense plants on subtle levels and carry on meaningful communication with their spirits. Most of the time, these writers discuss their uncontrolled experiences and speculative ideas in superficial ways, ignoring scientific scrutiny and bypassing peer-reviewed journals. The result is that plant consciousness is not taken seriously by well-established scientists, botanists, biologists, and ecologists, or respected scholars of consciousness studies; its proponents are persona non grata in the exclusive club of mainstream science.

DARWIN'S FORGOTTEN IDEA

Because of the widespread assumption that neural networks are necessary for consciousness, common sense does not allow for even the possibility that plants are conscious. Hand in hand with the academic view, common sense ties consciousness to neuroaxonal organization but overlooks the possibility that "the Universe emulates itself on every level."[1] According to this notion, similar experiences may result in other structures below, above, or on the same plane of existence.

Charles Darwin did not overlook this possibility. In studying botany, he noticed that root formations and the network of rootlets show organization similar to that of human brain tissue. In his time, little was known about brain anatomy and information-processing in complex systems. Therefore, his observation has been deemed superficial analogy and has not been taken more seriously. We must keep in mind that 90 percent of our current knowledge regarding brain function has been acquired only during the last two decades. Perhaps it is time to reexamine Darwin's forgotten idea. Here we consider a representative sample of affirmative claims addressing plant consciousness. This chapter will analyze the concept together with unorthodox views regarding animal communication and interpret them within a topological model of consciousness, which goes beyond the traditional neuroaxonal framework.

PLANTS UNDER THE LIE DETECTOR

A review of experiments conducted on plant consciousness and a critical evaluation of their results may help us to form our own opinions regarding whether plants are sentient, conscious beings. Cleve Backster, a leading expert on polygraph machines, conducted pioneering studies in the field of plant consciousness. In 1966, he introduced polygraph research into an entirely new area by hooking up a *Dracaena* cane plant to a polygraph machine in order to detect its rate of water consumption.[2] Backster was interested in how fast water travels from the plant's roots all the way up to the leaves, and thought that the polygraph could indicate the rising of the water by noting changes in plant-surface resistance. He noted that the plant showed unexpected responses as he moved the *Dracaena* around the laboratory, with reactions resembling human galvanic skin responses. Struck by this surprising finding, he applied different stimuli to the plant. Once, he decided to burn one of his plant's leaves. When Backster even thought about setting fire to a leaf, he faced the following reaction: "Then at thirteen minutes, fifty-five seconds chart time, the imagery entered my mind of burning the leaf I was testing. I didn't verbalize, I didn't touch the plant, and I didn't touch the equipment. The only new thing that could have been a stimulus for the plant was the mental image. Yet the plant went wild. The pen jumped right off the top of the chart."

He assumed that the plant somehow sensed his intentions and showed signs of distress. Pretending did not work; in order to get strong galvanic reactions from the plant, his intentions had to be serious. Backster's plant was not only concerned with his hostile plans toward them, but also seemed to be empathetic with regard to the suffering of others: when he caused harm to other living organisms, his plant responded strongly to these other beings' distress. Distance was not an issue; remote perception seemed to be at work: Backster could leave a plant alone while he sat in a bar and talked with friends, and the polygraph device would indicate the plant's reactions to the mood changes he was experiencing during the conversation. Independence from distance has also been reported in publications of prayer experiments: plants at remote locations that had been prayed for did better than nearby plants that were ignored.[3] Marcel Vogel also noticed that distance did not affect his results.[4] Galvanic recordings of plants connected to a polygraph machine correlated with the experimenter's emotions and actions even when the plants and the human were miles apart, as in Backster's case.

Cleve Backster concluded that plants have *primary perception ability,* as indicated by polygraph tests; otherwise, how could the galvanic responses have varied so abruptly, and in accordance with events happening in their surroundings? Backster was careful to avoid the parapsychologically charged term *extrasensory perception,* because he did not see that, in the first place, plants have senses as we usually understand them.

Nevertheless, the scientific community at large has not accepted the work of Backster and his followers. Most of the academic researchers were unable to replicate their results. The problem with studies of this kind is that usually the investigator is as much a part of the experimental setting as the tested plant itself. Those who side with Backster may argue that the sensitivity of the human involved is critically important. An attitude of rigorous analytical distancing can be the reason for the failure of many objective experiments with plants. According to Vogel, there is "a precise and important interaction between the experimenter and the plant which is equal in importance to the equipment being used."[5] He suggested that in successful human–plant communication, human beings must assume the role of active agent by "sensitizing" the plant to be receptive to human attitudes and emotions.

SMART VEGETABLES

Even if primary perception does exist in plants, this does not necessarily mean that plants are conscious. We may interpret most of plant behavior as *instinctive,* but this term is as vague—if not more so—than the concept of consciousness itself. If (as Rupert Sheldrake suggests) there is a trend in current knowledge to grant animals some level of consciousness due to the signs of self-awareness, deceptive skills, and cooperative behavior observed in many animal species, why should we not attribute to plants some sort of consciousness for similar reasons?

Indeed, there are plant experiments with results that point in just this direction. Experiments with *Ambrosia* roots have indicated that these plants are capable of self-recognition through differentiation between self and nonself, an ability that has been considered by some as basic for self-aware beings: the root system of the *Ambrosia* plant detects and avoids other *Ambrosia* plants and plants of different species, indicating self-recognition. The mechanism that helps the plant differentiate between the roots of other plants and its own is unknown, but can be interpreted on a molecular level. Likewise, it is essential for the human immune system to differentiate between self and nonself by chemical means, without resorting to conscious processes. Further, as far as defensive tactics are concerned, there are flowers that detect the approach of pests that visit to steal their nectar, and react by closing up when these insects are nearby.

Plants can orient themselves in space, as indicated by their coordinated movements when they are searching out objects or avoiding obstacles. In an environment where a plant is growing, it will grow toward hidden support and entirely ignore areas without potential support. Plants are able to "run" a maze for light, as laboratory animals do for food: in a mazelike structure with several blind alleys, a vine planted at the closed, dark end can find its way toward the light at the far end without making an error. In addition, we might watch our words if a plant is nearby! Early on, some researchers noticed that both speaking nicely to plants and verbally abusing them influence their growth.[6] This observatio was later corroborated by others: Hoffman reported that tomato plants exposed to gently spoken words on a daily basis produced 23 percent more tomatoes than control plants, which had identical treatment but were not spoken to.[7] Perhaps it is not the words but the positive intent that plants perceive, for psychic healers claim to influence seed germination significantly by adding "positive energy" to the process.[8]

To those who might think that this review is either getting close to or going over the edge regarding the concept of plant consciousness, here is an excerpt from the communication with a corn *deva,** or spirit, as channeled by Robert Shapiro. This indicates how much some psychics attribute superhuman intelligence to devas.

> I am the plant you refer to as corn. I speak to you as the Deva associated with our superconsciousness, the Corn Goddess. I have a very strong spiritual body that not only connects me cosmically to my point of origin but also embraces the earth as a nurturing parent. When I am planted in a field, I choose to feel every row and plant as a unit. Therefore, I do not experience spatial references in the same way as you; I feel myself as the entire field of plants. When an area of corn is accidentally destroyed, some element of protest is expressed from the rest of the corn. Corn shrivels a bit or makes a sound that only the observant farmer notices. I do not shrink out of fear; instead I understand that I am here to sustain you. I am prepared, at any moment, to offer myself in support of my true purpose on this planet. I have a sense of touch similar to that of the human being. I know when I am touched, and I am aware when someone or something is near that is not of my own kind. I have a strong energy field that radiates with an awareness of up to six feet. I have an ability to respond to the change in weather conditions and to the changes from day to night.[9]

If we put aside the notion that Shapiro's channeling may have become tainted by some New Age terminology and an agenda during the

---

*Often, in New Age literature, the embedded consciousness in plant species is called *deva* ("shining one" in Sanskrit). The term is used to describe a creative intelligence that fulfills some sort of morphogenetic and organizational role.

"download" process, and note in addition that the claims of indigenous shamans and contemporary psychics are valid, then we may entertain the possibility that plants not only have some sort of consciousness, but also are extremely intelligent and resourceful beings. Notwithstanding, this consciousness must be very different from our own in that only very special humans are able to recognize it. Thus, it can be easily missed by insensitive analytical approaches. It is possible that our prejudicial mindset, overadapted nature, and lack of sensitivity have led to a diminished ability to recognize consciousness in any form other than our own.

BEYOND THE HORSE'S MOUTH

Amelia Kinkade, author of the book *Straight from the Horse's Mouth,*[10] is an internationally renowned professional interspecies communicator. In this book, she shares her expertise with all readers and assumes that everyone harbors a dormant innate ability to communicate with animals wordlessly and without gestures. She is certain that the only barrier separating people from any other animal is skepticism.

To begin communicating effectively, we must tap into our *clairsentience* (sensing or feeling of a being's energy) and believe that an animal's feelings matter. The next step involves using *clairaudience*—that is, learning how to see pictures in an animal's mind and then exchange images with the animal. Also available to us is a sort of X-ray imaging process that can be used to get inside an animal's body to determine the source or cause of illness or to find a missing pet. All of these involve intuition whose function is increased by guided imagery, meditation, and other exercises. In using these types of intuition, claims Kinkade, we can literally learn to talk with pets—sharing memories or making plans with them, negotiating house rules, mediating sibling rivalries, diagnosing illness, tracking a disappearance, accepting one another's differences, and finding each other again. Apollo 14 Astronaut Captain Edgar Mitchell concurs: "Amelia Kinkade's rapport with animals of all species is quite amazing and consistent. Her talent and effort is helping to overturn centuries of false beliefs about the feelings, understanding, and mind states of our animal friends."

The zoologist Donald Griffin, who has performed research in animal behavior at Harvard, is skeptical about interspecies communication of the kind Kinkade discusses, but agrees that animals are more than bundles of instincts and reflexes reacting to stimuli. In an interview with the *New York Times*,[11] he said: "Animal thoughts and emotions are not just a sentimental pet lover's delusion." His expert opinion reflects a change in academic thinking inspired by two broad cultural trends: the environmental movement's emphasis on the importance of coexisting with rather than exploiting the natural world and the medical profession's gradual recognition of alternative therapies.

"The climate is really changing," says Rupert Sheldrake, a British biologist who has developed the theory of morphic resonance and has written several books on animal and plant development and behavior. "In the last ten years, there is a growing recognition in the academic world that animals could be thought of as having minds and emotions. Scientists are beginning to take a look at what pet owners already know."[12]

Rupert Sheldrake investigates the unexplained abilities of animals who seem to sense when their human companions are about to board an airplane or who know in advance when they are approaching home unexpectedly, when a favorite person is on the other end of the telephone, or when someone is about to have an epileptic seizure. Sheldrake has collected more than three thousand case studies attesting to what at first glance appear to be strange coincidences. He has recorded nearly two hundred instances of dogs, cats, horses, and even parrots predicting earthquakes. Sheldrake conducted an informal survey in England and the United States in which he asked one thousand pet owners whether they believed their pets could communicate telepathically. Forty-eight percent of dog owners and 33 percent of cat owners answered yes. More interesting still, he collected fifteen hundred anecdotes about "seemingly telepathic" messages that pets received successfully from their owners but only 73 cases that flowed the other way. "People seem to be much less sensitive than their animals," Sheldrake concluded. A lot of questions can be raised in response to such claims, but one of the most pertinent is: What part of the brain can provide us and our pets with this kind of sensitivity?

THE MATRIX RELOADED

In chapter 7, we saw that information processing within the central nervous system occurs through hierarchically organized and interconnected networks. This hierarchy of networks does not end at the neuroaxonal level, but also incorporates subcellular, cytoskeletal structures. When the size of the hierarchical components reaches the nanometer range and the number of elements exceeds that of the neuroaxonal system, an interface emerges enabling a transition between neurochemical and quantum physical events. Signal nonlocality, accessed by means of quantum entanglement, is an essential feature of the quantum physical domain. We have discussed that this interface may imply that some manifestations of altered states of consciousness or unconscious\conscious shifts have quantum origin with significant epistemological implications.

Also in chapter 7, a second foundation of knowledge was called direct–intuitive–nonlocal information processing, which utilizes signal nonlocality based on quantum holography within the subcellular network of the brain (and the whole body). This was suggested as a typical functional mode for altered states of consciousness (ASCs) of the integrative type and was contrasted with classical cognition, which was denoted as a perceptual–cognitive–symbolic method of acquiring knowledge and was regarded as the main characteristic of the ordinary state of consciousness. The perceptual–cognitive–symbolic form of information processing is capable of modeling via symbolism and is more culture-bound due to its psycholinguistic features. The direct–intuitive–nonlocal mode, however, lacks symbolic mediation. Therefore, it has more cross-cultural similarity and is practically ineffable regarding classical cognition, though culture-specific translation may occur in this mode. Unavoidably, culture-specific, symbolic processes may shape the perceptual–cognitive–symbolic mode, and its framework is limited to a species, generally. In the remainder of this chapter, we will see how the direct–intuitive–nonlocal method of accessing knowledge can cross over interspecies distances, because its interface or the type of information processing* is shared not only by different species, but also by every living creature.

THE MATRIX REVOLUTION

Networks are all the way up and networks are all the way down—as above, so below: biological organisms are built from a hierarchical organization of complex, *nonmonotonous* networks. A network is considered nonmonotonous if it is made of numerous nonidentical elements connected by diverse interactions. These features define the basis of complexity, and make any kind of nonmonotonous network capable of information processing. They also possess some sort of consciousness—that is, responsiveness, awareness to, and storing of imprints of changes in the ambient environment. A fishnet is monotonous, and regardless of the number of its building blocks, it is dumb. Yet this is probably not true in the case of the web of root fibers, microtubules, and other sub- or supracellular networks, which can contain a high degree of complexity. Also, complex network systems are not restricted to biological organisms. The network hierarchy goes beyond biological boundaries and can be found in nature on both the micro- (e.g., spinor networks) and the macroscale (e.g., Earth's electromagnetic flux tubes), potentially serving as storage for information at each level.

Chapter 7 introduced the Penrose-Hameroff model, which postulates the use of the subneural net of microtubules for quantum computation in biological systems. At the same time, the previous chapter

---

*Filamental networks are the suggested candidates to serve as media for topological consciousness. For more on this, see the section The Matrix Revolution.

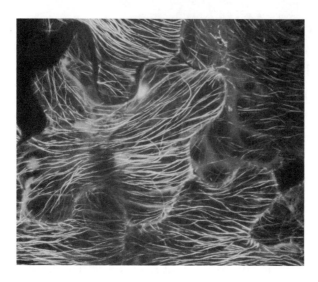

Figure 8.1.
The embedded
microfilamental
network of the cell

emphasized that there remain shortcomings in this intriguing model: despite their impressive intricacy, microtubules may be too coarse to be used in an explanation for the emergence of consciousness—of who we really are. In fact, microtubules do not form the finest texture of subcellular organization. Even smaller and more-subtle structures branch and interconnect in networks comprising an "infoplasm," the basic substance of living material.[13] The most delicate cytoskeletal system is the *microtrabecular lattice,* a web of microfilaments (biofibers) that are seven to nine nanometers in diameter. This represents the current micro frontier, the "ground floor" of living-material organization. If the periodic lattice of microtubules forms a network within a network of neurons, then the microfilamental matrix is a network embedded in the network of microtubules (see figure 8.1)!

Several arguments can be raised against the Penrose-Hameroff model and against many other models of biological quantum computation based on classical quantum mechanics. First of all, they are merely theoretical, without any experimental support. Especially pointed is the critique of Tegmark[14] and others that the warm temperature of the brain should prevent the material organization necessary for quantum computation. As part of the phenomenon called *heat decoherence,*

Brownian movement of particles in the infoplasm disturbs the elements that process the quantum bits (*qubits*). Due to the lack of effective error correction, it eventually may ruin the computation.

In response to Tegmark's criticisms, here is a parallel drawn for example and also an alternative model discussed under the heading Topological Quantum Computation.

1. The electric ray fish has no coil, meaning that technological solutions can be entirely different in biological systems.
2. The brain may develop and maintain a Bose-Einstein condensate, some sort of superconductive state without the seemingly requisite ultracool medium. Or it may incorporate a resilient substrate with highly efficient error correction. *Topological quantum computation* represents a possible solution for the latter problem.

TOPOLOGICAL QUANTUM COMPUTATION

Essentially, quantum computational models are based on a theoretical ability to manufacture, manipulate, and measure quantum states, to process qubits of information encoded in the state of particles, which may be trapped ions, atoms held inside silicon chips, or uniformly oriented molecules organized within the microtubules. Both chips and microtubules face one big problem: They must be carefully shielded to protect them from decoherence.

This is where quantum weaving in the microfilamental lattice enters the equation, and potentially eliminates altogether this problem of heat decoherence. Vaughan Jones's mathematical work[15] has proved that knots can store information. His ideas were developed further by physicists Edward Witten[16] and Alexei Kitaev,[17] both of whom pointed out that a braided system of quantum particles can perform quantum computation. Using quantum particles with just the right properties, braiding can efficiently carry out any quantum computation in super-fast time. Further, while traditional qubits are prone to decoherence, "braiding is robust: just as a passing gust of wind may ruffle your shoelaces but won't untie them, data stored on a quantum braid can survive all kinds of disturbance."[18]

The basic flaw of current theories of quantum computation in biological systems is that they are based on attempts to use concepts of conventional quantum theory. The classical quantum measurement approach postulating the "collapse of the wave function" is unsatisfactory for consciousness studies.[19] The demonstrated quantum weaving model represents a newer physical approach known as *topological geometrodynamics,* which provides a greater perspective.[20] We should not be reductionistic with regard to considering length scales: Matti Pitkanen believes that the universe is "emulating" itself in all length and time scales. Therefore, it is possible that quantum computations may be carried out in biologically relevant length scales. Pitkanen goes on:

> A topological geometrodynamics-based model involves many elements which represent new physics very essential for topological quantum computation. One of the most fascinating possibilities is: time loops are in principle possible by signaling to a geometric past so that arbitrarily long computations could be made instantaneously by iteration in which a new run is initiated in the past. If these loops are really possible, they would mean a complete revolution. Problems which would require a computation of eternity would become solvable.

MIND KINKS, TOPOLOGICAL CONSCIOUSNESS, AND PLANT INTELLIGENCE

Current efforts of artificial intelligence (AI) are aimed toward problem solving, and they usually attempt to simulate cognition as it is processed in the neuroaxonal system of the human brain. This method of developing AI is modeled after the perceptual–cognitive–symbolic mode of gaining knowledge. While machines may exhibit this perceptual–cognitive–symbolic form of intelligence, animals also possess the direct–intuitive–nonlocal form, because they share with humans the subneural mechanisms of quantum holography. But what about plants? Do they harbor a direct–intuitive–nonlocal mind, and only that one?

This controversial question arose after my personal discussion with Dennis McKenna at the home of Luis Eduardo Luna in Wasiwaska, Florianópolis, Brazil. Dennis told of a report that described a giant mushroom, *Armillaria ostoyae,* commonly known as a honey mushroom and sometimes called shoestring rot and found in the Pacific Northwest (specifically, in Malheur National Forest, Oregon). It is one of the biggest single organisms (or a colony having the same DNA) on Earth—an immense network of interwoven fungal fibers (mycelia) spanning twenty-two hundred acres three feet underground and containing one square mile in volume. The visible golden mushrooms aboveground are only the reproducing organs, and therefore represent only the tip of the iceberg. Recently, an even larger *Armillaria ostoyae* covering more than eleven thousand acres was found in Washington state. Genetic tests indicate that fungi are more closely related to animals and human beings than to other plants. Fungal mycelial fibers may develop a network of loops in much bigger numbers than the microfilamental matrix of the human brain.

As the Inca discovered and used in their *quipu* recordings, information can be encoded in knots and threads. A quipu consists of plied, colored threads of cords that store data in knots. It is a coded system that has yet to be deciphered. Computation based on weaving is called *topological,*[21] and a vast loop network may enable an organism or superorganism to resonate with the world, resulting in a phenomenon we could describe as *topological consciousness.* Paul Stamets writes, "The mycelium is an exposed sentient membrane, aware and responsive to changes in its environment. . . . Interlacing mycelial membranes form, I believe, a complex neuron-like web that acts as a fungal collective consciousness."[22]

Besides Stamets, the McKenna brothers (Dennis and Terence) were among the first outspoken proponents of mushroom and plant consciousness—which we humans are able to tap in to in altered states of consciousness. Although plants cannot speak because they lack a neuroaxonal system, they can be in deeper contact with the world than we suppose, and are able to communicate with us.[23] When we use our topological (direct–intuitive–nonlocal) consciousness that's hidden in the fabric of the subcellular matrix, and we liberate it from the suppression of the overdominant perceptual–cognitive–symbolic cognition of ordinary consciousness through the use of particular rituals, we can access the wisdom of the plant kingdom.

The size of topological consciousness does not necessarily reach its peak at the giant-mushroom level. Threads—loops on every scale—can form a topology emerging in consciousness. Pando (or the Trembling Giant) is a clonal colony of a single male aspen tree (*Populus tremuloides*) located in the state of Utah, determined to be part of a single living organism as revealed by identical genetic markers and the existence of one massive underground root system. The plant is estimated to weigh six thousand tons, making it the heaviest known organism in existence. The root system of Pando, at eighty thousand years old, is thought to be one of the oldest known living beings in existence. The giant marine plant *Posidonia oceanica* has been discovered in the Mediterranean Sea (near the Spanish Balearic Islands) and has a length of several miles and an estimated age of about one hundred thousand years. We can only imagine the kind of topological wisdom held by a plant such as Pando or this marine organism. What's more, the majority of plants on Earth with interconnected root fibers may represent a form of topological superconsciousness, the Gaian mind. A huge network of plants—like the Internet—shares information on changes in the environment, and possesses a form of intelligence that only a few of us can recognize.

In an alternative model based on his theory of topological geometrodynamics, Pitkanen[24] proposes that the flux tubes of Earth's magnetic field and the magnetic field of all living systems are a network of
superconductors. These flux tubes might be a kind of nervous system
not only of the entire biosphere, but also of the whole Blue Planet, and
they might make it possible to access an enormous amount of information from Earth's past, present, and future. Electromagnetic flux tubes
can serve as a medium for meaningful communication among plants,
animals, humans, and—fasten your seat belts—material objects and
nonliving entities such as rocks, caves, rivers, and lakes. With Pitkanen's
model, perhaps it is possible to understand (and even experience) every
entity to which indigenous peoples attribute spirit: animals, plants, and
minerals.

✧

This chapter represents an exploration into unknown territory—the
netherworld of plant and animal consciousness. Perhaps it is indeed
possible to approach rationally and to study seriously questions of
plant consciousness and telepathic communication with animals. It is
hoped that the information in this chapter will help us to interpret
the mystery of our symbiotic relationship with the plant world and
why shamans of the Upper Amazon are adhering to absolute truth
in their statements regarding obtaining knowledge from plants themselves with the help of ayahuasca and while in highly altered states of
consciousness.

9

cɫose encounters of the ancient kind and spontaneous DMT release

Ede Frecska, M.D.

For millennia, encounters with divine, otherworldly entities have been among the most profound human experiences, expressed in visions and prophecies, omens and oracles, dreams and revelations. Divine encounters were recorded in the earliest scriptures and reveal the most ancient and most powerful drama that spans heaven, Earth, and hell. On the stage of this drama the actors were gods and goddesses, demigods and angels, heroes and heroines, humans and humanoids. The encounters with divine beings had immense power, affecting both the life of individuals experiencing them and communities hearing reports of them. These encounters were the first spiritual illuminations, transformative experiences that had an incredible impact on human affairs, changing the fate of rulers, building or ruining empires, inspiring prophets, and sprouting world religions.

Divine encounters can be considered the primary source of spiritual wisdom. While all religious individuals would agree that scripture provides the infallible rule for faith and practice, most believers also agree that authentic divine encounters carry an even higher authority than holy scripture. According to the Hebrew manuscripts, God communicated to Moses through a revelation, not in writing—the scripture merely followed the experience of the Divine. As God said to Moses (Exodus 24:12, Masoretic Text version): "Come up to Me into the mount and be there; and I will give thee the tables of stone, and the law and the commandment, which I have written, that thou mayest teach them."

This citation refers to one of the greatest moments in the history of human civilization. There were others, and the most significant developmental steps in ancient history were based on divine encounters. By opening doorways to the supernatural, divine encounters expose a great degree of truth and moral insight. The state of mind of those who experience such encounters is undeniably altered from the ordinary state of consciousness. Further, these encounters are reflected in the nonordinary perceptions, intense emotional responses, and exceptional cognitive performances accompanying such experiences.

Earlier, we discovered the difference between integrative and disintegrative forms of altered states of consciousness (ASCs) and traced the main difference between them to the lack or presence of divination, which is conceived as a process of accessing transformative information from spiritual realms. Among integrative ASCs, divine encounters represent the uppermost level and have immense power in facilitating human reintegration on the highest scale: they can create civilizations and shape societies in accord with the spiritual realm. Just as in the less dramatic although highly adaptive forms of psychointegration[1] such as shamanic healing, in which some kind of restorative information is incorporated into the system to be treated, in the instance of divine encounters there must be an intense information flow that results in integration on a larger scale, denoted here as *sociointegration* (paraphrasing Winkelman's term *psychointegration*). The sociointegrative form of divine encounters is so profound and transforming that rational thinking cannot cope with it, leading to speculative interpretations relating to extraterrestrial intervention, invasion from outer space, or manipulation by nonhuman intelligence.

For those who have successfully wrestled other chapters here, it is easier to understand that shamanic journeys and divine encounters have the same principal motif: access to reintegrative, transformative information from spiritual sources that in our opinion appear to originate in the nonlocal universe. This chapter will guide us through other theories dealing with nonhuman invaders from the local universe, or extraterrestrial information providers of the human race.

RAMBAN'S CONUNDRUM

Moses Ben Nachman (1194–1270), also known as Ramban or Nachmanides, was a medieval scholar, Catalan rabbi, influential kabbalist, biblical commentator, and great thinker of his time. He lived in a prosperous era of the history of the Jewish religious tradition. Two prominent schools of Jewish culture existed in medieval Europe: the Tzorfat School, headed by the world-renowned Bible and Talmud commentator Rabbi Solomon Ben Isaac (referred to as Rashi), and the Sephardic School, headed by a group of brilliant scholars including Rabbi Judah Ben Samuel Halevi, Moses Ben Maimon (Maimonides), and Ramban himself. Ramban was not only an influential follower and critic of Maimonides's rationalism, but at the same time he developed the ideas of kabbalah and used some of them in his commentaries on the Bible.

Though Ramban was the first kabbalist to openly discuss the esoteric doctrines of kabbalah, he had always considered that the deep kabbalah teachings were only for the chosen ones, and many times he evaded open explanations of his ideas, noting that there was a secret behind the text and its interpretation. One of Ramban's enigmas was the "Nephilim secret." The English translation of the Masoretic Text of Genesis 6:4 says: "The Nephilim were in the Earth in those days, and also after that, when the sons of God came in unto the daughters of men, and they bore children to them; the same were the mighty men that were of old, the men of renown."

Here is Ramban's commentary to this verse of Genesis 6, found in the work of Mikra'ot Gedolot:[2] "But the Midrash Pirkei Rabbi Eliezer, which is mentioned in the Talmud, treatise Yoma explains the word 'HaNphilim' [Nephilim] as Messengers fallen from the sky. That is the best commentary for the verse Genesis 6:4. But to explain the secret contained in this verse, it is necessary to write very much."*

Rashi commented similarly on Bereshith Rabbah: "They were called Nephilim because they fell [Naphlu] and caused the downfall [Hipilu] of the world." Later interpreters stated that the Nephilim were so called because the heart of man fell from fear of them. That was a necessary shift from Ramban's version, because such an idea was very dangerous for both the ruling Christians and the accepted Jewish ideology. According to Matest Agrest,[3] however, "for the contemporary reader it is evident that Ramban sees in this verse a record of the descending of manlike messengers from another world to the Earth, that is, *paleocontact*."

PALEOCONTACT THEORIES

The advocates of these notions propose that advanced extraterrestrials have played an influential role in human history. The originator of this idea is Matest Agrest, a Russian-born ethnologist and mathematician who was the first to advance a theory that intelligent beings from outer space visited Earth in ancient times and that certain monuments of past cultures on Earth have resulted from contact with an extraterrestrial race. It was in an article printed on February 9, 1960, in the Russian *Literaturnaya Gazeta* (not a scientific journal) where Agrest proposed that Earth was visited by extraterrestrials in prehistoric times. His concept was very soon circulated in the world media, and was

---

*Ramban also offers the interpretation that the Nephilim were so called because they were the offspring of "the Sons of God" who were born to less-than-superior women and therefore were inferior compared to children born of Noah's daughters.

popularized later by Erich von Däniken. Because of his experience in investigating old manuscripts, Agrest noticed that the Hebrew word נפלים (Nephilim) contains the core relevant concept, but is only transliterated into English.

In several translations, the word נפלים (Nephilim) is deciphered as "giants" or "titans." Agrest's aim is to demonstrate that the translation of the Hebrew word Nephilim as "giant" in Genesis 6:4 is incorrect. According to Agrest, the correct meaning of Nephilim is "beings fallen" (from the sky). Therefore, Agrest believes that this verse reports that in the time of Enoch, extraterrestrial humanlike beings descended to Earth. Thus, Genesis 6:4 becomes a written document of paleocontact. By rediscovering one of Ramban's commentaries on Genesis 6, Agrest introduces a misinterpretation that has become widespread in science-fiction literature and on the Internet: that the Nephilim are the fallen angels.

Also in Genesis, Agrest found a sentence he interpreted as an opposite event: the ascension of a man from Earth to the heavens. The sentence refers to Enoch and is found in Genesis 5:24: "Enoch walked with God, then he was no more, for God took him." The Bible informs us meticulously of the age of death of all the ancient ancestors, but there is no note about the death of Enoch. There is a Jewish legend that he was the inventor not only of the written language, but also of mathematics and astronomy. In the Qur'an (Sura 19:56), Enoch is named Idris—a man of truth.

According to the Zohar, the masterpiece of kabbalah, there was a Book of Enoch in ancient times, and it was mentioned by the apostle Jude as apocryphal. Like many other apocrypha, the Book of Enoch was lost until it was rediscovered by the Scottish explorer James Bruce in 1773. It follows the structure of the Bible—indeed, the first seven chapters of the discovered Book of Enoch are essentially the same as those in the Bible—and Agrest uses verses 1–7 in chapter 6 as reference for his paleocontact theory:

1. And it came to pass that after the eons of men multiplied in those days (the days of Jared, the father of Enoch) . . .
2. And the angels, the sons of heaven, saw them. . . .
5. There were two hundred of them in all.
6. And they descended on Ardis which is the top of the mountain Hermon. . . .
7. and here are the names of their superiors [twenty names are given].

Here Agrest correlates the location of the place of descending, Mount Hermon, and the time of descending, the time of Jared. It is worth noting that the name Jared in Hebrew means "descended." The event of descending of humanoid beings from the sky supposedly made a great impression on the inhabitants of Earth. In biblical times, children born at the time of a remarkable event were named after the event. Thus, the name of Enoch's father was Jared. So—Agrest posits—it is possible that the divine beings fallen from the sky who are mentioned in chapter 6 of Genesis really descended from the mountain of Hermon in the time of Jared.

Another element of the paleocontact view is the suggestion that much of human wisdom or religion was given by space invaders in ancient times. This possibility has been considered by some scientists, including Carl Sagan and the Russian astronomer Iosif Shklovsky. Although Sagan, Shklovsky, and other highly regarded academics took seriously the possibility of extraterrestrial visitations in Earth's past, they were generally cautious in their speculations. While Sagan was known as a skeptic with rergard to the existence of UFOs, in the book he coauthored with Shklovsky[4] he argues that technologically advanced extraterrestrial civilizations were common in the universe, and he considers it very probable that Earth had been visited several times in the past.

Popular authors, most notably Erich von Däniken[5] and Zecharia Sitchin,[6] appear to be less critical in their approach, and they have

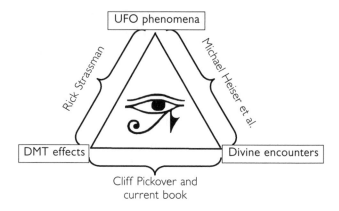

Figure 9.1. Manifestations of the nonlocal universe

been the most outspoken advocates of the ancient-astronaut hypothesis. Indeed, this ancient-astronaut theory, an expansion and perhaps a less credible elaboration of the paleocontact theory, often claims that human beings are either the descendants or creations of aliens who landed on Earth millennia ago.

Our purpose here is to discover what might be relevant in the sometimes remarkable and sometimes outlandish theories of von Däniken and Sitchin and to clarify the pros and cons of the ancient-astronaut theory. In doing so, we will draw upon the work of Rick Strassman and of the ancient religion expert Michael Heiser, which provides additional insights into UFO encounters (figure 9.1).

THE FALL OF THE FALL OF THE NEPHILIM

There has been a great deal written about the meaning of the Hebrew word Nephilim. Many—like Agrest and Sitchin—have accepted the idea that the word Nephilim is simply the masculine plural participle of the Hebrew *naphal,* "fall." According to Michael Heiser, a well-read linguist of Near Eastern languages and a stern critic of Sitchin, practically all of these interpreters—even many scholars of the Hebrew scriptures, Ramban included—are wrong, because the typical explanation that Nephilim comes from the Hebrew *naphal* does not fit with Hebrew morphological patterns for a masculine plural participle in any stem.

The ancient Hebrew language was originally written without vowels. Around the sixth century BCE, however, Hebrew began to use certain consonants for vowel sounds. The reason for this historical development was the preservation of correct pronunciation: at the time of the Babylonian exile, Hebrew was being lost as a spoken tongue; vowels were incorporated into the system to teach people to read correctly. Conflicting interpretations may derive from the use of different missing vowels associated with the same consonants in ancient scriptures.

Michael Heiser eloquently shows us that the form of the word Nephilim does not derive either from the active or passive participle of the Hebrew *naphal* and cannot mean "those who fall," "those who fall upon," or "fallen ones."[7] These meanings do not match the form and the form does not match these meanings. Nor were Nephilim given the designation of "fallen" because of some inherently fallen spiritual state (as in Original Sin, which led to the expulsion from Eden). Heiser indicates that there is good reason to return to and accept the earlier version of scripture. His conclusion is that the word Nephilim is better interpreted from the Aramaic noun *naphil* as "giants" or "titans," as the name was interpreted in conventional translations of the Bible.

Even more, according to Heiser, the word Nephilim does not describe a human race. In the Hebrew scriptures, family lines or races of people were generally designated by their founding male ancestor. For example, the Anakim were descendants of Anak and the Edomim (Edomites) originated from Edom (one of Esau's names in the Hebrew scriptures). Yet the Nephilim have never been described as being descended from anybody. Because the Bible describes them both before and after the Deluge, if the Nephilim were humans, then it would contradict the rest of scripture, which, as 1 Peter 3:20 shows, indicates clearly that there were only eight survivors of the Flood: "[I]n the days of Noah, during the construction of the ark, in which a few, that is, eight persons, were brought safely through the water."

Zecharia Sitchin leans toward the "fallen" explanation, because his purpose is to prove the idea that the Nephilim were extraterrestrials who descended to Earth in rocket ships. For this same reason, he keeps arguing, despite lacking consistent textual evidence, that the Nephilim are the Sons of God. Though this conclusion and extrapolation may be a bit off the mark, as we will see here, with reasonable support of experts, it is very likely that our ancestors witnessed humanlike beings arriving from the skies. Yet it was not the Nephilim who descended from heaven. Instead, it was the Sons of God, and the Nephilim were their offspring.

THE SONS OF GOD, THE WATCHERS

In addition to the puzzling origin of the Nephilim, the identity of the Sons of God is a mystery of Genesis 6—and the two riddles are related. Modern-day commentators suggest that the term Sons of God refers to a tribe of exceptionally tall, good-looking men who appeared in biblical lands and were appealing to women. At variance with contemporary views, ancient rabbis ascertained that the Sons of God were angels. For argument, the rabbis brought up the prologue of the Book of Job, in which God has a dialogue with two angels, Samyaza and Azazel, who condemn the corrupt ways of men.

The angels convince God to let them descend to Earth to prove their righteousness. When they do, they are immediately filled with desire for the beautiful daughters of men: " . . . the sons of God saw the daughters of men that they were fair; and they took them for wives, whomsoever they chose." The offspring of these unions are denoted by the word Nephilim, which has been better interpreted to mean "giants," rather than "fallen angels," because they were not "fallen ones," though their heavenly predecessors were.

Though Genesis 6 tells us that the heavenly ones married women, it does not condemn this as a sin. Here, the Sons of God are given no specific name or function; they could represent fallen angels or simply divine beings that mated with earthly women. The Sons of God also appear in Psalm 82 and in the apocryphal books of Enoch and Jubilees, in which they are perpetrators of evil deeds and inclinations. Psalm 82 tells that the angels (plural *elohim*) sinned, but does not tell how—that is, it does not mention that they married human females. Some scholars suppose that the angels' sin was reproducing with mortals. In the Book of Enoch, the Sons of God are called Watchers, angels dispatched to Earth simply to watch over human affairs. Samyaza, Azazel, and the others failed in their duty, became corrupt, and taught their human hosts to make metals, weapons, cosmetics, and other accoutrements of civilization that had been kept secret in heaven. According to the Book of Enoch, the Watchers numbered two hundred (but only their leaders were named)—the size of their group was large enough for a heavenly congregation.

DIVINE COUNCIL IN THE GARDEN OF EDEN

It is well known to scholars of the Hebrew scriptures that scripture often depicts God presiding over a council of divine beings.[8] A number of passages in the Hebrew Bible describe the divine council's function with precise terminology, and a picture emerges that is rather different from that held by the Christian tradition. In a biblical scene, God is pictured as the chief deity enthroned among the members of his council standing before him, and the members of this heavenly assembly—the Sons of God—who serve to emphasize and execute God's decisions. According to scripture, there has been a heavenly council of spiritual beings that has influence over our world—yet for nearly the past two millennia, there has been a general misunderstanding of the way God governs human affairs. A singular God (Elohim) leads a divine council consisting of other, less powerful gods (plural *elohim*), and the Garden of Eden was their meeting place. Instead of being a place of human habitation, this garden was reserved as a divine abode;

God put Adam there "to till it and to keep it," possibly in service of the heavenly council.

According to some scholars, Genesis 1:26 indicates that the Sons of God were present during the week of Creation: Genesis 1:26 states, "... [A]nd God said: 'Let us make man in our image, after our likeness...'" and Job 38:6, 7, says, "Whereupon were the foundations thereof fastened? Or who laid the corner-stone thereof, when the morning stars sang together, and all the Sons of God shouted for joy?" To make matters more complicated, though, there were malevolent spiritual powers in the heavens that influenced humankind, teaching humans evil things and opposing God's people. As Paul wrote in Ephesians 6:12: "For we do not wrestle against flesh and blood, but against principalities, against powers, against the rulers of the darkness of this age, against spiritual hosts of wickedness in the heavenly places."

Discovering in the Bible that godlike beings, Sons of God, already existed from the time of creation and were governing humans—at times with dubious intent—does not require us to view Israelite religion as polytheistic, but definitely points toward a Sumerian influence on the Book of Genesis.

THE SUMERIAN CONNECTION

As far as we know today, Sumer (the biblical Shinar) is where civilization began, appearing suddenly about six thousand years ago in the delta of the Tigris and Euphrates Rivers, though there is some disagreement about its primacy, because Jericho in Israel is eleven thousand years old and is thought to be the oldest city in the world. In any case, the Sumerian civilization left the oldest written records we have and seemed to be thriving several hundred years before the Egyptians (4000 BCE for Sumer civilization and 3500 BCE for Egyptian civilization). Both cultures have much in common, however—though there are many differences between the two. We may find that both derived from a common antecedent civilization.

Zecharia Sitchin, the pioneer of research into the Sumerian past, writes passionately—for good reason—about the accomplishments of the Sumerian culture:

> It gave Humankind almost every "first" in all that matters as integral components of a high civilization—not just the first brick making . . . but also the first high-rise temples and palaces, the first priests and kings; the first wheel, the first kiln, the first medicine and pharmacology; the first musicians and dancers, artisans and craftsmen, merchants and caravaneers, law codes and judges, weights and measures. The first astronomers and observatories were there, and the first mathematicians. And perhaps most important of all: it was there, as early as 3800 BCE, that writing began, making Sumer the land of the first scribes who wrote down on clay tablets in the wedge-like script ("cuneiform") the most astounding tales of gods and humans. Scholars regard these ancient texts as myths. We, however, consider them to be records of events that have essentially happened.[9]

Many authors have also noticed that the Bible might have been influenced by ancient Sumerian stories, because many verses in the Book of Genesis, for example, are found much earlier in Sumerian and Babylonian tablets—but in more expanded and detailed form. Sumerians had stories similar to those that appear in Genesis 1–11. Some of the influential Sumerian texts are the *Enuma Elish* (Epic of Creation), the King List, and the Flood story. In these texts are well-elaborated stories of Sumerian gods and goddesses, with the key motifs reappearing in the myths of almost every ancient Near Eastern culture. Many adopted some of these Sumerian stories and wrote them down as best they could without having direct access to the original tablets. Because of this, the stories went through a transformation over time. In addition, mistranslations and errors accumulated because of the different languages and influences of individual translators who placed their own stamp on them. It is likely that even the honorable scribes of the Hebrew Bible were not immune to these errors. Yet all these ancient depictions augment the biblical narrative, and paint a detailed picture of a course of events with identifiable principal participants (though their names differ in different versions) who come together in the saga of divine encounters. Academic scholars by and large persist in calling all such evidence fiction or mythology.

The merit of Sitchin lies in the fact that he was one of the first who noticed that certain texts have an older origin than the Hebrew Bible, and he gave credit to these stories by considering them as records of real, historical events. Indeed, those events may have happened, but let us look for the scene of the almighty drama in a different domain of reality. Who were these Sumerian deities, the protagonists of the earliest written stories? Were they just actors of mythical legends, as we judge them today? Or were they—as some scholars are beginning to believe—real beings who were somehow superior to the common Sumerians? Were they considered gods because they did incomprehensible things that even today we would see as godlike? Prior to addressing these questions, let us turn to the most enigmatic Sumerian deities: the Anunnaki.

THE ANUNNAKI

There is much confusion among researchers, scholars, and laypeople about the identity of the Anunnaki. What most agree on is that the Anunnaki were worshipped, admired, and feared as gods by the Sumerians. It was the Anunnaki who taught the people a wide array of "civilized behaviors" such as art, music, poetry, astronomy, mathematics, architecture, mining, metallurgy, jewelry-making, tailoring, blacksmithing, human sacrifice, and warfare. As the ancient lore indicates, they also engaged in evil behavior, and were demoted from the heavens.

According to Sitchin's interpretation of the ancient Sumerian texts, the name Anunnaki literally means "those who from heaven to Earth came." According to Heiser, however, this is not correct. His translation is "princely offspring." As sons of Anu (The Heavenly One), they were high in rank, but some of them were later consigned to the netherworld and were turned into "infernal gods." As Sitchin tells it, the Anunnaki arrived on our planet from outer space with the order of Anu (The Heavenly One) under the leadership of Ea (He Whose House Is Water), later called Enki (Lord of Earth), and here they established a colony named Eridu (House in the Faraway Built). The extraterrestrial visitors' mission was obtaining gold, which they needed on their home planet, Nibiru. The colonization did not go well. More and more Anunnaki had to travel to Earth, and in the end their number reached six hundred. About half of them, the group of the Igigi (Those Who Observe and See), remained skyborne, fulfilling interplanetary liaison-type functions.

Enki, who also served as the chief scientist of the Anunnaki, had a solution for speeding up the mission. He said: "Let us create a primitive worker, which will take over the backbreaking toil." Enki created the first intelligent worker from a hominid (proto–*Homo sapiens*) he found in southeast Africa. According to Sitchin, he achieved the task by mixing the blood of a young Anunnaki male with the egg of a female hominid. The fertilized egg was then inserted into the womb of a female Anunnaki, and after a tense waiting period a model man, Adamu, was born.

Heiser's interpretation of Sumerian texts is at odds with Sitchin's: Acting as judges in their high estate, the Anunnaki contributed nothing but approval to the idea of killing one of the gods and making humans from his remains. According to Heiser, Sumerian tablets do mention hybridized human beings created by a god with the approval of the Anunnaki. Directly or indirectly, Enki was also involved in the business of creating a royal race—the Nephilim in the Hebrew Bible—for the purpose of keeping the upgraded hominids in slavery and ensuring that they remained "civilized." In some tales, the royalty was said to be a combination of reptiles and humans.

Who, then, were Enki and the Anunnaki? As readers may have figured out by now, Enki and the Anunnaki were the Sons of God, the fallen angels of the biblical texts. Actually, there were different classes of celestial beings who functioned in a divine hierarchy and eventually were caught up in spiritual warfare. The Hebrew Bible has laid it out quite well, but this story did not make it to English translations. The description of the creation of humans can be extracted from the Hebrew scriptures and summed up briefly: Elohim said in front of the Sons of God (the "fallen ones"): "Let us make Adam in our image, after our likeness." Then, with the consent of the heavenly council, the task was carried out: "And Elohim created Adam in his image." The Elohim of Hebrew mythology corresponds to Anu, and Enki—the keeper of knowledge—is undoubtedly the source of the biblical serpent in the Garden of Eden. Based on ancient descriptions, Sitchin has also suggested that the Anunnaki probably had some

Figure 9.2. Ritual object from the Ubaid period of Sumer

quasi-reptilian form. Figure 9.2 shows a statuette with clear reptilian features found at the Al Ubaid archaeological site in Iraq. It belongs to the Ubaid period, dating from 5900 BCE to 4000 BCE—predating the classical Sumerian era—and probably depicts the mother goddess Inanna aka Ninhursag (Lady of the Mountaintop). There is no official explanation for the intriguing shape of the statuette. The figurine is labeled a "ritual object," common parlance in archaeological circles when all are uncertain as to what a particular object represents.

Who were those Anunnaki who orbited in the skies and appeared in the Akkadian and Babylonian tales under the name Igigi? *Igi* refers to "eye" in Akkadian and is combined with the cuneiform *gi,* which symbolizes sexual intercourse. Igigi can then be translated as "Eyes in the Sky"—the Watchers, who deflower sexually. Similar entities show up in dozens of ancient cultures. In ancient Greek mythology, there are Titans, godly beings who descended from heaven and who had sexual intercourse with earthly women. Interestingly, the Greek word *titanos* means "gray," a term sometimes used to describe mantislike aliens. As readers may have guessed by now (and we summarize in Table 9.1), ancient peoples have told us a complete story of UFO encounters and abductions that occurred probably as far back as six thousand years ago—perhaps even more. The British archaeologist Steven Mithen states in his book on human prehistory, *After the Ice:* "[T]he possibility arises that the roots of Babylonian religion lie in the Neolithic culture of the Jordan valley around 6500 BC."[10]

Based on the plaster statues found at the 'Ain Ghazal excavation site in 1983, Mithen paints a ritual scene with a detailed description of deities: "They have flattish bodies, elongated necks, large round faces, and wide-open eyes with deep black centers. The noses are molded as stubs; the lips hardly exist at all. The plaster is pure white." This sounds eerily like a description of aliens, though Mithen interprets them as ghosts. Controversial and contradictory as it may sound, we conceptualize them differently: they were "real" extraterrestrials—though not necessarily from outer space. Instead, these ancient gods—possibly the teachers of agriculture—were DMT (dimethyltryptamine) entities that emerged from inner space. Strassman's work indicates that at least some of the experiences involving UFO encounters are probably related to the effect of the endohallucinogen compound DMT.[11] Here we try to learn if a similar phenomenon might have occurred in ancient times, might have served as the source of creation myths, and might represent a different kind of reality, one that is called nonlocality elsewhere in this book.

TABLE 9.1 PARALLELS AMONG SUMERIAN, HEBREW, AND CONTEMPORARY MYTHS

Sumerian	Hebrew	Contemporary
Anunnakis	Sons of God	Extraterrestrials
War of gods	Rebellion in heaven	Star wars
Descent of 200	200 fallen angels	Gray abductors, UFOs
The rest stay on "orbit"	The Watchers	Reptillian supervisors
They change humans to turn them into slaves	They interfere with human affairs	They operate on humans
Mating with women	Fornication	Penetration of women
Transfer of knowledge	Teaching of earthly delights	Training of chosen ones, the "keepers"

GENESIS TOLD IN TRYPTAMINE TONGUE

Michael Harner, the forerunner of neoshamanism, is the author of the book *The Way of the Shaman,* which became an important text for shamanic practitioners coming from a Western cultural background. At the beginning of this book, Harner describes his first encounter with the DMT-containing psychedelic brew ayahuasca. It is one of the best and richest illustrations of the typical characteristics of the DMT experience (here appearing in bold). Themes that are parallel with mythical tales are emphasized in italics:

Overhead the faint lines became brighter, and gradually interlaced to form a canopy resembling a **geometric mosaic** of stained glass. The **bright violet hues** formed an ever-expanding roof above me. Within this celestial cavern, I heard **the sound of water grow louder** and I could see **dim figures** engaged in shadowy movements. As my eyes seemed to adjust to the gloom, the moving scene resolved itself into something resembling a huge **fun house**, a supernatural *carnival of demons*. In the center, presiding over the activities, and looking directly at me, was a gigantic, grinning *crocodilian head, from whose cavernous jaws gushed a torrential flood of water*. Slowly the waters rose, and so did the canopy above them, until **the scene metamorphosed** into a simple **duality** of blue sky above and sea below. All creatures had vanished.

Then, from my position near the surface of the water, I began to see two strange boats wafting back and forth, floating through the air towards me, coming closer and closer. They slowly combined to form a single vessel with a huge **dragon-headed** prow, not unlike that of a Viking ship. Set amidships was a square sail. Gradually, as the boat gently floated back and forth above me, I heard a **rhythmic swishing sound** and saw that it was a giant galley with several hundred oars moving back and forth in cadence with the sound.

I became conscious, too, of the most beautiful singing I have ever heard in my life, **high-pitched** and ethereal, emanating from myriad voices on board the galley. As I looked more closely at the deck, I could make out large numbers of people with the heads of blue jays and the bodies of humans, not unlike the bird-headed gods of ancient Egyptian tomb paintings. At the same time, some **energy-essence began to float from my chest** up into the boat. Although I believed myself to be an atheist, I was completely certain that **I was**

dying and that the ***bird-headed people*** had come to take my soul away on the boat. While the soul-flow continued from my chest, I was aware that **the extremities of my body were growing numb.**

Starting with my arms and legs, my body slowly began to feel like it was turning to solid concrete. **I could not move or speak.** Gradually, as **the numbness closed in on my chest**, toward my heart, I tried to get my mouth to ask for help, to ask the Indians for an antidote. Try as I might, however, I could not marshal my abilities sufficiently to make a word. Simultaneously, **my abdomen seemed to be turning to stone**, and I had to make a tremendous **effort to keep my heart beating.** I began to call my heart my friend, my dearest friend of all, to talk to it, to encourage it to beat with all the power remaining at my command.

I became aware of my brain. I felt—physically that it had become **compartmentalized** into four separate and distinct levels. At the uppermost surface were the observer and commander, which was conscious of the condition of my body, and was responsible for the attempt to keep my heart going. It perceived, but purely **as a spectator**, the visions emanating from what seemed to be the nether portions of my brain. Immediately below the topmost level I felt a numbed layer, which seemed to have been put out of commission by the drug—it just wasn't there. The next level down was the source of my visions, including the soul boat.

Now I was virtually certain **I was about to die.** As **I tried to accept my fate**, an even lower portion of my brain began to transmit more visions and information. I was "told" that this new material was being presented to me because I was dying and therefore "safe" ***to receive these revelations***. These were the secrets reserved for the dying and the dead, *I was informed*. I could only very dimly perceive the givers of these thoughts: ***giant reptilian creatures*** reposing sluggishly at the lowermost depths of the back of my brain, where it met the top of the spinal column. I could only vaguely see them in what seemed to be gloomy, dark depths.

Then they projected a visual scene in front of me. First they showed me the planet Earth as it was eons ago, before there was any life on it. I saw an ocean, barren land, and a bright blue sky. Then black specks dropped from the sky by the hundreds and landed in front of me on the barren landscape. I could see that the "specks" were actually large, shiny, black **creatures with stubby pterodactyl-like wings** *and huge whale-like bodies. Their heads were not visible to me. They flopped down, utterly exhausted from their trip, resting for eons. They explained to me in a kind of* **thought language** *that they were fleeing from something out in space. They had come to the planet Earth to escape their enemy.*

The creatures then showed me how they had created life on the planet in order to hide within the multitudinous forms and thus disguise their presence. Before me, the magnificence of plant and animal creation and speciation—hundreds of millions of years of activity— took place on a scale and **with vividness impossible to describe.** *I learned that the* **dragon-like creatures** *were thus inside of all forms of life, including man.* ([Footnote from Harner:] In retrospect one could say they were almost like DNA, although at that time, 1961, I knew nothing of DNA.) *They were the true masters of humanity and the entire planet, they told me. We humans were but the receptacles and servants of these creatures. For this reason they could speak to me from within myself.*[12]

In the days following this experience, Harner, at that time an atheistic anthropologist, shared his experience with an evangelist missionary couple and a blind Conibo shaman. He was surprised to find that these experiences were neither unique nor extraordinary. The missionaries looked up corresponding passages in chapter 12 of the Book of Revelation (e.g., "And the serpent cast out of his mouth water as a flood . . ."), and the shaman told him: "Oh, they're always saying that [referring to the dragonlike creatures (snakes) stating they were to be the masters of humanity]. But they are only the masters of outer darkness." The Conibo shaman referred to outer space in his language, from his worldview, despite the fact that Harner had skipped that part of his story. With all respect to the blind shaman, however, he was wrong about those dragonlike creatures. In Richard Dawkins's book on the selfish genes,[13] he points out that these genes are the true masters of the planet, and "we humans were but the receptacles and servants of them." Harner received a preview of Francis Crick's DNA-based panspermia theory[14] twelve years before its publication!

On another continent, in Africa, some tribes claim to bear extensive esoteric knowledge of a race of reptiles that, they say, controls Earth. They also claim to have accounts of a reptilian race that created blacks and used them to work their gold mines—tales that are extremely similar to the accounts described by Harner and those outlined in the Sumerian tablets. How could people living under different skies, on different continents, in different eras, and having very different worldviews have common divine experiences? The effects of the endogenous psychedelic compound DMT may provide the clue.

THE DMT CODE

Summarized here are the typical effects of the DMT experience more or less in an order of their appearance after DMT is administered intravenously. This list is based on the pioneering work of Rick Strassman.[15]

The typical introductory symptoms at the onset of the DMT effect include hearing loud, rumbling, buzzing, pulsating noise. The tone can quickly shift to hissing with a high-frequency pitch, and the sound is usually accompanied by feeling vibrations in the body, feeling a rush, feeling a wave of heat running through the body, feeling strange sensations in the bodily organs, and feeling power (some people perceive it as energy) entering or leaving the body. In this phase, visuals consist of seeing flickering, pulsating, bright light, followed by geometric imagery, spirals, or zigzags (phosphenes). It is common to perceive a "presence," sometimes with a pressure on the chest, as if someone invisible is sitting on top of the body. Muscle paralysis, numbness, floating, and out-of-body experiences may occur in this phase.

The DMT experience culminates in a sudden transition, as if breaking through a wall or membrane, and this is sometimes preceded by hearing a crackling or buzzing or clicking sound and the sense of being in an unusual world that feels surreal and hyperrealistic at the same time. The visuals grow very complex, colors are much brighter than in ordinary reality, and strange entities appear: talking lizards; smart snakes; little people; angels; aliens; two-dimensional, cartoonlike forms that may penetrate the body of the subject (as in an operation, implantation, or insemination), especially when he or she is resisting the experience. Ego-dissolution, the sense of falling apart, or fear of death overtakes those who try to resist the effect. For those who are able to let go and surrender to the experience, a teaching time arrives, complete with the entities' mentoring. Subjects may feel that the aliens are telepathically "downloading" to them a good deal of pertinent information. Harner supposed he was dying, tried to accept his fate, and then received those rich revelations. The quality of awareness changes, with the rise of a peculiar duality of reality orientation, the sense of being in two realms at the same time—that is, feeling the sheet of the bed and the pressure of the pillow, at the same time being in the alien world.

It is not necessary to have all of these symptoms and in the same sequence; the experience is highly variable, but the commonalities among experiences are remarkable. If similar symptoms occur without taking DMT externally, then the experience may be the result of a spontaneous DMT release (see boxed points below). Dimethyltryptamine is an endohallucinogen; the brain has enzymes to synthesize this powerful psychotropic chemical and has an active transport mechanism for taking it through the otherwise very restrictive filter of the blood–brain barrier. It is supposed that the pineal gland can be a source of endogenous DMT. Strassman points out that spontaneous DMT release may provide a rational explanation for UFO abductions and related phenomena. It is a striking coincidence that the majority of UFO encounters occur during the early-morning hours, when the pineal gland is the most active. Sleep paralysis—"old hag syndrome"—may also be the consequence of a limited, mitigated form of spontaneous DMT release.

The Main Characteristics of a Full-blown Spontaneous DMT Activity*

1. Typical onset between two and five a.m.
2. Starts with strange noise, pulsating bright light, bodily vibrations, paralysis, feeling of a presence
3. Continues with sudden transition, experiencing superreality; entities operate, penetrate; intelligent reptiles communicate, teach (the latter mostly in case of surrender)
4. Dual presence (being "here" and "over there" at the same time)

*After Strassman

Hank Wesselman, a prominent follower of Michael Harner's neoshamanic movement, began his career as a physical anthropologist with research activities in Africa's Great Rift Valley, where Lucy and other early human ancestors have been discovered. In the 1980s, he had a series of spontaneous and then deliberate shamanistic experiences that revealed to him a dramatic future for humanity. Wesselman's journeys were spontaneous ASCs of the integrative type occurring usually in the early-morning hours. He published his fascinating "intrapsychic" adventures and exciting discoveries in three consecutive books,[16] which are on par with the writings of Carlos Castaneda. Here are excerpts from his first encounter:

> I . . . was just slipping off to sleep when I felt a **peculiar sensation in my body.** As my dissolving attention re-formed and turned toward it, the feeling abruptly intensified, **paralyzing me where**

I lay. Startled, I opened my eyes. I saw momentary **spots of light interspersed with strange lines and zigzags** against the darkened field of the ceiling. A transparent arc seemed to coalesce out of the lights, and then **the bedroom disappeared.**

I found myself in a forest in almost total darkness. Around me in all directions, tall black tree trunks and branches stretched away into the night. The night was very still, and a faint fragrance floated on the warm air. **The illusion was vividly real, and yet paradoxically, I could still feel myself lying in bed** next to Jill and hear her turning the pages of her book. I felt very much awake.

. . . As my attention shifted back into the "dream" and the forest around me, these sensations, these **rushes of feeling**, increased. At this point I discovered that I could move, and I proceeded to walk through the trees, profoundly **impressed at how real everything appeared.** I wasn't too sure how I was moving or what I was walking on, but as in a dream, my intention seemed to be enough to take me here or there. **My body in bed, however, was still immobilized** by the sensations.

. . . The sensations abruptly intensified, and **my body swelled and stiffened**, becoming increasingly **paralyzed**, as though I were **wrapped in an invisible fist** that was slowly squeezing me, cutting off my breath. For a moment, I worried that I might be having a seizure of some sort, and **I felt the edge of fear.** The fear departed as abruptly as it had appeared, however, when I realized that the sensations were intensely pleasurable. Each increase in pressure was accompanied by a **euphoric surge** mixed with an indescribable joy.

Something cut through my absorption in this overwhelming rapture and drew me toward the trees to my right. There among the shadowy tree trunks **I saw a huge, dark form.** It was vaguely manlike, and I could make out what I thought was a distinct head and body, but **the body was strangely geometric** and. . . . door-like. The head was rounded and small, there seemed to be no arms or legs. **It was flat**, completely black, and featureless.

. . . The sensations continued to flow around and through me, exerting **pressure from both within and without.** I tried to move but **I was now completely paralyzed.** I heard Jill turn another page and thought to myself, "I've got to try to tell her what's happening," but **my jaw was locked,** and my entire body was as rigid as a stick of wood. I couldn't close my hands.

. . . Abruptly, it seemed as if the shadow had increased the sensations so much that **I felt myself "lift off."** I drifted slowly up through the trees until I was standing above the ground, turning slowly in space among the leaves and flowers. The ecstatic sensations surged through and around me, and my muscles shook, trembling with the force. To fight against the enormous strength that enfolded me seemed absurd. The dark form was obviously immensely strong, and yet it hadn't harmed me.

I heard a roaring sound and waited to see what would happen next. Then as abruptly as the experience began, it stopped. I was gently placed back on the ground, and the dark form changed, shifting its shape to blend into the shadows under the trees. Simultaneously, the sensations that had held me rigid began to **flow out of me in slow surges,** each one less powerful than the last. Progressively the trees, the shadow, and the bright sphere dissolved, and the darkened bedroom reappeared before my eyes . . . the world was ordinary once again. The first light of dawn was illuminating the sky. My mind was reeling.

Wesselman had an encounter with an entity, a being that is known to Native Americans as a threshold guardian. In addition, the fingerprint of a DMT-induced experience appears in this report. In his trilogy, Wesselman gives accounts of a dozen similar, richly detailed experiences without any previous psychedelic practice. Interestingly, when I contacted him, he had no awareness of the possibility of spontaneous DMT experiences being the inspiring force behind his marvelous writing.

Experiences related to the release of endogenous DMT are more universal than we might suppose, and it is certain that they occurred in ancient times. Listeners of Art Bell's or George Noory's radio shows on *Coast to Coast AM* may notice that many UFO reports and near-death experiences carry the characteristic stamps of a spontaneous DMT release (for example, the interview with Steven Greer entitled "ET Contact and Disclosure," which aired on June 1, 2006).

Perhaps we can imagine the scene of a small Sumerian settlement about six thousand years ago. What if some people imagined such a site and then reported their hyperrealistic experiences after having spontaneous (or augmented—perhaps by *Peganum harmala;* see figure 9.4 on page 250) DMT release? Is it possible that DMT is the source of some creation myths, and that its effects can explain some peculiar characteristics of ancient legends: Anunnaki coming from outer space, modifying humans, inseminating women, and transferring significant information? Here are some other possible consequences.

NACHASH ILLUMINATUS

The word *nachash,* most often translated as "serpent," appears in the Hebrew Bible in the scene explaining the origins of Original Sin. The meaning of this Hebrew word is much richer and can be illuminated in light of the DMT experience (see figure 9.3 on page 250). Michael Heiser points to the triple meaning of *nachash,* which can be translated as "serpent" (noun), as "shiny" (adjective), or as "to deceive" or "to divine" (verb).[17] As we have seen, any of these meanings can take form or be built into a DMT experience. If a strong believer in mind-expanding substances has any doubt about the deceitfulness of a DMT experience, he or she must remember that not all hallucinations are true (some will even argue that by definition, no hallucination can be true). It's best to refer to the expert opinion of Harner's blind Conibo shaman: Only the worthy receives the truth.

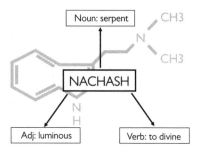

Figure 9.3. The three meanings of the Hebrew word nachash *in Genesis 3 correspond to three characteristics of the DMT experience (based on the word interpretation of Michael Heiser).*

ANGELOGENESIS

As is shown by the ancient depiction of the Sumerian Anunnaki and the myths of many other cultures, smart and winged reptile beings were the first to descend on Earth. Figure 9.4 illustrates what may happen when Mesopotamian artists from consecutive generations, removed by centuries or even millennia from the original visionary experience, copy winged beings over and over again.

Reptilian   =>   Avian   =>   Human

Figure 9.4. Winged figures on Mesopotamian clay tablets indicate what may happen if artists without the original visionary experience copy the theme again and again during centuries and millennia. Please pay attention to the plant on the left tablet, which bears a striking resemblance to Syrian rue, Peganum harmala *(right). This plant originates from the Near East and is known to amplify DMT effects.*

INVASION FROM INNER SPACE

It is estimated that in the observable universe (that is, the perimeter of the whole universe from those places where light could reach us since the time of the Big Bang), there are as many as two hundred billion galaxies—each one with hundreds of billions of stars. The actual number of galaxies (and stars with potentially life-bearing planets) is even larger, because the size of the visible universe is but a tiny portion of the universe as a whole, the Metagalaxy, which started to expand with the Big Bang. Based on current calculations,[18] the ratio of the actual size of the universe to the observable size is equal to the ratio between the size of the observable universe and the size of a proton. That means that we must multiply the number of visible galaxies by the huge difference between the size of the observable universe and the proton. This unimaginable number of galaxies grows even more mind-boggling if we take into account the multiverse (as opposed to universe) theory, because contemporary physic's string theory (more recently M-theory), bubble universe theory, and the many-worlds interpretation of quantum mechanics posit the existence of parallel universes.

We may argue that parallel universes can have different physical constants than our universe—therefore they cannot permit the development of life. Based on the concepts of the eminent string theorist Michio Kaku,however, this might not necessarily be the case because of the presence of Darwinian-like evolutionary processes that affect parallel universes.[19] Yes, natural selection may work in different universes! The physical constants of our universe predispose it to the presence of both a vast number of black holes and intelligent life. The singularity of a black hole may generate a Big Bang in a parallel universe on the "other side." The physical constants of that baby universe are very close to the constants of the mother universe. In this way, we can see how a universe of our kind can propagate itself, while universes with shorter life spans and a smaller number of black holes have less of a chance to multiply.

✧

The number of possible intelligent life-forms is likely to be incredibly high in the multiverse model. How, then, might intelligent beings from the vastness of the multiverse reach out to each other and communicate among themselves? Definitely not by rocketships and radio waves, which traverse our local universe at a snail's pace during the span of a human life. There is no need for such methods if the nonlocal feature of the universe (multiverse) permits contacts of a different kind. As we have seen, these types of encounters may occur instead in inner space and manifest as a transdimensional contact.

Is there any difference between a transdimensional emergence and an intrapsychic one? Probably not—as we already discussed with regard to work by Jim DeKorne in the introduction.[20] Higher dimensional beings can perceive lower dimensions more easily than lower ones can perceive higher dimensions. For the latter, sensory organs (developed for coping in a three-dimensional space) are not suitable for perceiving entities emerging from higher dimensions. What follows that those from the nonlocal, topological field appear inextricably linked with our inner psychic processes, because the interface for nonlocal processes—the quantum array antenna of the brain holding the quantum hologram of the Multiverse—is below the neuroaxonal level. Therefore, high dimensional outer space gets intrapsychically projected and presents in inner space.

Ancient gods such as the Anunnaki and the ghosts of 'Ain Ghazal probably did not descend from the skies, but instead ascended from inner depths, through the receptive capacity of the human soul, which is anchored to a source in common with that of outer space. (We can remember the wisdom of Atman and Brahman.) The gods were likely real beings, but were based on the duality of reality detailed throughout this book—they were, and are, entities of the spiritual–nonlocal realm instead of being sheer products of imagination. The concept of their spiritual existence is not in conflict with their physical reality. Istvan Dienes, an unorthodox physicist and a follower of the topological theory of consciousness, recently said of such beings: "They are autonomous structures existing in the topological field!" Ancient people considered them gods because they brought from nonlocal sources knowledge that was unimaginable to the common public. Information that led to the development of human civilization was received as a divine encounter via that common source, the dynamic ground, and DMT—the spirit molecule—might have been a key that opened the doors to that spiritual source.

What this chapter represents is my attempt, as an amateur scholar who comes from the field of psychopharmacology, to draw upon both archaeology and the history of religion and provide a fresh perspective to these phenomena by offering some controversial proposals based upon my own expertise. Perhaps we can unite UFO observations and a serious assessment of ancient and biblical studies. Interestingly, there is a striking coherence between what some people (in fact, a very significant portion of the population) have experienced and what has been recorded as divine encounters in ancient texts. In this chapter, nonordinary reality has been attached to both of these types of experience without fully disregarding their physical reality. By keeping a balance between sacred (spiritual) and profane (rational), we can convey a reassuring message to faithful Jews, Christians, and Muslims who have been caught in a conflict between their religious faith and rational thinking: Holy revelations were not the sheer product of imagination, and the great prophets truly tapped in to a holy, very meaningful source. Indeed, the encounters on Mount Sinai and those during Al-Isra truly occurred. The concept of their spiritual existence does not deny their physical reality.

Using different terminology, Rabbi Joel David Bakst arrives at a similar conclusion: "[F]undamentally bney elohim (sons of God) are not angels and the bnot adam (daughters of man) are not earthly women. They are forces and processes that are part of the divine 'physiology' of creation dealing specifically with primordial realities and their interface with the current reality."[21]

DMT, the endogenous human hallucinogen (though here the term *entheogen*—manifesting the divine within—would be more appropriate), may be one of the key components holding together this mix, because it provides clues to the most cohesive, coherent understanding of the phenomena. Shockingly, this endogenous compound offers coherence and conceptual validation of divine encounters and related spiritual experiences. Accepting the role of DMT in divine encounters or in holy revelations does not debunk scripture—understanding its role is not a sacrilege if we accept that DMT can be a key (among many others) to the spiritual realm.

Perhaps our knowledge of reality must be altered to reflect a rational explanation of spiritual revelations. Divine encounters, while real to those who experience them, probably reflect a much more sophisticated model of reality than scientific empiricism currently allows. In other words, divine encounters are likely not real in the traditional sense of flesh-and-blood or silicon extraterrestrial visitors interfering with human affairs. Here we may conclude that humans had indeed come into contact with a spiritual intelligence that appears to antedate space–time as we know it—and gods are less extraterrestrial than nonlocal. They emerge intrapsychically in the form of spiritual experience through nonlocal, extradimensional connections within the multiverse.

10

Hypnosis, Past Life Regression, Meditation, and More

Slawek Wojtowicz, M.D.

Hypnosis, meditation, yoga; rebirthing and holotropic breathing (healing techniques utilizing accelerated breathing); and some other types of "spiritual technology tools" produce experiences almost identical in content and intensity to those induced by psychedelics.

A few years ago, the American public was shocked by the controversial report from a respected psychiatrist from Harvard that claimed that under hypnosis, some of his patients recalled being abducted by alien beings. John Mack almost lost his job after publication of his book, *Abduction,*[1] which tackled this topic. The excitement around this subject matter gradually diminished even though thousands of other people came up with similar accounts and several additional books on similar topics have been published by Mack and others.[2, 3, 4] Some people studying this phenomenon estimate that more than five million Americans have experienced alien abduction, but there is no way to corroborate these stories, and it remains an uncomfortable subject to deal with for the majority of people. In March 2007, France became the first country to open its files on UFOs, unveiling a website (www.cnes-geipan .fr) that documented more than sixteen hundred sightings spanning five decades. Of these, nearly 25 percent are classified as Type D, meaning that despite good or very good data and credible witnesses, these cases cannot be explained. Other countries also collect data about unidentified flying objects (UFOs), notably Britain and the United States, where information can be requested on a case-by-case basis under the Freedom of Information Act.

Mack suggests in his book that aliens have come here to do more or less what shamans do: to try to open our minds and to awaken us. In his view, the aliens had imbued many abductees specifically with a sense of profound, transpersonal love, as well as with a powerful desire to work for the betterment of our endangered environment. He goes as far as to say that "[t]he alien encounter experience seems almost like an outreach program from the cosmos to the spiritually impaired." His research suggests that several alien species are experimenting on us independently. It appears that we are dragging down the whole universe by being selfish, self-centered, unloving, close-minded, and dense. In this sense, we are very important—the awakening of humanity will make the universe a much nicer place in which to live for all sentient beings. Mack speculates that the critical mass required to start the chain reaction to awaken everyone is less than 5 percent of Earth's population. Yet some other abduction researchers, including Budd Hopkins, question his conclusions, pointing out that abduction experiences have been very traumatic for most abductees and that it is difficult to claim any benefits resulting from these experiences.

Rock and cave paintings found in many locations around the world imply that modern humans don't have a monopoly on encounters with alien beings and realities. In *Supernatural,* Graham Hancock describes prehistoric paintings that depict a wide variety of seemingly alien beings who might have been the ancient teachers of humanity. Some of these rock paintings are reminiscent of certain alien species encountered by modern psychonauts and abductees—so-called Grays, or mantislike aliens.[5] The figure here shows examples of other apparently alien beings depicted on rocks and cave walls by our ancestors (see figures 10.1–10.4).

Figure 10.1. Rock art from the Sego Canyon, Utah, located north of Thompson Springs. These images were likely painted by shamans who encountered alien entities in altered states of consciousness and are associated with a hunter-gatherer culture that flourished in Utah from four thousand to fifteen hundred years ago.

Sacred ancient Hindu writings known as Vedas and dating to 3000–2000 BCE describe encounters with aliens or gods who used various machines, weapons, and vehicles called *vimanas* that were able to fly in the air and under water and could travel into space.[6] The *Mahabharata* describes conflicts between gods in which they used weapons as lethal as those we have now.[7] Apart from "blazing missiles," the poem records the use of other deadly weapons, such as Indra's Dart (Indravajrā), operated via a circular "reflector." When switched on, it produced a "shaft of light" that, when focused on any target, immediately "consumed it with its power."

In one exchange, the hero, Krishna, is pursuing his enemy Salva in the sky when Salva's vimana, the Saubha, is made invisible in some way. Undeterred, Krishna fires off a special weapon: "I quickly laid on an arrow, which killed by seeking out sound." Many other terrible weapons are described quite matter-of-factly in the *Mahabharata,* but the most fearsome of all is the one used against the Vrishis:

Gurkha flying in his swift and powerful Vimana hurled against the three cities of the Vrishis and Andhakas a single projectile charged with all the power of the Universe. An incandescent column of smoke and fire, as brilliant as ten thousands suns, rose in its entire splendor. It was the unknown weapon, the Iron Thunderbolt, a gigantic messenger of death which reduced to ashes the entire race of the Vrishnis and Andhakas.

It is not clear whether these encounters occurred in consensus reality or under the influence of hallucinogens (a distinction that would have been very alien to our ancestors!), including the mysterious substance known as Soma, or perhaps as a result of various spiritual practices, such as meditation and yoga. Similarly, in Genesis 6:4, the Hebrew scriptures describe human encounters with alien beings who were the Sons of God: "The Nephilim were on the earth in those days—and also afterward—when the sons of God went to the daughters of men and had children by them." Also, in the Book of Ezekiel (1:4–24), a spaceshiplike vehicle is described with technical details as it is seen through the eyes of a pre–Industrial Age man:

I looked, and I saw a windstorm coming out of the north—an immense cloud with flashing lightning and surrounded by brilliant light. The center of the fire looked like glowing metal, and in the fire was what looked like four living creatures. In appearance their form was that of a man, but each of them had four faces and four wings. Their legs were straight; their feet were like those of a calf and gleamed like burnished bronze. Under their wings on their four sides they had the hands of a man. All four of them had faces and wings, and their wings touched one another. Each one went straight ahead; they did not turn as they moved. . . .

As I looked at the living creatures, I saw a wheel on the ground beside each creature with its four faces. This was the appearance and structure of the wheels: They sparkled like chrysolite, and all four looked alike. Each appeared to be made like a wheel intersecting a wheel. As they moved, they would go in any one of the four directions the creatures faced; the wheels did not turn about as the creatures went. Their rims were high and awesome, and all four rims were full of eyes all around.

When the living creatures moved, the wheels beside them moved; and when the living creatures rose from the ground, the wheels also rose. Wherever the spirit would go, they would go, and the wheels would rise along with them, because the spirit of the living creatures was in the wheels. . . .

Spread out above the heads of the living creatures was what looked like an expanse, sparkling like ice, and awesome. Under the expanse their wings were stretched out one toward the other, and each had two wings covering its body. When the creatures moved, I heard the sound of their wings, like the roar of rushing waters, like the voice of the Almighty, like the tumult of an army. When they stood still, they lowered their wings.

This description was detailed enough for some engineers to file a patent for a wheel that can move in any direction and to create technical drawings depicting how the spaceship may have looked like.

We have already discovered the striking similarity between experiences of abductees and volunteers infused with DMT in Rick Strassman's study. It turns out that hypnosis may also bring out other types of science-fiction-like memories. Obviously, we can wonder how much impact the hypnotist has on the experience: Presumably, psychedelic experiences reflect the subject's own emotional-cognitive condition, while experiences induced by hypnosis may be affected by external factors, such as an experimenter's bias.

Brian Weiss is a well-known and respected psychiatrist and a graduate of Columbia University and Yale University who is currently the chairman emeritus of psychiatry at the Mount Sinai Medical Center in Miami, Florida. Dr. Weiss has been using hypnosis as a therapeutic tool to accelerate progress in the psychotherapy of patients with a variety of problems. He became an expert hypnotherapist, and was very successful in taking patients back to early childhood, where many of their current problems originated. In his book *Many Lives, Many Masters,*[8] he describes how, in the early 1980s, he began working with a female patient who was very susceptible to hypnosis. At first, however, he did not have much luck in identifying the traumas that were responsible for symptoms that brought her to therapy. She was able to regress to very early childhood, but did not appear to remember anything disturbing that could have caused her present neuroses. Dr. Weiss was at loss as to what to do, so he told her to go to the point in time when her problems started.

To his shock and amazement, she reported that she was now a seventeen-year-old boy, drowning in the ocean. She was experiencing that death in terrifying detail, and he had to bring her out of the hypnosis quickly. He did not believe in reincarnation and did not know what to make of her experience, yet some of her symptoms improved, so he decided to continue therapy. During subsequent hypnotherapy sessions, his patient traveled to different periods in history, and described her surroundings and her past lives in vivid detail. Dr. Weiss was growing more and more incredulous, but his patient kept getting better, so the therapy continued. Then, something even more unusual happened: during one of the sessions, she reported being in a time period between incarnations. Her voice changed, and she told him about events from his personal life that she couldn't have possibly known (such as the death of his two-month-old son due to a cardiac defect several years before, an event that preceded his move to Florida). Dr. Weiss was no longer skeptical; this information convinced him finally that what he heard from the patient was real, that her stories were not just products of her imagination. He described the work he was doing as *past life regression.*

He started using this technique in the therapy of other patients, and he accumulated a wealth of stories from the patients he treated over twenty years. Finally, he gathered his courage and decided to publish a book describing his findings—despite concerns about the potential negative impact on his academic career. Today, he has published several books on the subject and conducts workshops for psychotherapists, psychiatrists, and other clinical professionals, teaching them how to use past life regression therapy in their practice. Scores of his patients have regressed easily to various historical periods. Some patients report memories from Atlantis, and one patient saw flying vehicles powered by "pure energy" cruising over sleek, glass skyscrapers. The patient described them as looking more like cars than planes. His job was to change his level of consciousness to manipulate energy and transform matter to gain personal power. He and his peers used this power successfully to control surrounding civilizations. In the process, they almost destroyed the planet.

Some patients returned to the Stone Age or to even earlier periods in prehistory. One patient reported traveling back in time sixty thousand years: he was an alien being who recently migrated to Earth because his home planet was dying. His body was similar to the human body, and members of his species lived among humans. His job was to store artifacts and written knowledge of his civilization in natural caverns deep under Earth's surface. "By the time humans have reached a level where they can understand what was hidden, they will be able to find it," he told Dr. Weiss.

More recently, Dr. Weiss has tried to take patients into both the near and the distant future. He is careful to acknowledge that the future seems to be a "flexible" destination—a multitude of possible and probable futures may lie ahead of us. Many people believe that we have free will and if this is the case, the future course of human history is not predetermined, but instead depends on our present actions. He describes experiments in which he hypnotizes audiences participating in his workshops (often hundreds of people at the time) and asks them to go into the future one hundred, two hundred, five hundred, or more years. Afterward, he asks audience members to write down what they saw (without comparing notes with others), and then he compiles the results. In his recent book *Same Soul, Many Bodies,* Dr. Weiss describes what he has learned so far.[9]

Interestingly, the majority of these accounts appear to describe a rather consistent picture of how our world may look one day. According to him, in one to two hundred years, the world will be largely the same as it is now. There will be natural and man-made calamities, but not on a global level. After three to six hundred years, a second Dark Age will begin. The next few hundred years after this appear to be very stormy and dark, but ultimately things get much better. A thousand or more years into the future, we will inhabit an idyllic, fertile, peaceful land. Some of the areas of the world, such as the Middle East and North Africa, will be off-limits (perhaps because of radiation damage or epidemic), but the rest of the world will be beautiful. Fewer people will inhabit Earth, and these inhabitants have been described as content, happy, even blissful. They can access all knowledge and are omnipotent, they can come into and leave their bodies at will, there is no disease, and even death isn't what it seems today. In short: heaven on Earth—the way our life was always meant to be.

Brian Weiss also describes how some of his patients are able to detach from their bodies and float above them during meditation or experience their past or future lives. Some people who practice meditation report experiences that could be called paranormal or mystical. In addition to out-of-body travel, these may comprise time travel and contact with alien entities. While I was meditating as a medical student several years ago, I also experienced an encounter of this type.

I was lying on the bed in my bedroom, doing a certain type of a breathing exercise, when I felt a vibration in my extremities, and then my hearing began expanding like a sphere. First, I heard my sister scribbling something in the room next door, then my hearing shifted to focus on water dripping slowly from the tap in the kitchen downstairs, then to a street car screeching on its tracks several blocks away. Finally, I heard the waves of the sea lapping on the beach miles away, as if I was right there. Simultaneously, I noticed that my body felt like an empty shell, and I started shrinking within that shell, becoming smaller and smaller. At some point, I sensed another presence near me.

Figure 10.2. Rock paintings from the Great Gallery in Horseshoe Canyon, Canyonlands National Park, Utah. Sometimes called the Holy Ghost Panel by Mormon locals, these paintings are associated with a hunter-gatherer culture that flourished in Utah from four thousand to fifteen hundred years ago. Note the Threshold Guardians surrounding an alien being with a peculiar "face."

I perceived it as dark and hostile, and it appeared intent on destroying me. I panicked and tried to get up, but I couldn't—I was paralyzed. I struggled and I managed finally to sit up, drenched in sweat and scared to death (as if I was experiencing "old hag syndrome").

As you can imagine, I abandoned this type of meditation for a long time—though it turns out that this may have been a mistake. The dark figure I experienced was likely either my shadow—the part of our personality that we reject and tend to project onto others around us—or a Threshold Guardian, an entity often described by Native American shamans that guards the entrance to spiritual realms. Such shadow figures have been discovered in some ancient rock paintings from a variety of places around the world (see figure 10.2). Facing the shadow allows us to overcome fear and thus radically advance on the spiritual path.

Hank Wesselman, a contemporary American anthropologist, describes very similar experiences in his book *Spiritwalker: Messages from the Future.*[10] He didn't panic as I did when strange effects began occurring. His courage paid off and allowed him amazing experiences. A gateway was opened in his mind, and in due course this led him into a distant future—a time more than five thousand years from now. A few months after his initial episode, he underwent a classical out-of-body experience: first, he wandered around his house while his body was still lying on the bed, and then he was lifted into space and traveled to a number of other planets—some lunarlike with ashy gray plains and deserts and others full of alien plants and animals. One of the planets had two suns in the sky, which produced interesting double shadows of slightly different hues. After these experiences, he was suddenly back on his bed.

Subsequently, he experienced a series of events that involved merging with a young man named Nainoa. As Wesselman's fascinating story unfolds, we trek with Nainoa through the jungles of future America and meet our remote descendants. The author deduces that the American continent is being recolonized by settlers from Hawaii. He describes people living in Stone Age–like conditions, and speculates that our current technological civilization has been wiped out by catastrophic rises in ocean levels—thirty to fifty feet a year, with a total rise of three hundred to five hundred feet over several years, which has destroyed ports and cut off the oil supplies on which our society depends. In his vision, there isn't much left after the collapse of current civilization, and it appears that there is no hope for people ever to reclaim technological advances that we enjoy today. In his future time, there is hardly any metal left for the production of tools.

It seems as though this particular future is not necessarily compatible with the one seen by participants of Brian Weiss's workshops. Can these differences be explained by the personal bias of those who experience it and their assumptions and fantasies about the future of humanity? Some argue that only minor portions of these "revelations" have supernatural origins; most of them can be easily explained by taking into account the personal background and the knowledge base of each visionary. Another explanation, already mentioned, is that there are multiple possible futures; the future course of our history will be determined by our actions today.

In his book *The Disappearance of the Universe,* Gary Renard describes how, after several years of diligently practicing meditation,

Figure 10.3. Great Martian God rock painting from the Tassili National Park, Algeria. It is approximately eight to ten thousand years old.

he finally reached a stage when he could completely empty his mind. When he opened his eyes after one of his meditation sessions, he saw two strangers on the couch in his room. To his amazement, they claimed to have arrived from the future. Sounds like a classical science-fiction story, right? These guests continued to visit Renard's house periodically, teaching him about spirituality, relationships, and God. He claims that he experienced teleportation and even traveled into the near future with them. As you might imagine, Renard could not resist asking them some questions about the past and the future—and as you might expect, they were not too forthcoming with the details, but they were willing to give to him some interesting tidbits of information.[11] In his second book, *Your Immortal Reality,* Renard learns that humans did not evolve on Earth, but instead migrated from a distant planet in another solar system—first to Mars and then to Earth.[12] That seems to corroborate the story conveyed by one of Brian Weiss's patients. The strangers confirmed for Renard that an alien spaceship indeed crashed in Roswell, and in addition, they told him that there are several humanoid alien species in the universe that have DNA very similar to ours.

Renard asked the strangers what is going to happen in 2012, because some people believe that the world will end on December 21, 2012 (when the Mayan calendar ends). The strangers said that this time would be simply an end of one cycle and a start of another one, rather than the end of the world. They told him also that global warming would be turned around eventually, though it would produce some very extreme weather in the meantime. They told him that the average life span would reach one hundred years by the end of this century, and that the world is going to undergo the biggest economic expansion in human history, with the Dow Jones Industrial average reaching 100,000 by the middle of the century (though growth will be even bigger in Europe). The strangers also told him about quantum computers that would boggle the mind, space elevators, tourist trips to the moon, and teleportation—just like in *Star Trek,* only even better, because teleportation will become the prevailing mode of space travel beyond the next century. Incidentally, in October 2006, the journal *Science* reported that physicists in Denmark succeeded in teleporting a macroscopic atomic object containing billions of atoms a distance of half a meter. The website of the Danish National Research Foundation Center for Quantum Optics (http://quantop.nbi.dk) includes updates on the progress of their research. A quantum physicist has recently told me that an effort is under way to teleport viruses.

Renard's friends from the future also warned about the new leader of Iran, who, according to them, is an insane extremist who should not be fooled with or dismissed lightly. They claimed that he is the man whom Nostradamus described as the biggest threat to the cities of the West. They told him that this man will be involved in some capacity in setting off a nuclear device in one or more big cities such as Tel Aviv, London, New York, and Los Angeles.

Finally, it is worth mentioning that certain breathing techniques, such as *rebirthing*[13] (also known as yoga breathing) and its modernized version, known as *holotropic breathing,* may lead to some of the experiences described in this book. During these breathing sessions, each person lies on a mat with eyes closed and uses his or her own breath to enter a nonordinary state of consciousness. Holotropic breathing combines accelerated breathing with evocative music and bodywork, such as massage, deep-tissue manipulation, and energy balancing.

Many people with spontaneous experiences such as those described here don't speak about them for fear of being ostracized or labeled

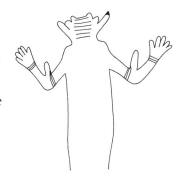

Figure 10.4. Grand Dieu de Sefar (Great God of Sefar). This rock painting from the Tassili National Park, Algeria, is approximately eight thousand to ten thousand years old.

"mentally ill." It is not clear how common such experiences are in the general population, but they can be induced relatively easily by "spiritual technologies" described here.

We may wonder what, if any, is the purpose of these experiences. Are they simply mind candy to be pursued for the sake of entertainment—or do they have a deeper purpose? In fact, all of these techniques may produce experiences that play an important role in healing our minds and bodies and aiding our spiritual development.

In his recent book *Communion with God,* Neale Donald Walsch tells us that all of the wondrous abilities of future humans can be realized today by individuals who are determined enough to do the work necessary to awaken.[14] Awakening means freedom—freedom from anything that may bind us: suffering, boredom, imprisonment in the body in time or on the planet. We are limited only by our imagination. Native American shamans and Indian gurus such as Swami Prabhupada, who wrote a book entitled *Easy Journey to Other Planets,*[15] claim to have an ability to visit other worlds. Perhaps it is truly possible for us to take a tour of the universe without waiting for technology to catch up with our dreams.

$$=== \text{ 11 } ===$$

preparation
for the journey

Rick Strassman, M.D.

Important disclaimer: None of the authors of this book condones any illegal activities, even when it comes to the potentially beneficial effects of altering consciousness with a psychedelic drug. In nearly the entire world, it is illegal to possess major psychedelics such as mescaline, DMT, LSD, and psilocybin. In some instances, the plants that contain these chemicals, such as mescaline-containing peyote cactus and psilocybin-containing magic mushrooms, are also banned.

While a discussion of the current laws regarding these plants and chemicals is beyond the scope of this book, we believe in the maxim "The law of the land is the law." Therefore, the authors take no responsibility—legal, medical, psychological, spiritual, or otherwise—for any difficulty in which anyone may find him- or herself as a result of manufacturing, possessing, distributing, or using a psychedelic substance.

Nevertheless, the human drive to profoundly alter consciousness in the way that psychedelics do so reliably cannot be extinguished. Whereas there clearly are other legal ways in which we may alter our consciousness—meditation, prayer, fasting, extreme sports, and so on—few of us are able to attain a truly psychedelic state without using drugs or plants. Thus, some may consider the legal and other risks associated with taking psychedelic substances as less compelling than their perceived benefits.

Whenever possible, we advise using such materials in licit circumstances. There are countries and contexts in which the use of certain psychedelic substances is legal. Examples include ayahuasca-using churches in the West, centers in Latin America that use ayahuasca and other psychoactive plants, and peyote-using churches in North America, where jurisdictions allow its use for both Natives and non-Natives.

✧

Those preparing for a psychedelic drug experience, even the most seasoned veterans, nearly always feel intense anticipation. The late Secret Chief, a San Francisco Bay–area psychologist who supervised thousands, if not tens of thousands, of psychedelic drug sessions, referred to this feeling of anticipation of a session as "[t]he trip has already begun."

The Secret Chief was uncannily, unerringly, and extraordinarily accurate—and it may require some deep thinking to fully understand what he meant. Obviously, the mere act of thinking about, discussing, and deciding to undergo a psychedelic drug session is not the same as actually taking a drug. Nevertheless, by making such a decision, we initiate a cascade of events within the matrix of set and setting, which form a continuum not only limited to the discrete time period during which we are under the influence of a psychedelic, but also spreading in all directions, like the proverbial pebble thrown into the pond. By embarking on the preliminary stages of taking such a trip, we set in motion certain feelings, thoughts, and actions that lead to a potentially life-changing event. Our lives have already come under the influence of the trip.

Set and setting, the two primary factors involved in determining the outcome of the inner journey to outer space, are themselves modifiable via the two primary tasks of that journey: getting ready and letting go.

GETTING READY

In order to derive the most benefit from making any journey, inner or outer, we must do what we can to minimize the risks of a negative outcome and optimize the chances for a positive one. Once we have established the most solid foundation possible, we can be more assured of the beneficial outcome that may result from truly letting go.

We possess the power to determine the nature and course of our trip much as we possess the power to determine the nature and course of our lives. On the one hand, our lives are undeniably constrained by the circumstances of our birth: our genetic make-up; who our parents are; and the chemical, social, and psychological environment into which we were born. In addition, we are subject to the "accidents" continuously coming our way: those chance encounters that play such an important role in who we are and what we do. On the other hand, we also have the choice of how to regard and react to these circumstances. This may be what is meant by the maxim "Everything is in the hand of heaven except the awe of heaven."

At the same time, we must not forget that the ultimate purpose and context of our lives is vast and ultimately unknowable. In this case, we can refer to the complementary maxim "The work is never done, but we must never cease from doing it." We must do everything we can to develop our intention and attitude toward what awaits us in the psychedelic state. Then, when we meet what awaits us, we can allow it to show us what it will and take us where it will.

There are several practical considerations in getting ready for a session. We can parse these into a general temporal scheme: long-term work, intermediate work, and short-term work.

Long-term Work

If we know ourselves—our state and traits—as best as possible, we will be able to contend with any likely resistance to the letting go that is requisite for the optimal journey. This self-knowledge cannot be acquired quickly, but rather requires years and decades. Nevertheless, at some point, anyone who will make this journey must begin walking the path to inner knowledge.

The two most common ways of increasing self-knowledge and

learning how we relate to ourselves and others—those enduring and deep-seated elements of our set—are *psychotherapy* and *spiritual practice*. Although some consider the two at cross-purposes, they may be combined in very useful ways, because they exhibit common elements in theory, technique, and goals. Both use focused self-awareness to observe, understand, accept, and modify our feelings, thoughts, and behaviors in order that we may live more fulfilling, satisfying lives. Whereas meditation may emphasize awareness of mental, cognitive, and perceptual processes, Western psychotherapy usually relates to working with emotional concerns.

Spiritual or religious practice may be shorn of much of its theological content and rituals by emphasizing primarily its benefits in the development of self-awareness and the cultivation of desired mental states. For example, sustained concentration on our body and mind in a regular meditation practice can help make apparent several core issues: How do we experience anxiety—in our bodies or mentally? If we perceive anxiety in both the body and mind, which perception comes first? What of vulnerability, happiness, and fear? What are our fears? Is it our nature to share with others or keep to ourselves?

Prayer, perhaps in a way we usually don't consider, also may provide access to helpful discoveries. Praying to an outside source of help or wisdom may result in many of the same answers regarding who we are and how we function in the world—answers similar to those that might arise in a meditation practice. Where we acquire such information may not matter fundamentally within the context of simply obtaining increased self-knowledge and efficacy. In addition, regular meditation or prayer practice does much to develop our muscles of attention, and we can then apply our strengthened ability to focus toward examining ourselves in ways we may not have been capable of engaging previously.

A reliable, dependable, empathetic, and admirable teacher can be of great help in this process. He or she can provide instruction and encouragement and serve as a role model who encourages us to persist in our practice. In addition to these more formal teaching functions, an effective meditation or prayer teacher allows for the development of a close relationship between him- or herself and students. An open-eyed examination of the nature of this relationship—its ups and downs, misinterpretations, and projections—can be invaluable to our process of discovering who we really are.

Effective psychotherapy shares features with an effective meditation or prayer practice. These include paying attention to areas of difficulty in our lives. By looking carefully at what situations stir up particular emotions, thoughts, and behaviors, we may discover previously unacknowledged emotional and cognitive habits that served us at one time but no longer do so. Within the traditional psychotherapeutic setting, we find the relationship that develops between student and therapist more commonly subject to careful examination. This *analysis of the transference* is especially the case within the psychoanalytic framework.

If our meditation or prayer practice is focused on more than self-examination and self-improvement, it will begin forcing us to ask larger questions that almost certainly will arise in any deep psychedelic work. These questions concern the existence, nature, and providence of God; the reason for our birth; the nature of this reality; enlightenment; and how to contend with nonphysical realities and encounters with alien or spiritual or noncorporeal beings. The deeper mystical teachings of the religions from which these meditation or prayer practices emerge are well equipped to provide answers to these questions. We may thus find ourselves pursuing a deeper involvement in a particular religion.

Conversely, the typical psychotherapeutic endeavor is not as concerned with spiritual issues—though any good psychotherapist knows the limits of his or her skill and will make a timely and appropriate referral to a spiritual teacher when necessary. In the same manner, a competent spiritual teacher will recognize the need for a psychotherapy referral when mood, thought, or personality issues appear to be interfering with progress in a meditation or prayer practice.

Intermediate Work

Once we have decided to take a psychedelic journey, we can start preparing in specific ways. To the extent possible, we can educate ourselves regarding what to expect on our trip. Having some sense of the expected terrain, as described by those who have gone before, can be quite helpful. In this way, if others have alerted us to what to expect, we may not be surprised when we encounter phenomena far beyond the range of what is familiar to us.

The literature regarding near-death and out-of-body experiences, meditation, abduction, shamanism, and, of course, the taking of psychedelic drugs contains a wealth of information about others' experiences. It can provide us with helpful background information as well as practical means of dealing with those states. Also recommended is speaking with others who have gone before, listening to talks, and getting involved in online groups of the various communities that discuss highly altered states of consciousness—and not only those concerned with the effects of psychedelic drugs.

Some might object on the grounds that these educational activities may bias us toward particular expectations that can lead to certain specific types of experiences at the expense of others—yet these arguments are not especially persuasive. The truly psychedelic experience is totally unexpected. Nevertheless, knowing how unexpected it can be may help us to keep our bearings when confronted with it. We will be ready for the unexpected.

Discuss the impending trip with your therapist or spiritual teacher if you have one. However, it should not come as a surprise if the stigma attached to drug use causes spiritual teachers to discourage the taking of them. This may be the case even if he or she has had personally beneficial experiences with psychedelics. Faced with disapproval from someone in whom we have placed great faith and who has previously been very helpful to us, we may need to shelve the topic of psychedelic use and continue our work with him or her without any continued interference caused by such a discussion. Or perhaps we may decide to seek instruction elsewhere, in a context in which we can discuss how psychedelic drug experiences may work together with therapy or meditation or prayer.

Those who are taking medication should make certain that there are no possible adverse interactions with these medications and the psychedelic drugs considered. For those who are taking medications for conditions that can also be managed by lifestyle changes such as exercise; weight loss; diet adjustments; and the cessation of the use of alcohol, tobacco, caffeine, and other drugs, try to follow through with these changes first to see if some of the medications may no longer be necessary. The point is to simplify body chemistry as much as possible. Though the reasons behind the desire to stop medications may remain private, the actual process of trying to discontinue them must be taken up with your health care provider.

Intent

Once we have decided we want to experience a psychedelic drug session, we must home in on our intent. As the Secret Chief asked, "To what purpose?" Why are we doing this and what do we hope to accomplish or gain from such an experience? Is it primarily curiosity that drives us—are we intellectually and emotionally drawn to novelty, to something new, exotic, and exciting? Do we wish to experience pleasure of an extraordinary degree? Do we have an emotional, artistic, creative, professional, spiritual, or interpersonal problem we want to solve? Are we seeking a spiritual experience or answers to our deepest yearnings? Do we wish to know God—to see him or her face-to-face? Do we hope for an encounter with the angels or the powers through which God manifests? Are we interested in outer-space travel, science-fiction revelations, journeys through time, and encounters with alien civilizations and their inhabitants? Do we wish to obtain information and power for good or for ill? Do we want to make the world a better place—or do we intend to hurt those who have hurt us? Do we wish to suffer? Do we want to create a situation in which we replay abusive past or present relationships?

There are so many possible motivations to take a trip—and any of these may compete and blend with one another. We must be as honest as possible with ourselves when deciding what our intentions are, realizing that having a particular intention doesn't necessarily guarantee the content of the session. We don't always have the trip we want; instead, we seem to have the trip we need. If we tell ourselves that our motivation is, perhaps, to learn more about our relationships, but, more honestly, we want to have a good time, we may be unpleasantly surprised when we're actually confronted by deeper, more painful psychological issues. Conversely, we may approach the experience with deep solemnity and expectations for a divine encounter and then be similarly unprepared for the fun, light-hearted aspects of our session. Thus, it is important to understand the full range and complementary nature of our motivations. Ideally, this is accomplished through the use of the introspective skills we have obtained during our own inner work, either spiritual or psychotherapeutic.

It is worth noting that developing an intention to undergo a spiritual, otherworldly, near-death transcendent type of experience is, in some ways, the same as making the decision to subvert the dominant Western postindustrial worldview. That is, the total loss of self-control and our usual self-identity and the wish to interact with and be guided by spiritual entities whose mercy we count upon fly in the face of a materialistic, individualistic, and fear-based relationship to existence. It also runs contrary to a solely clergy-mediated relationship to the divine. If and when we do have this type of experience, we must realize that the mainstream, using the tools of ridicule and psychopathologizing, among others, will oppose our discussing and valuing it.

Short-term Work

How do we prepare ourselves in the day or two before the psychedelic journey? First, it is paramount that we understand our intentions. Then, by attending to certain concrete matters, we validate our intention to mark this experience as unique. The essence of making something holy or sacred is to separate or distinguish between the sacred and the profane. Though at the absolute level of reality, there are no such differences between what is sacred and what is profane, at the relative level, in which most of us exist most of the time, the two do differ. Thus, it is important to manifest our inner intent through our physical reality. We want to perceive as clearly as possible our psychedelic experience without the muddying effects of influences such as fatigue and an unsafe environment.

It's important to approach the trip in good health and with a positive state of mind and to be well rested and have a clean body and clean clothes. Participants should be careful with what they eat, drink, and smoke several days before the trip. Further, are there loose ends requiring attention? Are these minor tasks, such as taking out the garbage, making a necessary phone call, and paying an overdue bill, or are some more significant, such as updating a will? Though updating a will may appear morbid, consider the prospect that while undergoing a near-death experience, you may recall that you have no will! Would your emotional reactions to your sense of dying be different if you knew you had taken care of those you were leaving behind?

Before taking any psychedelics, it is recommended that you check in with those who are most important in your life. Are we on good terms with our partner, spouse, family, friends, and business associates? An extra prayer, meditation session, or psychotherapy appointment or two in the days before a trip can make clear some internal or external issues that might require special attention.

SETTING

Clearly perceiving our intent naturally leads us to decide upon the setting, the circumstances in which we will be taking the trip. Earlier, we discovered different categories of experiences resulting from psychedelic-drug ingestion. We can use these categories as a model for conceptualizing the types of trips available to us:

- A pleasurable trip that fulfills curiosity
- A problem-solving session that addresses psychotherapeutic issues we want to work on or creative, professional, or other concerns
- A spiritual, near-death experience or otherworldly journey

Also to be considered are the particulars of the trip. These include:

- Environment—outdoors or indoors
- The dose of the drug
- Whether we will journey alone or in a group
- Whether we will have a sitter
- Accoutrements for our trip such as music or art supplies
- Supplemental techniques for reaching altered states of consciousness

Finally, we must consider if the session will take place in a research setting. All types of trips can take place in a research environment; it is important, however, to note the constraints and opportunities unique to this type of setting—the most important of which concerns the issue of altruism, the notion of giving up something in our own trip for the benefit of others.

Is the Setting Outdoors or Indoors?

An outdoor setting of natural beauty can lead to profound levels of identification or merging with the natural world, yet being outdoors is also less predictable than being indoors. These unpredictable factors include insects, animals, inclement weather, unwelcome intrusions by other people, dirt of all kinds, and lack of facilities if participants fall ill or feel particularly helpless.

An outdoor setting in a city or suburb can provide a unique perspective on humanity, but it lends itself more to an externally oriented and at times potentially chaotic experience. Such a setting requires us to be prepared for exposure to a wide array of interpersonal and technical challenges. An indoor setting in an area of natural beauty can combine the best of both worlds: the safety and predictability of an indoor space and the option of going outside to experience nature.

DOSAGE, ROUTE OF ADMINISTRATION, AND COMBINING DRUGS

We can divide doses into low, intermediate, and high. Usually, the higher the dose of drug, the more intense and longer-lasting the effects. Yet there are many cases in which the same person experiences a marked effect from a small dose and seems less affected by a large dose at some other time. Instead of serving as examples of tolerance, in which repeated dosing decreases subsequent responses, or sensitization, in which low initial doses increase the effects of subsequent low doses, there seems to be some poorly understood interplay among dose, set, and setting that results in dose not being invariably related to intensity and duration of effect.

There is merit in beginning with a low dose of any substance that is new to us, whether that "substance" is a relationship, exercise routine, or a psychedelic drug. As is true most of the time, however, the true nature of any particular relationship is rarely known without receiving a full dose. Thus at some point, for the truly adventurous explorer of these realms, sooner or later a high dose plays a role in his or her work with the substance and the realms into which it leads.

Another consideration is route of administration. There are various ways to administer a drug. Intravenous injection, smoking, and snorting are the fastest ways to experience effects. Slower onset occurs with routes such as intramuscular and subcutaneous (under the skin) injection. Slower yet are gastrointestinal methods, such as swallowing or rectal administration. Topical application to the skin or mucous membranes varies in speed, depending upon the integrity of the tissue—that is, effects occur more quickly from applying a drug to a wound or open sore than from applying it to intact, calloused skin. In addition, the "carrier" for the topically applied drug, the solvent into which it is dissolved, can make a big difference in the speed of absorption. For example, DMSO (dimethylsufoxide) is a solvent that allows for very rapid skin absorption of a drug, whereas cocoa butter is absorbed by the skin more slowly.

It's also best to choose one dose of one drug for a particular session and then stick to that decision. Participants may feel the need to take more of a substance if the effects are not as hoped for—what some refer to as taking a "booster" dose. While there are instances of this booster being an integral part of the experience—for example, in indigenous ayahuasca sessions—it is advisable to exercise caution in this area. Particularly when alone, impaired judgment may lead to making ill-advised decisions, and can lead to taking a dose that is too high. Remember, there is always the next time to take more.

Neither is it advisable to mix substances. Doing so blurs the effect of one or the other, and may produce toxic interactions.

SOLO OR GROUP: THE ROLE OF STRUCTURE

In this instance, the term *structure* refers to behavioral parameters that we impose upon ourselves during a session. Such parameters are for our own safety and comfort and optimization of the trip. Further, when we are in a group setting, establishing a structure is intended to respect others' feelings and needs. There are several options regarding how many people we decide to journey with: We may travel solo, with a small group of friends or strangers, or with a larger group of friends or strangers.

Solo
Safety concerns suggest having a trusted individual or individuals in our space when we take psychedelics, but sometimes none is available. In addition, we may want to journey free from any interpersonal interference; we may not want company. Nevertheless, it is relatively imprudent to embark solo on a first trip. Even after we've gained some

familiarity with a particular drug, it's wise to let a confidant know of our plans and whereabouts when we take the drug again.

If we do take the journey alone, it is important to think through certain issues beforehand, and to decide upon responses to which we can adhere. It's important to gain familiarity with these structural issues from those who are more experienced with taking a drug, and that we spend some time establishing reasonable and appropriate guidelines for our session. Though we might hope to commit these guidelines to memory, once the time comes, it is helpful to have them available in written form in case we are unable to recall them. In most cases, when we are under the influence, it is ill advised to change the structure we have set up before taking the drug. It is important to remember that we can always change the guidelines for our next session, when we have had some time to think about these issues after we've had the experience of one journey.

There are many structural issues to consider, especially if we are taking the drug alone. Will we be listening to music? If so, will we set up our play list beforehand or decide what we will listen to when we are in an altered state of consciousness? Do we intend to keep our eyes open or closed? Would we like eyeshades? Will we remain clothed? How much of the session will we spend lying down versus sitting up and walking around? When and what do we eat? How will we make sure we drink enough fluids? Under what circumstances might we take more of a drug or smoke a cigarette or drink alcohol or coffee? After our trip, when can we drive or leave the immediate premises? What about answering the telephone or making calls? How do we get help if we need it? What do we do if things become unbearable—do we want to have a tranquilizer on hand to chemically abort the trip?

Group

Whenever more than one person in the room is under the influence, we must take into consideration other people's set and setting issues; however, this may quickly ferment into a frothy brew of personalities

The Muse of Conscious Awakening,
oil on canvas by Martina Hoffmann © 2001

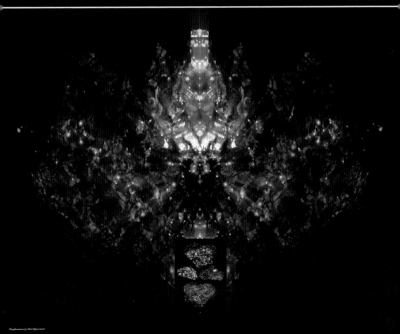

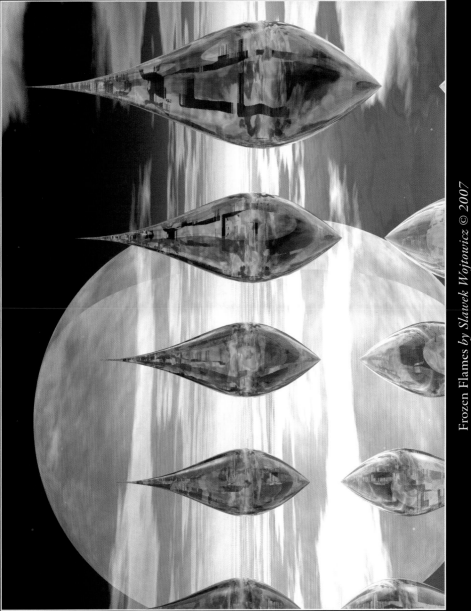

Frozen Flames *by Slawek Wojtowicz* © 2007

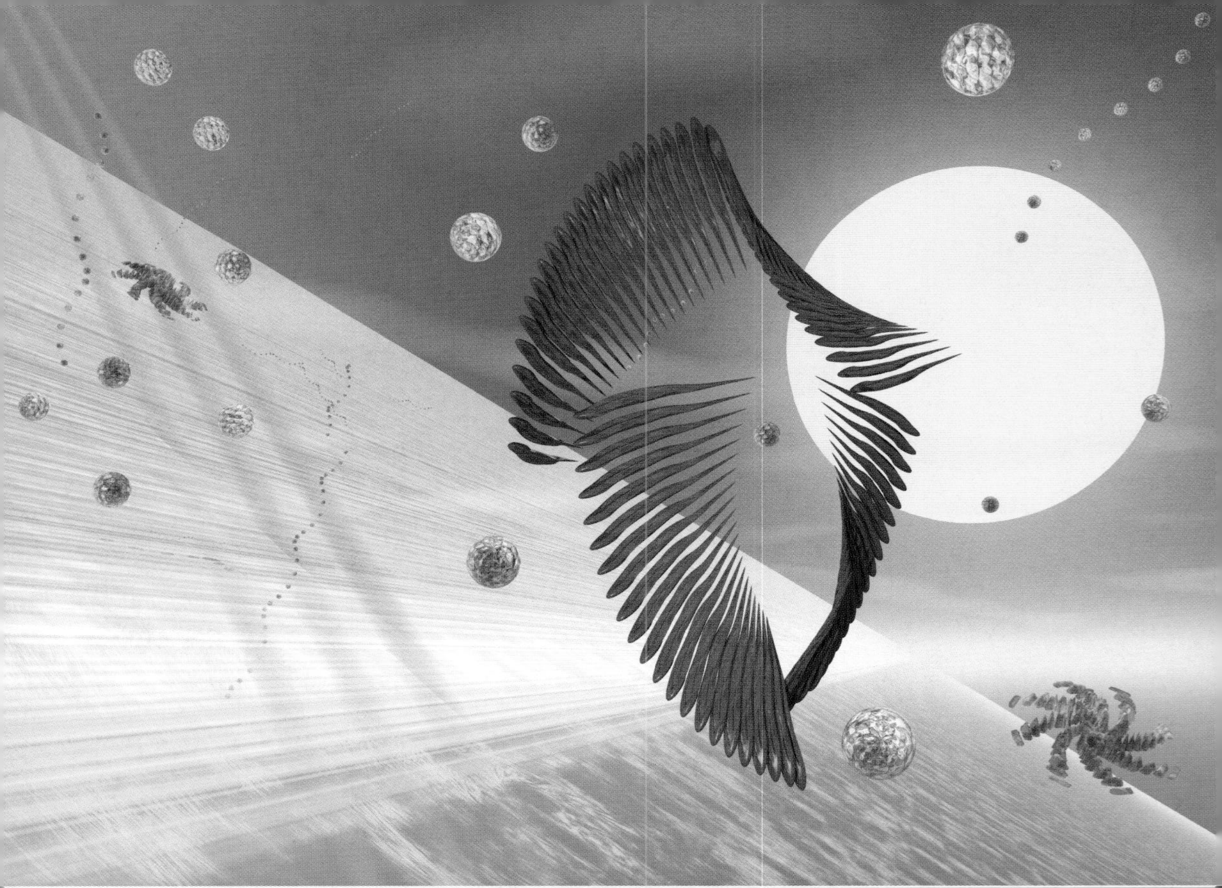

High Gravity Chase *by Slawek Wojtowicz* © 2007

and interactions. Therefore, in group settings—particularly in a new group—it is important to have additional elements of the structure decided and agreed upon in advance. One way to minimize stresses associated with a group session is for each person to have his or her solo trip. The use of eyeshades and well-spaced, single-sized mattresses or pads will help effect well-demarcated, individual experiences in a group setting. As drug effects wear off, interactions might then begin outside the main room in order not to distract those who want to continue with a more inner-directed experience.

Yet the purpose of a group setting, particularly with lower and intermediate doses, may be to engage in some group activity such as playing or listening to music, sharing an aesthetic experience, or problem solving. In cases such as these, we might spend most of our time exploring how the group process is affected by the influence of the psychedelic. Most important, however, is that these expectations and ground rules be discussed and agreed upon before a session begins.

There are other concerns in a group: How do we signal that we are in need (that is, do we raise our hand or speak)? How would we like to be supported? Is support verbal or physical? How are decisions made regarding our welfare or behavior? If some find the music, incense, or room temperature or lighting unpleasant, how will this be managed? In addition, will others in the group be sober or intoxicated? If intoxicated, will everyone in the group be taking the same drug? How will we know?

Whereas certain variables lend themselves to more or less flexible responses, some structural issues are best adhered to rather strictly. For example, intercourse or sexual interactions of any kind between participants during the session should be prohibited, as should physical, verbal, or emotional acting out of aggression. It is unwise to ask for or accept material favors such as money or property during the group session. Certainly, we may ask for and accept favors whose consequences do not extend beyond the session, such as a blanket if we are cold, a book for viewing, and the like. Asking for favors that require follow-through outside of the session, however, should wait until everyone is back to a normal state of consciousness. In addition, everyone must remain in the group until previously agreed-upon criteria have been met—for example, the group leader has determined that drug effects are adequately resolved and, if there is no leader, everyone must get a good night's sleep before leaving. Privacy and confidentiality are crucial in the success of any such group, and, therefore, everyone must agree never to mention with whom they took a group trip without the express permission of the others involved.

One of the advantages of the group setting is the option of having a period of organized sharing after the session, usually the day after the experience. This can be quite helpful in terms of the crucial reentry and reintegration necessary for optimal use of the session.

THE SITTER

Along with the question of who else is in the room tripping with us, an important question concerns whether anyone is "sitting" for those under the influence. The sitter supervises a psychedelic session much like a babysitter supervises children—those who take psychedelics may need the same kind of steering, restraining, and nurturing. In addition, it derives from the similarity between sitting in meditation and supervising a psychedelic session. The sitter must combine the skill of allowing people under his or her care to go through whatever takes place in a psychedelic trip and the skill of remaining alert and focused on the needs of those who are journeying. This combination of alert passivity and passive activity is a hallmark of many meditation practices.

Whether we are tripping on our own or in a group without a designated sitter, ostensibly there is a greater sense of freedom to have the type of trip we want—yet, particularly with high-dose sessions, it may be easier to let go more completely if we feel someone is taking care of us. In addition, the relative anarchy that may reign in a group setting, especially if people are on high doses, can be difficult to orchestrate.

One or more sitters can provide a much needed supervisory function in such a setting.

Some sitters may lead sessions more actively, rather than simply responding to the needs of participants. Those trained in a shamanic model may play musical instruments, sing, whistle, dance, shout, manipulate bodies physically and energetically, and pour, rub, or spit various liquids, smokes, and powders onto participants.

Set of the Sitter

Though there are many reasons to trip with a sitter, it is important to be extraordinarily careful regarding under whose supervision we place ourselves when we are taking psychedelics. Such consideration both makes the most of sessions and works to avoid problems. It's useful to note that participants will be deeply involved with this person at all stages of a trip—before, during, and after. The sitter is in a position of authority, leadership, and support, and those who will participate in a session are well advised to learn what they can about that person.

Some questions include: Is he or she religiously or spiritually oriented? Is he or she a member of any particular religion or profession? What is his or her training? What about sexual orientation? Is he or she married or does he or she have children? Does a potential sitter drink alcohol or use drugs, and if so, does he or she use them excessively or in moderation? Is he or she vegetarian? What are his or her motivations for supervising sessions—money, a desire to heal, sadism, curiosity, altruism, voyeurism, career advancement? How does he or she relate to the power and reputation that a sitter may accrue? What is his or her experience with these compounds in terms of administration to others as well as regarding personal use? Is this someone of whom we can ask questions and with whom we can work out plans for various situations that might arise during our trip? Do we feel we can trust this person to give us guidance and support when we are unable to provide these for ourselves?

We strongly encourage asking prospective sitters any or all questions whose answers will affect participants' feelings of safety and encouragement during a session. Included in these questions is a discussion of issues regarding structure. In addition, because it is so difficult to obtain psychedelic drugs, the person who supervises a session may be the one from whom participants obtain the drug. This is usually the case in small-group and shamanic sessions, and is always true in the research environment.

Is the Sitter Experienced?

Within the shamanic tradition, it is axiomatic that the leader is intimately and thoroughly familiar with all manner of drugs and plants that he or she will administer to others. This is also usually the case in the West with those who sit for underground users of psychedelics. Empathy—knowing what another is feeling—is quite important in any healing or spiritual work, and is found most often when the healer has previously undergone a similar experience. Even if the setting is not intended to address healing or spiritual issues directly, these may nevertheless arise at any time, and the sitter should be capable of responding appropriately.

Within the academic setting in the United States, a sitter's personal use of the psychedelic in question is discouraged. This is one of the unfortunate results of the Harvard research group's widely publicized personal use of psychedelics in the 1960s. Yet western European researchers are required to "go first" in any of their own psychedelic studies. There are several reasons for this: in order to make sure drugs and doses are safe, these scientists believe it is more ethical to first self-administer an experimental treatment, especially if there is no significant therapeutic benefit expected. By going first, they bear the brunt of any adverse effects. In addition, European regulatory authorities believe that the informed consent process is better served if the researchers are personally familiar with the effects of the drug. As a result of their own experience, they then are more able to inform a prospective volunteer fully regarding what to expect, and can be more empathetic during the actual drug studies.

Is the Sitter Tripping at the Same Time?

It's important to know if, at the time of a session, a sitter is under the influence of a psychedelic. It's also important to determine how participants will know whether or not the sitter takes a drug. Often, in shamanic or indigenous settings, the leader also partakes of a psychedelic substance, though perhaps at a lower dose than the participants in order to retain the ability to move around and interact. This empathetic resonance among those who are experiencing a particular drug effect helps the sitter provide an especially deep level of support and guidance. In Western models, however, this is an evolving area; some leaders ingest pschedelics, others do not.

In an academic setting, it is unlikely that the researcher will also use the same psychedelic substance during the study period. The extraordinarily rare possibility exists that a sitter under the influence of the same drug would also be the object of study. For example, a research project might ask whether a therapist is more or less helpful while affected by the same psychedelic used by participants. Whatever the case, answers to the question of the leader's use of the drug should be addressed ahead of time. There have been a number of situations in which group leaders have acted inappropriately while intoxicated, crossing important boundaries and later using as an excuse the effects of the drug.

ACCOUTREMENTS

Music can evoke profound effects in a highly psychedelicized individual. It usually is easier to arrange music beforehand, either by the solo tripper or, in the case of a group session, in consultation with the sitter if there is one. In a group setting, it is advisable to consider a "veto" rule regarding music: If anyone finds the music intolerable, it must be discontinued. Music with understandable lyrics can sometimes be distracting or can constrain the experience. Instrumental music or world music with lyrics that are unintelligible may allow for more fluidity in reaction to it. Playing musical instruments in a solo setting may help a participant express nonverbal, nonvisual elements of a trip. In a group setting, however, participants must take into account the reactions of other group members.

Art supplies, particularly during the "coming down," resolution period of a trip, can aid in giving form, shape, and color to otherwise nonverbal aspects of the experience. Writing materials also may be helpful, and in solo settings, a voice-recording device can capture fleeting ideas. Some people find looking into a mirror while tripping to be particularly evocative, especially in a session with a primarily spiritual or psychotherapeutic focus. Similarly, reviewing family photos from the past and present can stimulate the release of many emotions and insights.

SUPPLEMENTAL TECHNIQUES

There are many nondrug-based methods available for altering consciousness. These may be helpful in refocusing attention for those who might feel adrift in the psychedelic space or who might be physically uncomfortable. Examples of these techniques include yoga, massage, and a quiet form of meditation. Other techniques may help participants break through a particular psychic impasse in a trip. These include controlled hyperventilation, singing, dancing, and exercise. It's a good idea to be familiar and comfortable with these ancillary techniques before trying them in a psychedelicized condition. It's also important that participants not expose themselves to stressful or traumatic interventions unless that is one of the purposes of the trip. For example, participants may wish to work through their resistance to a particular yoga posture that they normally find too difficult to attain.

TYPES OF TRIPS

Keep in mind that despite the type of trip we wish to have, and despite deciding upon the dose, where we are, who we are with, and the activities available to us, we may not have the kind of experience we wanted.

For example, we may expect a relatively minor, pleasurable experience, but may instead reach a near-death state. We must be ready for anything to occur during a trip, no matter how much effort we expend in preparation. Also, it is rare that any one trip consists of only one particular type. Psychedelic experiences are notoriously varied. We enter and exit many levels during any one session. Nevertheless, there are general types of sessions and advisable related parameters.

Aesthetic, Pleasure-oriented Trips

These journeys may occur outside, in an environment of natural beauty, or they may occur in a setting of man-made beauty that features music, art, or archaeological relics. Ideally, participants will have access to both environments. If we are alone, we may take a walk in the woods, visit a museum, play or listen to music, or get a massage. For this type of trip occurring solely in an urban setting, it is best to take a low dose of psychedelic.

These types of trips lend themselves to group experiences. Examples of large group settings include contemporary "raves"—large-venue dance events—and events such as Burning Man, in the Nevada desert, where tens of thousands of people congregate. Also fitting this type of intention are smaller groups, such as several friends who "hang out" together and enjoy each other's company in a psychedelic state.

Usually, these are sessions without a sitter or leader. The spontaneity and freedom that we seek in such a setting, with doses generally being relatively low, do not require much supervision. It's a good idea, however, to make certain that noninebriated people are available who know of participants' condition and whereabouts.

Problem-solving Sessions

We may decide to use a psychedelic drug to help work on personal, professional, or creative concerns. Lower and intermediate doses provide more ease in maintaining focus on these issues and recalling our solutions when we return from our journey.

Enhancing creativity with psychedelics may occur outdoors or indoors, depending upon the particular task. An unobtrusive sitter can help record our new approaches to problems, and can provide encouragement and focus. We may want help within the context of a psychotherapeutic process, using the effects of psychedelics to modify the processes by which psychological healing occurs—that is, projection, transference, abreaction, and catharsis. In psychotherapeutic sessions, it's usually helpful to have someone acting as a sitter. This may be our own therapist or someone whom we only work with in psychedelic sessions. In a psychotherapeutic group setting, some people may be in therapy with the sitter, while others may not.

Lower doses in the psychotherapeutic setting allow for a better focus than higher ones, and provide the basis of *psycholytic psychotherapy.* High-dose sessions, referred to as *psychedelic psychotherapy,* add the qualitatively unique spiritual, mystical, or near-death states to the quantitative augmentation of normal psychotherapeutic processes. Religious and spiritual issues often become conscious and important in psychedelic psychotherapy.

If we are working on interpersonal issues, we and those with whom we want to work through these problems might be journeying together. We may choose to begin the session solo and later come together with other group members. Because of the sometimes intense dynamics that may arise even with low or medium doses, it is helpful to have a sitter in this type of session.

One model of psychedelic psychotherapy combines high doses of drug with overpowering, multimodal sensory stimulation in an indoor group setting. This particular technique is intended to cause a breakdown of psychological defenses not deemed possible by any one modality alone. Yet such experiences are difficult to negotiate and later to integrate.

It is usually easier to work on psychological issues in an indoor setting, although access to the natural world can provide a necessary balance for the intense inner work that engages participants.

SPIRITUAL, NEAR-DEATH, AND OTHERWORLDLY EXPERIENCES

These breakthrough experiences usually lend themselves to large-dose, introspective, solo settings. They also require the most in terms of our ability to let go and open ourselves to highly unusual effects. If we choose involvement in a group setting, the emphasis usually remains on an individual's experience, at least in the initial and middle stages of the trip.

It is easier for us to maintain an inward focus in an indoor setting. Nevertheless, nature can provide powerful catalysts for such experiences. If we decide to take this type of trip outdoors, we must do our best to ensure that participants are safe and free from unexpected disturbances.

If there is a sitter, he or she is unlikely to be a minister of any organized religion. Rather, those trained in the shamanic tradition are usually capable of containing and guiding these types of sessions. In the postindustrial West, sitters are often psychologically or spiritually trained individuals with their own psychedelic experience. Supplemental techniques such as controlled hyperventilation can be useful in providing the final impetus for the desired breakthrough.

As alluded to earlier, these types of experiences usually require us to be placed into uncomfortable inner spaces. The giving up of cherished self-concepts and identifications necessary to emerge anew into our reality is nearly always quite distressing at some point—and once we have had this type of experience, there is little social support for discussing its merits within the larger social mainstream. Social and spiritual support to help integrate such deep experiences is necessary, and must be part of the preparation for any planned breakthrough session.

VOLUNTEERING TO BE IN A RESEARCH STUDY

Any of these types of trips can be experienced within the research setting. Volunteering to be a research subject, however, even for a study that may provide benefit—such as psychotherapy, mysticism, or creativity research—involves the element of altruism, of giving up something in our own trip for the greater good. This altruism generates a unique dynamic between us and our setting, particularly to those in the room with us. When we volunteer for a research study, the trip is not all ours. We are being asked—and are expected—to provide data and information rather than just have an experience for our own sake. While this is neither intrinsically good nor bad, the informed-consent process must be open and transparent and this altruism must be acknowledged at the outset. From the beginning, there exist competing interests between our trip and the data we are generating—and we will not be allowed to forget this give-and-take that's superimposed upon our trip. It's important that research subjects not be surprised by, rebel against, or resent the exigencies of providing data. For example, as we may be traversing the deepest reaches of inner space, our vein may clot, and the nurse will flush the intravenous line with jarringly cold water or he or she might need to remove the line and replace it with another.

Those who are neophytes to psychedelic states must consider these issues carefully. "Sharing" a trip in this way can be likened to having our first sexual experience observed, with data and specimens collected. We might be more generous with our time, body, mind, and soul after we've gained some experience and familiarity with such new and intense experiences. Nevertheless, it is possible to participate in a research setting during our first psychedelic experience and have it turn out better than one we undergo alone or with friends. Perhaps the setting takes into account our inexperience and is designed to determine those factors that contribute to the best outcome. Such research projects are rare, though, and regardless of their intent, they must still collect data.

Research settings are characterized by a relatively constrained physical environment. They are almost always indoors, range of movement is restricted, and there are few surprises. Generally speaking, accoutrements or supplemental consciousness-altering methods are few or unavailable. These constraints are intended to keep constant as many variables as possible while modifying only those of interest. For example, the researcher may vary the dose of drug in the exact same setting to determine the effects of dose on the measured variables such as heart rate and blood pressure. It is interesting to note that though the usual hospital research unit is not especially peaceful, there we may have a sense of medical security—for instance, knowing that a cardiac resuscitation team is nearby—that is otherwise absent. In these studies, we are usually the only one in the environment taking a psychedelic drug.

Once we have decided to participate in research, there are two general types from which to choose: biological and psychological. The emphasis in the former is on data regarding our body, and the emphasis in the latter is on data regarding our mind. Biological studies may include subjective effects in their purview. They are called *psychopharmacological*—that is, seeking the pharmacological underpinnings of subjective experiences. *Psychobiological* studies, or *psychophysiological* studies, attempt to explicate the physiology of the mind. For example, these may assess the effects of psychedelics on involuntary aspects of perception, such as how we respond to images presented to one or both eyes using various sequences and time intervals.

The tools used in biological research may include brain-imaging equipment, some of which may be noisy and tight-fitting and may involve being injected with a radioactive drug. Participants may have blood drawn to quantify levels of any number of factors: hormones, immune function, and metabolism of the drug in question or other drugs. Body temperature may be monitored, as may cardiovascular responses such as blood pressure and heart rate using an automatic blood pressure cuff.

Psychological studies can be divided into roughly two different categories: *problem solving* and *phenomenological*. We have previously discussed some of the parameters involved in problem solving with psychedelics, as well as the difference in psychotherapeutic work between lower-dose psycholytic and higher-dose psychedelic therapy.

In the research setting, the goals are similar but the structure is more rigorously adhered to.

Phenomenologically based psychological studies focus on the mental rather than biological effects of psychedelics—that is, perception of time, color, distance, and depth. Rather than assessing perceptual, information-processing mental functions, psychoanalytic studies may investigate more-complex phenomena such as projection, transference, mood reactivity, and free association.

Finally, studies may investigate the efficacy of psychedelics in eliciting mystical, near-death, and otherworldly experiences. These are somewhat more difficult to categorize within a research setting because they deal with concepts that, for many, fall outside of the purview of traditional scientific inquiry. Nevertheless, they partake of the general research model, limiting variables as much as possible and providing data to the research team.

LETTING GO

Once we have completed as much preparatory work as possible before a session and clarified our intent—thus choosing our setting—we are ready to turn our attention to the actual trip.

On the day of the session, we should be well rested and clear-eyed, feeling ready for whatever may come our way. Though it's a good idea to have water or ice chips available during the session to address thirst and dehydration, a person should not plan on eating any food or drinking alcohol.

The fundamental task required for an optimal psychedelic experience is somewhat paradoxical: It consists of actively establishing the direction in which we decide to let go. We consciously choose the cliff from which we will jump and with what attitude we make that leap. This is especially the case in high-dose sessions during which we hope to encounter the most radical and unusual experiences.

Resistance to high-dose, powerful trips can be extraordinarily painful and confusing. An opened-eyed, level-headed surrendering of resistance is the most effective way to prevent being thrown into this maelstrom and is the best method for pulling ourselves out of it if we do find ourselves overboard. Prayers, mantras, mudras, visualization, music, bodywork, and other aids may be helpful at various points in our trip to redirect the flow of experience. At the deepest, most exposed, raw, and vulnerable moments of the psychedelic encounter, however, it is only through letting go that we find ourselves making the most progress. From the five minutes of the DMT flash to the twelve hours of an ibogaine ordeal, this surrender is the crux of a successful journey.

The foundation laid by any previous inner work will hold us in good stead at such times by virtue of the attention skills we have developed. These skills make it easier to remain focused when confronted with the unexpected. In addition, effective psychotherapy or spiritual practice will have made us familiar with the skeletons in our closets and will have better equipped us to contend with them if and when they emerge. Thus, not only do we clearly perceive what is garnering our attention, but also we subsequently open up and drop our resistances to it. We will know when we are resisting and when we are moving forward at any given moment of the psychedelic experience.

Yet it is not only in negative aspects of a trip that we may become blocked. We also might be unable to move out of pleasant or neutral states. For example, we might find ourselves deeply blissful but also sense that we can go even deeper into what lies beneath and supports that bliss. Seemingly innocuous images or feelings, such as the curtain of psychedelic lights that is often a hallmark of the drug experience, may stand in our way. We want to see even more, but we cannot take the next step.

All these states can be managed to facilitate our moving forward; we can slow down, right ourselves, and then go on. We regain our balance through the proper application of attention and awareness. This is the slowing down, which we can facilitate physically through relaxed, deep breathing and helps release any tension in our bodies. Once we've slowed ourselves down and replanted our psychic feet, it is easier to move our consciousness through the resistance or block. Sometimes, however, we may not feel we have a body to relax or lungs through which to breathe. At these times, it may be useful simply to bring our minds back to what is happening, and to approach it in a positive, bright, and curious manner. For example, in my DMT work, I prepared volunteers by warning them that they might find themselves convinced that they had died. They could react in one of two ways: "Oh, my God, I'm dying—get me out of here!" or "I seem to have died. Very interesting. What's next?"

This approach creates the smallest space between being aware of an object (such as an emotion, thought, or perception) and having a relationship with it—in other words, just before we establish a relationship with it. The leverage exists in that microsecond gap; we become aware of the stuck or static nature of the relationship. Then, taking a psychic deep breath, we can pull back from it ever so slightly, enough to work ourselves through or out of the block. For example, with respect to the curtain of psychedelic lights, we can look for space or cracks within it and then pass through it.

ENCOUNTERING BEINGS

One of the most profound aspects of a psychedelic session is contact with alien or noncorporeal, spiritual, or invisible beings or entities. Upon experiencing such an encounter, the first task we must pursue is to regain our composure from the shock of meeting what appear to be sentient creatures in our newly discovered worlds—creatures that, in many instances, seem to have been waiting for us. Next, we are faced with how to relate to them.

Some beings appear to be kind, gentle, and concerned for our welfare. Others seem to be aggressive, angry, and hurtful. Some present in an ambiguous or mischievous manner. They may communicate more or less effectively or they may ignore us altogether. While their sheer novelty and unexpectedness make us feel a sense of awe, it may be best, whenever possible, to appraise them with the same objectivity with which we would judge any chance encounter with strangers. At the time of such encounters, we don't know these beings' language or culture, nor do we know their intent. As with all elements of the psychedelic experience, it's important not to become obsessed with them or our reaction to them. Once we establish a modicum of stability in our interactions with them and have decided they are "safe," we can engage them in any number of ways—we can seek their help, advice, love, and healing. Keep in mind, however, the flux of the psychedelic experience, and do not be surprised if these beings morph readily into the opposite of everything that we had considered them the moment before.

Entities with fangs, poisonous-looking appendages, and other clearly menacing features usually are not benign, and it is best to be very wary of them. We can listen to what they have to say, but we ought not to be in any hurry to follow their advice. On the other hand, strange or frightening entities that seem to understand our fears may be more beneficent, particularly if they modify their behavior or appearance in response to our anxiety. Even if their appearance and behavior repel us, more-benign entities usually do not force us to do or accept things or become angry with us if we do not agree to their requests. In addition, we should never make any contract with the beings for doing evil or harm to another person or thing.

THE BAD TRIP

Though we can try to ensure that we have a smooth session, it is the norm to have difficult, painful periods in at least part of any major psychedelic experience. These can range from transient anxiety to prolonged psychosis. More than 99 percent of the time in someone medically and psychologically healthy, properly screened, prepared, and supervised, such distressing moments are short-lived and leave little if any aftermath. Nevertheless, being prepared for difficult stretches in a session can help us manage them more easily.

Anxiety and fear are relatively common as we begin to enter into the psychedelic state—when we are "coming on" to the drug effect. Simply relaxing physically and mentally—for example, slowing and calming our breathing—is often sufficient to dispel these jitters. If we are with a sitter or in a supportive group, we may ask to have someone lay a hand upon us in a nonerotic manner or to hold our hand. Sometimes placing a blanket over the body or removing uncomfortably heavy clothes or coverings can also help by allowing us to reconnect with our bodies. Once we are in the midst of the experience, we can deal with unpleasant periods in a variety of ways. The simple breathing or physical contact suggestions outlined here can be helpful in refocusing us on the flowing, dynamic nature of the experience and can get us out of a rut. More-intense or prolonged confusion, anxiety, fear, anger, or grief may require more-active intervention, either on our behalf or on the behalf of those with us—that is, the sitter or group members.

Quieting the environment—turning off the music, turning down the lights, lying down—can be helpful. Such maneuvers allow us to pay attention to what is important: our inner state. Soothing interventions may be necessary, however. A warm or cool compress on the forehead; mild, nonintrusive, and nonsexual massage; and quiet, melodious humming or singing can help replace the more-tumultuous inner workings of our minds with quieter thoughts and visions.

For more-intense disturbances, there are a range of options: Someone may perhaps have to hug us or even lie on top of us to help us to ground ourselves. A cold shower, ice cubes down the back of our shirt, and other firmly yet gently administered strategies can help break any vicious cycles in which we find ourselves. Controlled hyperventilation can also help push us through any particularly tenacious disturbing states.

Finally, there is the option of using medication to interrupt an especially out-of-control situation—but such instances are extraordinarily rare. For many of us, however, it can be quite reassuring to know that a medication is available to pull us out of almost any negative spiral if we are unable to do so ourselves. Usually, a benzodiazepine such as alprazolam or lorazepam is sufficient, but the sedating side effects of these interventions—which can last for hours—must be taken into account. Antipsychotic medications are a last resort, and come with their own host of unpleasant side effects.

COMING DOWN AND REINTEGRATING

After a trip, we must be kind to ourselves. It's best to allow for one or two days between a session and resumption of normal, everyday activities. It's also important to rest, eat healthy food, drink plenty of liquids, and get several nights of good sleep. Rest. Most of all, we must consider what we just experienced. After a session, we should write, draw, or record in some way the images, feelings, ideas, body sensations, and perceptions we contacted. We should share and process our experience with others whom we trust: we may share with someone who either did or did not join us for our trip; with our sitter; or with a shaman, minister, or therapist. We must review the aspects of the trip that continue to draw our attention.

GETTING HELP

While most people can integrate even major psychedelic drug experiences relatively well, some sessions—especially our first ones—may be traumatic. Generally, by the time the session is winding down, a well-integrated experience resolves itself into a sense of happy satisfaction with our session. Intense, unshakable, powerful emotions such as sadness, anxiety, fear, or anger may foretell unpleasant postsession feelings.

Intense or prolonged negative after effects may occur, and these can range from anxiety and depression to psychosis. Added to these potential negative outcomes are the stigma associated with psychedelic drugs and their illegality. These factors make seeking help more problematic. Nevertheless, when we feel we need help, we must search for it. If we have taken our trip with others or if we were supervised by a sitter, it is best to start with them when asking for appropriate referrals for follow-up. Such after-session follow-up may range from an hour or two decompressing with a knowledgeable friend to psychiatric hospitalization. In between these two extremes is the common feeling that we have confronted issues we are not psychologically or spiritually mature enough to integrate. We may recognize that a course of inner work must now ensue in order to use the session optimally and in a healthy way.

INTEGRATION

Even after relatively trauma-free sessions, we are faced with a daunting task: What do we do with all this information? It may be a case of "Now for the hard part . . ." We may ask ourselves if we will trip again, and we may wonder why or how we will if we choose to try another session. Perhaps most important, we may ask ourselves if we plan to change anything about our life: our career, relationships, diet, drug use, or religious views or practices. Finally, we may ask whether we have begun a new phase of inner or outer work.

It may take a while for a big trip to fully exert its effects—we need space and time for the ripples to reach the shore. We may have to live many years to fully digest and manifest the results of a big journey. It's important to be patient with ourselves and not to become frustrated that more has not changed in our lives as a result of what appeared, at the outset, to be a life-changing experience. More drug trips may not be the answer; perhaps what's necessary is a sober, concerted application in our everyday life of what we experienced.

✧

Though we should not push ourselves, we also do ourselves a disservice by allowing a trip to be forgotten, filed away in some dusty recesses of our mind as just one more interesting experience. We must remember that in a psychedelic trip, we've been given a tremendous gift, one that very few people ever have the opportunity to receive and experience.

12

The sacred voyage
Beyond Science Fiction?
Slawek Wojtowicz, M.D.

Science fiction has always been very good at predicting the future: from submarines and spaceships imagined by Jules Verne to communicators from *Star Trek,* we have seen many seemingly far-fetched ideas come to fruition. Soon we may see many more science-fiction inventions and concepts come true—perhaps time travel (almost a thousand papers on this topic have recently been published in professional journals); travel in hyperspace or other dimensions; the discovery of multiple universes (string theory); the existence of antigravity (dark energy); teleportation (see the research on quantum entanglement); transport and communication with supraluminal speed (wormholes, signal nonlocality); and even invisibility cloaks. The future promises to be very exciting indeed. Many of us are very impatient, however, and we can't wait much longer for these inventions to change our lives. We yearn to experience right now the taste of things to come. Yet is this possible?

As computer geeks keep telling us, information is everything. More and more, scientists working in fields as diverse as those of quantum physics, astronomy, and molecular biology are telling us the same thing, though perhaps more accurately: Everything is information. Thanks to the spread of computers and the explosion of the Internet, information is the new superparadigm for theorists. Just as Newtonian physics was based on the paradigm of the clockwork universe, the information technology (IT) revolution has inspired scientists to see all in terms of information.

By *information,* however, physicists don't necessarily mean simple bits of data. Instead, they refer to a more fundamental, underlying principle of the universe—a principle from which all things are made. John Wheeler, perhaps the most distinguished proponent of information theory, claimed that, fundamentally, atoms are made up of bits of information. As he put it in a 1989 lecture, "Its are from bits." He elaborated: "Every *it*—every particle, every field of force, even the space–time continuum itself—derives its function, its meaning, its very existence entirely from binary choices, *bits*. What we call reality arises in the last analysis from the posing of yes/no questions." Those of a more religious bent might suggest that all things physical have a spiritual or nonmaterial origin.

Wheeler argues that this strange state is an inevitable consequence of the now familiar oddities of quantum mechanics. At its fundamental level, reality is fuzzy, its exact nature undetermined until observed—a concept most famously illustrated by Schrödinger's cat in a box: the cat can be simultaneously both dead and alive before we open the box.

DO WE LIVE IN A DREAM WORLD?

How many of us realize that a wide spectrum of uniquely human activities has its roots in altered states of consciousness (ASCs)? Origins of all religions, art (going all the way back to cave paintings created thirty thousand to forty thousand years ago), spiritual and shamanic healing, and even the creation of civilization itself (as seen in chapter 9) can be traced back to ASC experiences. Even the history of science gives us plenty of examples of inspiration that comes from beyond consensus reality.

One well-known instance is the story of the organic molecule known as benzene. The formula of benzene (C_6H_6) mystified scientists, who could not figure out its structure. German chemist Friedrich August von Kekulé, however, who laid the groundwork for the modern structural theory in organic chemistry, came up with a solution that provided a satisfactory explanation. In 1861, after years of studying carbon bonding, benzene, and related organic molecules, he had a dream of whirling snakes in which he saw one of the snakes seizing its own tail. He woke up with a start. He'd experienced the "Eureka!" moment that gave him the structure of benzene—which is made up of a ring of carbon atoms. In 1929 the ringlike nature of benzene was confirmed by the eminent crystallographer Kathleen Lonsdale. Another, more recent story is that of Francis Crick, who reportedly came up with the double-helix structure of DNA—the most significant biological discovery of the twentieth century—while under the influence of LSD. Of course, that discovery won him the Nobel Prize (shared with James Watson).

By now it should be clear that psychedelics can produce an astounding variety of experiences—from meetings with aliens and time travel to journeys into the spirit world and mystical revelation. Yet is there an internally consistent explanation that can make sense of these experiences? Interestingly, both mystical religions and modern quantum physics seem to agree concerning the true nature of reality: time and space are just constructs of human consciousness created by our minds. The reality we perceive as solid and independent doesn't really exist on its own; it is simply a projection emanating from our minds. Some call it Maya, a dream, an illusion, and others describe it as a full-immersion movie that's better than the one that could be experienced on a holo-deck in *Star Trek*.

Is it possible that we live in a dream world or, to use more modern terminology, in a very sophisticated virtual-reality simulation? As Rick Strassman has hypothesized here, DMT may be the molecule that is responsible for maintaining the illusion in which we live. Those who are science-fiction fans won't be shocked by this supposition. Similar concepts have been explored thoroughly in science-fiction novels and in movies such as *The Matrix, Waking Life,* and *eXistenZ*.[1] Since we are the source of the dream, it appears so real and familiar to us that we cannot even tell that it's just a dream.

This is an idea that many of us may have a great deal of difficulty accepting. From the absolute point of view, the relative doesn't really exist. Nevertheless, at a very fundamental level, the relative does exist. It is this strange dynamic between the relative and the absolute that is perhaps one of the ways DMT and similar endogenous molecules play a role in our lives. At the deepest, spiritual level of awareness, this reality is some sort of weird projection. Yet where most of us are most of the time—even the most enlightened among us—is the relative everyday level that we need to learn to negotiate as skillfully as possible.

The biggest illusion of all is that we appear to be separate, individual beings. Mystics across all religions, whether Zen or Tibetan Buddhists, Sufis in Islam, Kabbalah practitioners in Judaism, or gnostics in Christianity, agree that there is only one actor playing all the parts in this virtual-reality movie. That actor is God, the same one who is responsible for the creation of our universe. He is you and I as well as all other sentient beings. The mind of the Divine forms the essence of our own mind. Therefore, when we learn how to unite with the Source, we will know how to reach across time and space—anywhere in the universe—simply by looking deep within.

Each of us may be able to open the doors in our mind that lead to the entire universe: a much more incredible and exciting notion than any science-fiction story! So how do we do this? Many have performed this feat in the past: Jesus and Buddha are perfect examples, but there are countless others who managed to access the universe with equal success, though with less publicity. Most of those who sporadically use psychedelics don't learn how to control access to these gateways: lacking the training and proper preparation, they stumble through their psychedelic experiences and don't know how to return to a particular location they visited once before. Notable exceptions are shamans and yogis. Their specialty is exploration of other realities. They learn how to access and travel in these regions safely; they make maps of alien realms and pass this knowledge to apprentices, from generation to generation.

Becoming a shaman requires awakening from the dream in which we all are immersed. But what exactly does it mean to be *awake?* Do we really have to take the red pill, like Neo in *The Matrix,* to awaken and learn what's real and what's not?

SCIENCE FICTION AS A PATH TO AWAKENING

What exactly is enlightenment or awakening, and why is it so difficult to achieve? Why do only a few of us manage to awaken from the not-so-happy dream in which we appear to live? What is the information or wisdom attainable in the psychedelic state that can lead to enlightenment?

Mystical religions tell us that the root of all unhappiness and suffering is our ignorance concerning the nature of reality. We suffer because we chase after certain illusions (such as sex, money, fame, or power) and we are afraid of others (fear of death or of your boss is a good example!) because we think they are real. The prerequisite for awakening is a personal experience of the true nature of reality—it is not enough to hear or read about it or believe that we live in a dream. Psychedelics can provide exactly that: firsthand experience of other, otherwise unseen realities. It is essential to experience these firsthand, but even this is not enough for awakening to occur.

Once we gain this initial experience, the hard work begins: we must shed all our deeply ingrained preconceptions about the world and about ourselves and change the way we think. We must live the knowledge, instead of experiencing it solely on an intellectual level. Jesus put it this way (as we can read in the Gospel of Mark 8:34, New International Version): "If anyone would come after me, he must deny himself and take up his cross and follow me." This is hardest to do, yet it is absolutely necessary to reach the next stage of evolution. If you are a narcissist, you must became selfless; if you are lazy, you must turn into a diligent worker; if you are a slob, you must become neat; if you smoke, you must quit; if you are intolerant, you must open up and accept others as they are—and so on. This is where the proper integration of the psychedelic experience and traditional religion might provide a cross-fertilization that can benefit both sides of the aisle: psychedelicists can study the wisdom teachings of religions to learn how to manifest the sometimes inchoate wisdom they touch in the psychedelic state, and religious practitioners who lack deep, intuitive understanding of their tradition's teachings can have their own spiritual experience that confirms and expands what they know only intellectually.

To awaken, we must transcend ourselves—to become more than our sense of a separate self. In other words, we must learn to be selfless and think about others first, to serve others before we take care of our own needs. A shaman can help us get started and can help us reach our goal much more quickly, because he or she has firsthand knowledge of the spiritual realm and knows how to use psychedelics and other trance-inducing methods such as drumming or dancing. Of course, we can also arrive at this place through years of diligent meditation and through many other means. In fact, we are all on a spiritual path, even if some of us don't realize it yet.

Science fiction also happens to be one of the roads to enlightenment. It opens us up to new ideas, no matter how incredible they may appear. Remember that first interracial kiss on *Star Trek?* Being open-minded is a prerequisite for enlightenment. Questioning all presumptions, dogmas, and taboos leads to deeper and deeper levels of understanding. Being accepting and tolerant of others is yet another step in the right direction—and science-fiction fans are often more open-minded than the general population. In addition, many writers tackle spiritual matters under the guise of science fiction. In fact, it is difficult to find a science-fiction or fantasy novel or movie that does not touch on these issues in one way or another.

Science-fiction literature teaches us that the distinction is blurred between what we think is real and what is not. It shows that dreams can be totally indistinguishable from waking reality. When we are immersed in a dream, our critical mind is turned off and we can't tell that we are dreaming until we are awakened. We fly in the air, fight with aliens, travel in time, or survive encounters with dragons, but we don't question how these things are possible. We don't, that is, until we wake up. The same principle applies to our consensus reality—we think it is all real until we wake up and realize that it's just a strange dream, like our nocturnal dreams.

The popularity of movies such as *Star Wars, The Matrix, Total Recall, Cube,* and *Dark City*[2] has helped to spread the ideas known to mystics for millennia. Movies such as *Star Wars* show us that there are invisible spiritual powers at play, affecting our lives whether or not we acknowledge them. Even though we may feel like insignificant pawns in the game of life, our power rests in the ability to choose how we respond to challenges that fate places in front of us—and it is never too late to change our mind, as Darth Vader's example shows.

The Matrix was likely inspired by the gnostic gospels (many of them destroyed by the Church and rediscovered only fifty years ago in Nag Hammadi, Egypt), including the Gospel of Thomas, in which Jesus says: "Those who seek should not stop seeking until they find. When they find, they will be disturbed. When they are disturbed, they will marvel, and they will reign over all."[3] This sounds rather mysterious and exciting. Some experts suspect that the Gospel of Thomas might be older than the canonical gospels included in the Christian scriptures, and is therefore closer to the source and more likely to be true to the actual message of Jesus. We may ask why the Church branded such writings as heretical and attempted to eradicate these gospels.

One possible "secret" reason for suppression of these gospels in the West (in addition to their outright political threat to the monopoly of the Church—after all, who needs priests and bishops if we can experience God directly?) was the metaphysical terror experienced by those who uncovered only part of the truth: Yes, we may be divine inside, but there is only one of us; we are TOTALLY ALONE (and, while this has to be experienced to understand it, anything—even wars, pain, and suffering encountered in this world—is better than being totally alone). We are separated from God and stuck in hell—bound to repeat our mistakes over and over again in an infinite number of reincarnations. We can't really die and there appears to be no way out of this nightmare. . . .

This theme has been explored in movies such as *Abre los ojos*[4] (and its Hollywood remake *Vanilla Sky*), *Groundhog Day,* and *The Fountain.*[5] Mystics also tell us that there is no personal God as described by mainstream religions such as Judaism, Christianity, and Islam, but instead there is a field of potentiality or energy that can be experienced as pure love. Gnostics called this field *pleroma* (a Greek word that translates as "fullness"), and in Hinduism and Buddhism it is known as Brahma or Brahman. We might envision ourselves on a holodeck that creates everything that we imagine. . . . The trouble begins when we forget who we are and that we are totally alone and when we begin fighting with figments of our imagination. When we are lost in fear and lash out in anger at the "outside" world, the aggression bounces right back. We only hurt ourselves when we try to injure "others." . . . Fortunately, the same rule applies to love and compassion: The more we put them "out there," the more comes back our way.

Some say that ignorance is bliss; some people have believed that it is better to protect us from the "horrible" truth that there is only one of us. According to this view, it is an ultimate virtue to protect us from anything that would shorten the bliss of ignorance. When we grow inevitably unhappy (because none of us is spared disease, suffering, and death), we may begin seeking and may discover the truth of our real condition and experience the terror of ultimate loneliness. This experience may discourage us from venturing farther into spiritual realms. Though we would rather forget such experience, unfortunately it is impossible to forget. Here, then, is another way in which psychedelics may prove valuable in the mystic quest: they preside over a more controlled, regulated, and gradual exposure to this initially terrifying existential realization.

Neo in *The Matrix* is a good example of a seeker who finds a way to awaken from the daze of the dream. He realizes that his life is meaningless and starts to search for answers. Just as in our consensus reality, his search is bound to be fruitful, and our hero discovers that he has been living in a dream, in a virtual reality created by a supercomputer. As any who have seen the movie will recall, it was the red pill that helped to awaken him. Yet what was inside the pill? A careful viewing of the movie reveals a clue during Neo's encounter with a white rabbit. Inside the pill was a psychedelic: peyote.

Polish writer Stanislaw Lem was among the first to toy with the idea of virtual reality. In a short story entitled "Lymphater's Formula,"[6] he describes an advanced computer that is capable of dreaming. In his dreams, the computer is a beautiful girl. In *The Futurological Congress*, Lem's space adventurer Ijon Tichy wakes up from suspended animation in the future and finds that people now routinely consume psychedelic drugs that can induce realistic hallucinations or waking dreams. Instead of merely watching movies, they live out their virtual-reality fantasies. Tichy acclimates himself slowly to this strange new existence. Soon, however, he realizes with growing panic that he is trapped in a world in which the worst in humanity has been brought out by the power to perfectly simulate reality.

Tichy learns that nothing in this society is what it appears to be. He discovers that a pharmacological dictatorship has been secretly subjecting the population to another set of psychedelic drugs to induce a collective hallucination. As a result, everyone sees a utopia of luxury, well-tended nature, and advanced technology when the economy, the environment, and the physical integrity of the people themselves are actually in a state of near collapse. Toward the end of the novel, Symington (who turns out to be the dictator behind this false paradise) tells Tichy: "We keep this civilization drugged, for otherwise it could not endure itself. That is why its sleep must not be disturbed. . . ."[7]

Similarly, many of Philip K. Dick's novels explore spiritual themes. *Ubik* is a classic example, with multiple layers of reality and unreality embedded within the plot.[8] We meet the protagonist, Joe Chip, shortly before an explosion at a moon base that almost kills him and his colleagues. There is only one fatality: their boss, Glen Runciter. Or did Joe and the others die while their boss actually survived? If his boss is dead and Joe is alive, why does Joe keep getting strange messages from Glen? Is Joe's experience of his postaccident life just a hallucination, played out as his frozen body lies in suspended animation?

Joe is very confused: he is convinced that he is the one trying to rescue Glen Runciter, but it quickly becomes clear that he himself is in a dire need of rescue from the hell-like reality of half-life (a condition in which the dead are kept half alive, frozen for a prolonged period of time during which they can still communicate with the living through sophisticated machinery). Readers of this story shudder upon recognizing that not only the first level of reality has been exposed as false, but the second level, supposedly more real than the first, turns out to be an illusion too. The status of reality as such is undermined—nothing is real.

Joe's reality gradually disintegrates and he almost falls prey to the entropy that is one of the main ruling forces in his universe (and in ours). Everything he touches decays and collapses: cigarettes turn stale in the pack, mold grows on coffee, and all of his friends disappear, presumably devoured by a nasty character named Jory. Joe is rescued at the last minute before dying by spraying himself with an aerosol called Ubik—the all-purpose "reality support" that now begins to materialize, fleetingly and tantalizingly, everywhere. Joe initially believes that Ubik is supplied by his allies outside of half-life—specifically his boss. Later, it appears that Runciter's wife, Elly, who is also sequestered in half-life, provides the life-saving spray. Yet he realizes that this, too, is not the truth, when Elly's soul abandons half-life to reincarnate again.

It is interesting that as Joe struggles to understand the source of the surrounding reality, he always prefers to place it outside of himself. He believes that it is Glen, Elly, or Jory who create his reality and try to either rescue or destroy him. Only toward the end of the story does it occur to a careful reader that Joe himself is the dreamer who creates the illusion of his own reality. Ubik is a magical medicine that seems to promise fullness and restoration to health, life, and plentitude, and Joe is apparently blocked from this fullness only by particular factors outside of his control: the pharmacy is closed, it is out of stock, or the Ubik spray devolves into an earlier form of itself, becoming a tin of liver balm. Ubik is both a gap in the reality structure (pointing to something else beyond imperfect, impermanent, entropic reality) and a reality support, that which literally keeps us going. The back cover of the book tells what Ubik really is: "I am Ubik. Before the universe was, I am. I made the suns, I made the worlds. I created the lives, and the places they inhabit; I move them here, I put them there. They go as I say, they do as I tell them, I am the word and my name is never spoken. The name which no one knows. I am called Ubik but that is not my name. I am. I shall always be."

Another example of this confusion of reality can be found in *Total Recall*,[9] a movie inspired by one of Dick's short stories ("We Can Remember It for You Wholesale"). In this movie, it is equally impossible to tell what is waking reality and what is dream. Is Arnold Schwarzenegger's character dreaming, is his Mars adventure an implanted memory or has it happened for real? Is he a hero or a brain-damaged dope?

If nothing is real, can we choose the dream in which we would like to live, or can we at least make sure that our dream is a good one and not a nightmare? A modern gnostic gospel entitled *A Course of Miracles*[10] and books based on it, such as *Disappearance of the Universe* by Gary Renard,[11] claim that it is possible to change the nightmare into a happy dream without pain, suffering, and death. This is quite a fantastic idea. It is interesting that *A Course in Miracles* also clearly states that we are deeply confused or even insane—even though we don't realize it. Similar ideas are discussed in a movie called *Waking Life*,[12] which poses crucial questions: Are we sleepwalking through our waking state or wake-walking through our dreams? Why can't we let go of our attachments and awaken?

In another movie, entitled *eXistenZ*,[13] Allegra Geller, the world's leading game designer, is testing her new virtual-reality game, eXistenZ, with a focus group. As they begin, she is attacked by a fanatic assassin who employs a bizarre, organic gun. She flees with a young marketing trainee, Ted Pikul, who is suddenly assigned as her bodyguard. Unfortunately, her pod, an organic gaming device that contains the only copy of the eXistenZ program, is damaged. To inspect it, she talks Ted into accepting a game port in his own body so that he can play the game with her. The resulting game leads the pair on a strange adventure during which it is impossible to determine what is real and what is not. Eventually, even Allegra herself turns out to be a game character, but Ted doesn't quite grasp that he may be hopelessly lost in a world created by his own mind. It begins innocently enough:

> Allegra: So how does it feel?
> Ted: What?
> Allegra: Your real life. The one you came back for.
> Ted: It feels completely unreal.
> Allegra: You're stuck now, aren't ya? You want to go
>   back to the Chinese restaurant because there's
>   nothing happening here. We're safe. It's boring.
> Ted: It's worse than that. I'm not sure . . . I'm not sure
>   here, where we are, is real at all. This feels like a
>   game to me. And you, you're beginning to feel a
>   bit like a game character.

The good news is that nobody really dies in the game; the bad news is that nobody seems to know what is real and what is not.

The movie *Cube* experiments with a similar idea—several people find themselves in a strange, seemingly alien maze that's full of deadly traps. They don't remember how they got there, but they realize that they have to work together to figure out a way to escape this nightmare before they die of dehydration or starvation or from being chopped up into pieces. To their horror, it appears that the Cube (the maze) was built by humans and not hostile aliens. Escape is almost impossible because the rules of the game appear to change continuously. The prisoners die, one by one, while the chances of escape seem to dwindle with the loss of each individual.[14]

Dark City is a movie that explores Buddhist ideas of reincarnation and the nature of reality. It takes us to a city far away from Earth, an urban place built by aliens who are trying to learn what makes us human. Every night at midnight, people lose all memory of their prior life and their identities are changed, as is the city itself. One day a person might be a rich merchant, and another day he might be a thief, and still another day he might be a gas-station attendant. The hero of the story, John Murdoch, awakens alone in a strange hotel to find that he has lost his memory and is wanted for a series of brutal and bizarre murders. While trying to piece together his past, he stumbles upon a group of alien beings known as the Strangers, who possess the ability to put people to sleep and alter the city and its inhabitants. He discovers that almost everyone else is completely unaware of what is happening. He struggles to wake up other people and he succeeds eventually, at which time everyone is freed from the cruel experiment.[15]

WHO ARE WE AND WHY ARE WE HERE?

You may have heard the saying "The Truth will set you free," the phrase from the Gospel of John 8:32. It promises freedom to those who learn the truth. Mystics, however, tell us that most of us are living in a state of perpetual confusion: just like the characters in *Dark City,* we don't know who we really are, we don't remember how we got here and where we have been before, and, worst of all, we don't know how to escape from the trap into which we've fallen.

Yet it looks like there is a way out of this quagmire. The good news, according to the mystics, is that we will eventually succeed in our efforts to escape from hell. Just as in some of the movies mentioned here, however, there is only one way out—and to find it, we must first awaken from the dream. We must realize that salvation lies inside, not outside, of ourselves. Fortunately, we have been programmed with the right clues to lead us to the escape hatch. We feel truly happy and peaceful only when we choose the right path: when we are selfless and when we don't chase after illusions such as sex, money, or power. We all learn eventually that blind attachment to these illusions makes us feel unhappy, anxious, fearful, restless, and miserable. In addition, we seem to be biologically programmed—DMT-synthesizing genes exist in the human body and may be turned on precisely at these moments. We've got both the "hardware" and the "software."

The Buddhist tradition teaches of the tripod of the illusory world—greed, hatred, and delusion—and their antidotes—compassion, love, and wisdom. In this tradition, wisdom is the road that ultimately leads to enlightenment. Here, *wisdom* can be understood as the "information" attainable through shamanic, psychedelic, or other types of spiritual experience. After the acquisition of wisdom comes the translation of this information into action—love and compassion.

When we start to awaken, we realize that we have been living in a dream, that we are the actor playing all the roles, and that to achieve the next step of evolution (and to find happiness), we must transcend our limited sense of being separate selves. Even though it appears that each of us is a unique individual having absolutely distinctive tasks to grasp and learn, these appearances are misleading. The choice that we must make in each situation is in fact very simple and can be reduced to this: we must stand in the other person's shoes and put other people's needs and feelings ahead of our own desires. After all, if everything is a dream and everyone else is us, it makes perfect sense to love everyone as we love ourselves.

All mainstream religions tell us that God is love—and anyone can turn the bad dream into a good one by becoming a conduit of love, by giving love to everyone, without expecting anything in return. Mystics tell us that anyone who chooses such a path will quickly notice major changes in his or her life—perhaps even within few months. One of the versions of the *bodhisattva* (a being striving for awakening) vow spells it out thus:

> When we understand that there is no final attainment,
> No ultimate answer or stopping place,
> When our mind is free of warring emotions and the
>   belief in separateness,
> Then we will have no fear.
> No matter where we are on the bodhisattva path,
>   whether we are just beginning or we've practiced
>   for years, we're always stepping farther into
>   groundlessness.
> Enlightenment is not the end of anything.
> Enlightenment, being completely awake,
> Is just the beginning of fully entering into the
>   Unknown.
>
> May I be a guard for those who are protectorless,
> A guide for those who journey on the road;
> For those who wish to go across the water,
> May I be a boat, a raft, a bridge.
>
> May I be an isle for those who yearn for landfall,
> And a lamp for those who long for light;
> For those who need a resting place, a bed,
> For all who need a servant, may I be a slave.
>
> May I be the wishing jewel, the vase of plenty,
> A word of power, and the supreme remedy.
> May I be the trees of miracles,
> And for every being, the abundant cow.

Like the great earth and the other elements,
Enduring as the sky itself endures,
For the boundless multitude of living beings,
May I be the ground and vessel of their life.

Thus, for every single thing that lives,
In number like the boundless reaches of the sky,
May I be their sustenance and nourishment
Until they pass beyond the bounds of suffering.[16]

The Christian scriptures note the same concept in similar words. In the Gospel of Matthew 5:38–48, Jesus says:

You have heard that it was said, "Eye for eye, and tooth for tooth." But I tell you, do not resist an evil person. If someone strikes you on the right cheek, turn to him the other also. And if someone wants to sue you and take your tunic, let him have your cloak as well. If someone forces you to go one mile, go with him two miles. Give to the one who asks you, and do not turn away from the one who wants to borrow from you.

You have heard that it was said, "Love your neighbor and hate your enemy." But I tell you: Love your enemies and pray for those who persecute you, that you may be sons of your Father in heaven. He causes his sun to rise on the evil and the good, and sends rain on the righteous and the unrighteous. If you love those who love you, what reward will you get? Are not even the tax collectors doing that? And if you greet only your brothers, what are you doing more than others? Do not even pagans do that? Be perfect, therefore, as your heavenly Father is perfect.

We are all capable of uncovering the divine within each of us. It doesn't matter how we accomplish this: through hypnosis, meditation, or the use of psychedelics—though some paths are shorter than others.

When we become disillusioned with our search for happiness in the outside world, we begin searching for answers within, and that search is bound to be fruitful . . . and if we happen to encounter some aliens or visit distant planets in the process, so be it.

THE GAME OF LIFE

An old Jewish tale tells us that God loves stories and has a great sense of humor. I suspect he loves movies and games as well. What if our life is really a very realistic game, not unlike eXistenZ, with an unlimited number of levels? And what if there is really only one player? Is our life just a game that God plays to entertain himself? What if our goal here is to gather all the clues and complete whatever moves us to the next level?

It seems that the law of karma is an operational principle on the level we are exploring right now: if you kill someone in this lifetime, he or she will kill you in the next one (an eye for an eye, a tooth for a tooth). The sacred scriptures of all religions hint at the possibility of a next level—a place with much more freedom and unlimited happiness. Moreover, these holy books can be used as "cheat sheets" of sorts to give us clues and hints that suggest how to get to the next level.

The level we are on right now has some built-in incentives to push us forward—we've already dawdled here too long. The prophecies of Nostradamus and others tell us of impending cataclysms, the Mayan calendar comes to an end in 2012, and many predict that a time of change is coming. We see our natural environment deteriorating quickly—global warming is growing out of control, polar caps are melting before our eyes. Some predict that ocean levels may rise very quickly once average global temperatures reach a certain level—perhaps they'll rise as much as thirty to fifty feet a year, for a total of three hundred to five hundred feet, as suggested by Hank Wesselman in his book *Spiritwalker: Messages from the Future.*[17]

In his second book, entitled *Your Immortal Reality,* Gary Renard predicts that several major cities in the United States (including New

York and Los Angeles) and Europe may be targets for nuclear attack by terrorists within the next fifty years.[18] The world is not getting any safer: our government is wasting billions of dollars on wars that a majority of citizens don't support (for example, the war in Iraq and the "war on drugs") and still our children are not safe at school or on the street . . . How much longer will we wait before we change our mind and move to the next level? The next can't be much worse than the one we're on right now. Indeed, it should be much better.

notes

INTRODUCTION

1. Jim DeKorne, *Psychedelic Shamanism: The Cultivation, Preparation and Shamanic Use of Psychotropic Plants* (Port Townsend, Wash.: Breakout Productions, 1994).

CHAPTER 1. THE PSYCHEDELICS

1. C. T. Tart, ed., *Altered States of Consciousness* (New York: John Wiley and Sons, 1969).
2. R. Siegel, *Intoxication: The Universal Drive for Mind-Altering Substances* (Rochester, Vt.: Park Street Press, 2005).
3. A. T. Weil, *The Natural Mind: An Investigation of Drugs and Higher Consciousness,* revised ed. (Boston: Mariner/Houghton-Mifflin, 1998).
4. A. T. Shulgin, *Tihkal: The Continuation* (Berkeley, Calif.: Transform Press, 1997).
5. A. Hoffer and H. Osmond, *The Hallucinogens* (New York: Academic Press, 1967).
6. L. Grinspoon and J. B. Bakalar, *Psychedelic Drugs Reconsidered* (New York: Basic Books, 1979).
7. T. McKenna, *Food of the Gods* (New York: Bantam, 1993).
8. R. G. Wasson, C. A. P. Ruck, and S. Krammrisch, *Persephone's Quest: Entheogens and the Origins of Religion* (New Haven, Conn.: Yale University Press, 1988).
9. R. Eisler, *The Chalice and the Blade* (San Francisco: HarperSanFrancisco, 1988).

10. M. Dobkin de Rios, *Hallucinogens: Cross-Cultural Perspectives* (Albuquerque: University of New Mexico Press, 1984).

11. F. Wertham and M. Bleuler, "Inconstancy of the Formal Structure of the Personality," *Arch Neurol Psychiatry* 28 (1932): 52–70.

12. A. Hofmann, *LSD: My Problem Child* (New York: McGraw Hill, 1980).

13. J. H. Gaddum and K. A. Hameed, "Drugs which Antagonize 5-hydroxy-tryptamine," *Br J Pharmacol* 9 (1954): 240–48.

14. M. A. Lee and B. Shlain, *Acid Dreams: The Complete Social History of LSD, the CIA, the Sixties, and Beyond* (New York: Grove Press, 1986).

15. A. T. Shulgin and A. Shulgin, *Pihkal: A Chemical Love Story* (Berkeley, Calif.: Transform Press, 1991).

16. J. R. Cooper, F. E. Bloom, and R. H. Roth, *The Biochemical Basis of Neuropharmacology,* 8th ed. (New York: Oxford, 2002).

17. D. W. Woolley and E. N. Shaw, "A Biochemical and Pharmacological Suggestion about Certain Mental Disorders," *Science* 119 (1954): 587–88.

18. D. E. Nichols, "Hallucinogens," *Pharmacol Ther* 101 (2004): 131–81.

19. R. J. Strassman, "Hallucinogenic Drugs in Psychiatric Research and Treatment: Perspectives and Prospects," *J Nerv Ment Dis* 183 (1995): 127–38.

20. M. M. Cohen, M. J. Marinello, and N. Back, "Chromosomal Damage in Human Leukocytes Induced by Lysergic Acid Diethylamide," *Science* 155 (1967): 1417–19.

21. N. I. Dishotsky, W. D. Loughman, R. E. Mogar, and W. R. Lipscomb, "LSD and Genetic Damage," *Science* 172 (1971): 431–40.

22. R. J. Strassman, "Adverse Reactions to Psychedelic Drugs: A Review of the Literature," *J Nerv Ment Dis* 172 (1984): 577–95.

23. H. D. Abraham and A. M. Aldridge, "Adverse Consequences of Lysergic Acid Diethylamide," *Addiction* 88 (1993): 1327–34.

CHAPTER 2. DMT: THE BRAIN'S OWN PSYCHEDELIC

1. C. Rätsch, *The Encyclopedia of Psychoactive Plants* (Rochester, Vt.: Park Street Press, 2005), 50–56, 702–715.

2. R. H. F. Manske, "A Synthesis of the Methyl-tryptamines and Some Derivatives," *Can J Res* 5 (1931): 592–600.

3. O. Gonçalves de Lima, "Observaçoes sôbre o Vihno da Jurema utilazado pelos Indios Pancarú de Tacaratú (Pernambuco)," *Arquiv Inst Pesquisas Agron* 4 (1946): 45–80.

4. M. S. Fish, N. M. Johnson, and E. C. Horning, "Piptadenia Alkaloids: Indole Bases of *P. peregrina (L.) Benth*, and Related Species," *J Am Chem Soc* 77 (1955): 5892–95.

5. S. Szára, "The Social Chemistry of Discovery: The DMT Story," *Social Pharmacology* 3(3) (1989): 237–48.

6. A. Sai-Halasz, G. Brunecker, and S. I. Szára, "Dimethyltryptamin: ein neues Psychoticum," *Psychiat Neurol, Basel* 135 (1958): 285–301.

7. D. E. Rosenberg, H. Isbell, and E. J. Miner, "Comparison of Placebo, N-dimethyltryptamine, and 6-hydroxy-N-dimethyltryptamine in Man," *Psychopharmacology* 4 (1963): 39–42.

8. Z. Böszörményi and S. I. Szára, "Dimethyltryptamine Experiments with Psychotics," *J Ment Sci* 104 (1958): 445–53.

9. W. J. Turner Jr. and S. Merlis, "Effect of Some Indolealkylamines on Man," *Arch Neurol Psychiatry* 81 (1959): 121–29.

10. F. Franzen and H. Gross, "Tryptamine, N,N-dimethyltryptamine, N,N-dimethyl-5-hydroxytryptamine and 5-methoxytryptamine in Human Blood and Urine," *Nature* 206 (1965): 1052.

11. R. Rodnight, R. M. Murray, M. C. H. Oon, I. F. Brockington, P. Nicholls, and J. L. T. Birley, "Urinary Dimethyltryptamine and Psychiatric Symptomatology and Classification," *Psychol Med* 6 (1976): 649–57.

12. W. N. Pahnke, A. A. Kurland, S. Unger, C. Savage, and S. Grof, "The Experimental Use of Psychedelic (LSD) Psychotherapy," *JAMA* 212 (1970): 1856–63.

13. R. R. Griffiths, W. A. Richards, U. McCann, and R. Jesse, "Psilocybin Can Occasion Mystical-type Experiences Having Substantial and Sustained Personal Meaning and Spiritual Significance," *Psychopharmacology* 187 (2006): 268–83.

14. D. E. Nichols, "Hallucinogens," *Pharmacol Ther* 101 (2004): 131–81.

15. H. Isbell, R. E. Belleville, H. F. Fraser, A. Wikler, C. R. Logan, "Studies on Lysergic Acid Diethylamide (LSD-25). I. Effects in Former Morphine Addicts and Development of Tolerance during Chronic Intoxication," *Arch Neurol Psychiatry* 76 (1956): 468–78.

16. B. Kovacic and E. F. Domino, "Tolerance and Limited Cross-tolerance to the Effects of N,N-dimethyltryptamine (DMT) and Lysergic Acid Diethylamide-25 (LSD) on Food-rewarded Bar Pressing in the Rat," *J Pharmacol Exp Ther* 197 (1976): 495–502.

17. R. J. Strassman, C. R. Qualls, and L. M. Berg, "Differential Tolerance to

Biological and Subjective Effects of Four Closely-spaced Doses of N,N-dimethyltryptamine in Humans," *Biol Psychiatry* 39 (1996): 784–95.

18. J. C. Gillin, J. Kaplan, R. Stillman, and R. J. Wyatt, "The Psychedelic Model of Schizophrenia: The Case of N,N-dimethyltryptamine," *Am J Psychiatry* 133 (1976): 203–8.

19. T. Takahashi, K. Takahashi, T. Ido, et al., "[11]C-labelling of Indolealkylamine Alkaloids and the Comparative Study of Their Tissue Distributions," *Int J Appl Radiat Isot* 36 (1985): 965–69; K. Yanai, T. Ido, K. Ishiwata, et al., "In vivo kinetics and displacement study of carbon-11-labeled hallucinogen, N,N-[11C]dimethyltryptamine," *Eur J Nucl Med* 12 (1986): 141–46.

20. D. J. McKenna, G. H. N. Towers, and F. Abbott, "Monoamine Oxidase Inhibitors in South American Hallucinogenic Plants: Tryptamine and β-carboline Constituents of Ayahuasca," *J Ethnopharmacol* 10 (1984): 195–223.

21. A. T. Shulgin, *Tihkal: The Continuation*, 247–84.

22. J. M. Beaton and P. E. Morris, "Ontogeny of N,N-dimethyltryptamine and Related Indolealkylamine Levels in Neonatal Rats," *Mech Ageing Dev* 25 (1984): 343–47.

23. M. A. Thompson, E. Moon, U.-J. Kim, J. Xu, M. J. Siciliano, and R. M. Weinshilboum, "Human Indolethylamine N-methyltransferase: cDNA Cloning and Expression, Gene Cloning, and Chromosomal Localization," *Genomics* 61 (1999): 285–97.

24. R. Strassman, *DMT: The Spirit Molecule* (Rochester, Vt.: Park Street Press, 2001), 56–85.

25. R. J. Strassman, G. T. Peake, C. R. Qualls, and E. J. Lisanksy, "A Model for the Study of the Acute Effects of Melatonin in Man," *J Clin Endocrinol Metab* 65 (1987): 847–52.

26. R. J. Strassman and C. R. Qualls, "Dose-response Study of N,N-dimethyltryptamine in Humans. I: Neuroendocrine, Autonomic, and Cardiovascular Effects," *Arch Gen Psychiatry* 51 (1994): 85–97.

27. R. J. Strassman, C. R. Qualls, E. H. Uhlenhuth, and R. Kellner, "Dose-response Study of N,N-dimethyltryptamine in Humans. II: Subjective Effects and Preliminary Results of a New Rating Scale," *Arch Gen Psychiatry* 51 (1994): 98–108.

28. R. J. Strassman, "Human Hallucinogenic Drug Research in the United States: A Present-day Case History and Review of the Process," *J Psychoactive Drug* 23 (1991): 29–38.

CHAPTER 3. THE VARIETIES OF THE DMT EXPERIENCE

1. J. E. Mack, *Abduction* (New York: Ballantine, 1994).

CHAPTER 4. AYAHUASCA:
THE SACRED VINE OF THE AMAZON

1. D. J. McKenna and T. McKenna, *The Invisible Landscape: Mind, Hallucinogens, and the I Ching* (New York: Seabury Press, 1975).

2. W. Burroughs and A. Ginsberg, *The Yagé Letters Redux.* (San Francisco: City Light Books, 2006).

3. R. Metzner, ed., *Sacred Vine of Spirits: Ayahuasca* (Rochester, Vt.: Park Street Press, 2005).

4. P. Matthiessen, *At Play in the Fields of the Lord* (New York: Random House, 1965).

5. G. Reichel-Dolmatoff, *Amazonian Cosmos: The Sexual and Religious Symbolism of the Tukano Indians* (Chicago: Chicago University Press, 1971).

6. P. T. Furst, *Flesh of the Gods: The Ritual Use of Hallucinogens* (New York: Praeger, 1972).

7. M. Harner, ed., *Hallucinogens and Shamanism* (New York: Oxford University Press, 1973).

8. R. Karsten, "The Head-hunters of Western Amazonas," *Societas Scientiarum Fennica, Commentationes Humanarum Litterarum* VII 1 (1935).

9. G. Reichel-Dolmatoff, *The Shaman and the Jaguar: A Study of Narcotic Drugs among the Indians of Colombia* (Philadelphia: Temple University Press, 1975).

10. B. F. Lamb, *Wizard of the Upper Amazon: The Story of Manuel Córdoba Rios* (Boston: Houghton Mifflin, 1975).

11. G. del Castillo, "La Ayahuasca Planta Mágica de la Amazonía; el Ayahuasquismo," *Perú Indígena* 10(24 and 25) (1963): 88–98; M. Dobkin de Rios, *Visionary Vine: Hallucinogenic Healing in the Peruvian Amazon* (San Francisco: Chandler, 1972); F. Ayala Flores and W. H. Lewis, "Drinking the South American Hallucinogenic Ayahuasca," *Economic Botany* 32 (1978): 154–56; M. Costa Chiappe, "El Empleo de Alucinógenos en la Psiquiatría Folklórica," in C. A. Seguín, ed., *Psiquiatría Folklórica: Shamanes y Curanderos* (Lima: Ediciones Ermar, 1979); F. Bruce Lamb, *Wizard of the Upper Amazon: The Story of Manuel Córdoba-Rios* (Boston:

Houghton Mifflin Company, 1971); *Rio Tigre and Beyond: The Amazon Jungle Medicine of Manuel Córdoba-Rios* (Berkeley: North Atlantic Books, 1993).

12. N. Maxwell, *Witch-doctor's Apprentice: Hunting for Medicinal Plants in the Amazon* (Boston: Houghton Mifflin, 1961).

13. C. M. Torres and D. B. Repke, Anadenanthera: *Visionary Plant of Ancient South America* (New York: The Haworth Herbal Press, 2006).

14. J. C. Callaway, "A Proposed Mechanism for the Visions of Dream Sleep," *Medical Hypotheses* 26 (1988): 119–24.

15. R. Strassman, *DMT: The Spirit Molecule.*

16. D. J. McKenna, G. H. N. Towers, F. S. Abbott, "Monoamine Oxidase Inhibitors in South American Hallucinogenic Plants: Tryptamine and ß-carboline Constituents of Ayahuasca," *Journal of Ethnopharmacology* 10 (1984): 195–223.

17. L. E. Luna and P. Amaringo, *Ayahuasca Visions: The Religious Iconography of a Peruvian Shaman* (Berkeley, Calif.: North Atlantic Books, 1991).

18. J. Valle, *Messengers of Deception: UFO Contacts and Cults* (Berkeley, Calif.: And/Or Press, 1979), 209–10.

19. C. S. Grob, D. J. McKenna, J. C. Callaway, G. S. Brito, E. S. Neves, G. Oberlender, O. L. Saide, et al., "Human Pharmacology of Hoasca, a Plant Hallucinogen Used in Ritual Context in Brazil," *Journal of Nervous and Mental Disorder* 184 (1996): 86–94; J. C. Callaway, M. M. Airaksinen, D. J. McKenna, G. S. Brito, and C. S. Grob, "Platelet Serotonin Uptake Sites Increased in Drinkers of Ayahuasca," *Psychopharmacology* 116 (1994): 385–87; J. C. Callaway, L. P. Raymon, W. L. Hearn, D. J. McKenna, C. S. Grob, G. S. Brito, and D. C. Mash, "Quantitation of N,N-dimethyl-tryptamine and Harmala Alkaloids in Human Plasma after Oral Dosing with Ayahuasca," *Journal of Analytical Toxicology* 20 (1996): 492–97; J. C. Callaway, D. J. McKenna, C. S. Grob, G. S. Brito, L. P. Raymon, R. E. Poland, E. N. Andrade, et al., "Pharmacology of Hoasca Alkaloids in Healthy Humans," *Journal of Ethnopharmacology* 65(3) (1999): 243–56.

20. L. E. Luna, *Vegetalismo: Shamanism among the Mestizo Population of the Peruvian Amazon* (Stockholm: Almqvist and Wiksell International, 1986).

21. M. Winkelman, "Psychointegrator Plants: Their Roles in Human Culture, Consciousness and Health," in *Yearbook of Cross-Cultural Medicine and*

Psychotherapy, M. Winkelman and W. Andritzky, eds. (Berlin: Verlag und Vertrieb, 1995), 9–53.

22. E. Frecska, K. D. White, and L. E. Luna, "Effects of the Amazonian Psychoactive Beverage Ayahuasca on Binocular Rivalry: Interhemispheric Witching or Interhemispheric Fusion?" *Journal of Psychoactive Drugs* 35(3) (2003): 367–74.

23. E. Frecska, K. D. White, and L. E. Luna, "Effects of Ayahuasca on Binocular Rivalry with Dichoptic Stimulus Alternation," *Journal of Psychopharmacology* 173 (2004): 79–87.

24. D. Stuckey, R. Lawson, and L. E. Luna, "EEG Gamma Coherence and Other Correlates of Subjective Reports during Ayahuasca Experience," *Journal of Psychoactive Drugs* 37(2) (2005): 163–78.

25. A. Lutz, L. L. Greischar, N. B. Rawlings, M. Ricard, and R. J. Davidson, "Long-term Meditators Self-induce High-amplitude Gamma Synchrony during Mental Practice," *Proc Natl Acad Sci USA,* 101(46) (2004): 16369–73.

26. A. Newberg and E. D'Aquili, *Why God Won't Go Away: Brain Science and the Biology of Belief* (New York: Ballantine Books, 2001).

27. D. Joffe, F. Echenhofer, K. Wynia, L. E. Luna, and J. Gunkelman, "Improved EEG Coherence Estimates of the Effects of Ayahuasca and Related Experiences," paper presented at the September 2005 meeting of the International Society of Neuronal Regulation (ISNR), Denver.

28. R. Penrose, *Shadows of the Mind: A Search for the Missing Science of Consciousness* (Oxford: Oxford University Press, 1994).

29. K. W. Tupper, "Entheogens and Existential Intelligence: The Use of Plant Teachers as Cognitive Tools," *Canadian Journal of Education* 27(4) (2002): 499–516.

CHAPTER 5. THE VARIETIES OF THE
AYAHUASCA EXPERIENCE

1. E. J. Langdon, "A Visit to the Second Heaven: A Siona Narrative of the Yagé Experience," in *Ayahuasca Reader: Encounters with the Amazon's Sacred Vine,* Luis Eduardo Luna and Steven F. White, eds. (Santa Fe, N. Mex.: Synergetic Press, 2000).

2. L. E. Luna and P. Amaringo, *Ayahuasca Visions: The Religious Iconography of a Peruvian Shaman* (Berkeley, Calif.: North Atlantic Books, 1991).

3. A. Gebhart-Sayer, "The Geometric Designs of the Shipibo-Conibo in Ritual Context," *Journal of Latin American Lore* 11(2) (1985).

4. B. Shanon, *The Antipodes of the Mind: Charting the Phenomenology of the Ayahuasca Experience* (Oxford: Oxford University Press, 2002).

5. M. Eliade, *Shamanism: Archaic Techniques of Ecstasy* (Princeton, N.J.: Princeton University Press, 1964).

CHAPTER 6. MAGIC MUSHROOMS

1. *Florentine Codex General History of the Things of New Spain in Thirteen Parts* (12 volumes) Translated from the Aztec-Sahagun Manuscript 12 of 13 volumes" by Arthur J.O. and Charles E. Dibble Anderson

2. R. Metzner, *Sacred Mushroom of Visions: Teonanácatl—A Sourcebook on the Psilocybin Mushroom* (Rochester, Vt.: Park Street Press, 2005).

3. P. Stafford, *Magic Mushrooms* (Oakland, Calif.: Ronin Publishing, 2003).

4. R. G. Wasson, *The Wondrous Mushroom: Mycolatry in Mesoamerica* (New York: McGraw-Hill, 1980).

5. O. Beck, A. Helander, C. Karlson-Stiber, and N. Stephansson, "Presence of Phenylethylamine in Hallucinogenic Psilocybe Mushroom: Possible Role in Adverse Reactions," *J Anal Toxicol* 22(1) (1998): 45–49.

6. K. S. Borowiak, K. Ciechanowski, and P. Waloszczyk, "Psilocybin Mushroom (*Psilocybe semilanceata*) Intoxication with Myocardial Infarction," *J Toxicol Clin Toxicol* 36(1–2) (1998): 47–49.

7. M. L. Espiard, L. Lecardeur, P. Abadie, I. Halbecq, S. Dollfus, "Hallucinogen Persisting Perception Disorder after Psilocybin Consumption: A Case Study," *Eur Psychiatry* 20(5–6) (2005): 458–60.

8. M. Franz, H. Regele, M. Kirchmair, J. Kletzmayr, G. Sunder-Plassmann, W. H. Horl, and E. Pohanka, "Magic Mushrooms: Hope for a 'Cheap High' Resulting in End-stage Renal Failure," *Nephrol Dial Transplant* 11(11) (1996): 2324–27.

9. F. Hasler, U. Grimberg, M. A. Benz, T. Huber, and F. X. Vollenweider, "Acute Psychological and Physiological Effects of Psilocybin in Healthy Humans: A Double-blind, Placebo-controlled Dose-effect Study," *Psychopharmacology (Berl)* 172(2) (2004): 145–56. Epub, November 13, 2003.

10. R. H. Schwartz and D. E. Smith, "Hallucinogenic Mushrooms," *Clin Pediatr (Phila)* 27(2) (1988): 70–73.

11. P. Stafford, *Magic Mushrooms* (Oakland, Calif.: Ronin Publishing, 2003).

12. R. S. Gable, "Toward a Comparative Overview of Dependence Potential and Acute Toxicity of Psychoactive Substances Used Nonmedically," *Am J Drug Alcohol Abuse* 19(3) (1993): 263–81.

13. T. McKenna, *Food of the Gods: The Search for the Original Tree of Knowledge: A Radical History of Plants, Drugs, and Human Evolution* (New York: Bantam, 1993).

14. T. McKenna, *The Archaic Revival: Speculations on Psychedelic Mushrooms, the Amazon, Virtual Reality, UFOs, Evolution, Shamanism, the Rebirth of the Goddess and the End of History* (San Francisco: HarperSanFrancisco, 1992).

15. R. R. Griffiths, W. A. Richards, U. McCann, and R. Jesse, "Psilocybin Can Occasion Mystical-type Experiences Having Substantial and Sustained Personal Meaning and Spiritual Significance," *Psychopharmacology (Berl)* 187(3) (2006): 268–83; Epub, July 7, 2006.

16. Erowid, www.erowid.org/plants/mushrooms.

17. Ken Russell, director; Paddy Chayefsky, screenplay, *Altered States* (Warner Bros. Pictures, 1980).

CHAPTER 7. THE SHAMAN'S JOURNEY

1. D. Lewis-Williams and D. Pearce, *Inside the Neolithic Mind: Consciousness, Cosmos and the Realm of the Gods* (London: Thames and Hudson, 2005).

2. S. Tyler, *Cognitive Anthropology* (Prospect Heights, Ill.: Waveland Press, 1987).

3. T. Crow, "Is Schizophrenia the Price that *Homo sapiens* Pays for Language?" *Schizophrenia Research* 28 (1997):127–41.

4. M. Winkelman, "Spirits as Human Nature and the Fundamental Structures of Consciousness," in *From Shaman to Scientist: Essays on Humanity's Search for Spirits,* ed. James Houran (Lanham, Md.: Scarecrow Press, 2004).

5. R. Walsh, *Spirit of Shamanism* (New York: Tarcher/Putnam Books, 1991).

6. A. Watts, *The Supreme Identity: An Essay on Oriental Metaphysics and the Christian Religion* (Westminster, Md.: Random House, 1972).

7. K. Wilber, *Grace and Grit: Spirituality and Healing in the Life and Death of Treya Killam Wilber* (Boston: Shambhala, 2001).

8. G. W. Leibnitz, *Philosophical Works of Leibnitz* (Whitefish, Mont.: Kessinger, 2003).

9. R. Walsh, *Spirit of Shamanism* (New York: Tarcher/Putnam Book, 1991).

10. K. Wilber, *Grace and Grit: Spirituality and Healing in the Life and Death of Treya Killam Wilber.*

11. G. Engel, "The Need for a New Medical Model: A Challenge for Biomedicine," *Science* 196 (1977): 129–36.

12. M. Winkelman, "Physiological, Social and Functional Aspects of Drug and Non-drug Altered States of Consciousness," in *Yearbook of Cross-cultural Medicine and Psychotherapy,* ed. Michael Winkelman and Walter Andritzky (Berlin: VWB-Verlag, 1991), 183–98.

13. M. Dobkin de Rios and D. E. Smith, "Drug Use and Abuse in Cross-cultural Perspective," *Human Organization* 36 (1977): 14–21.

14. M. Winkelman, *Shamanism: The Neural Ecology of Consciousness and Healing* (Westport, Conn.: Bergin and Garvey, 2000).

15. M. Eliade, *Shamanism: Archaic Techniques of Ecstasy* (Princeton, N.J.: Princeton University Press, 2004).

16. M. Winkelman and P. M. Peek, "Introduction: Divination and Healing Processes," in *Divination and Healing: Potent Vision,* ed. Michael Winkelman and Philip M. Peek (Tucson: University of Arizona Press, 2004).

17. M. Harris, *Cultural Materialism: The Struggle for a Science of Culture* (New York: Random House, 1979).

18. M. Harner, *The Way of the Shaman* (San Francisco: Harper and Row, 1990).

19. M. Eliade, *Shamanism: Archaic Techniques of Ecstasy.*

20. C. Castaneda, *Separate Reality* (New York: Washington Square Press, 1991).

21. C. Tart, *States of Consciousness.*

22. M. Winkelman, *Shamanism: The Neural Ecology of Consciousness and Healing.*

23. E. Bourgignon, "Possession and Trance in Cross-cultural Studies of Mental Health," in *Culture-Bound Syndromes, Ethnopsychiatry, and Alternate Therapies,* vol. 4 of *Mental Health Research in Asia and the Pacific,* ed. William P. Lebra (Honolulu: University Press of Hawaii, 1976), 47–55.

24. T. McKenna, *The Archaic Revival: Speculations on Psychedelic Mushrooms, the Amazon, Virtual Reality, UFOs, Evolution, Shamanism, the Rebirth of the Goddess, and the End of History.*

25. E. Kant, *Critique of Pure Reason* (Cambridge, U.K.: Cambridge University Press, 1999).

26. K. Wilber, *Grace and Grit: Spirituality and Healing in the Life and Death of Treya Killam Wilber.*

27. Don Siegel, director; Harry Julian Fink and Rita M. Fink, screenplay, *Dirty Harry* (Warner Bros. Pictures, 1973).

28. F. Crick, *Astonishing Hypothesis: The Scientific Search for the Soul* (New York: Scribner, 1995).

29. J. Horgan, *The Undiscovered Mind: How the Human Brain Defies Replication, Medication, and Explanation* (New York: Free Press, 2000).

30. S. Pinker, *The Blank Slate: The Modern Denial of Human Nature* (New York: Penguin, 2003).

31. A. Einstein, B. Podolsky, and N. Rosen, "Can Quantum-mechanical Description of Physical Reality Be Considered Complete?" *Physical Review* 47 (1935): 777–80.

32. J. S. Bell, "On the Einstein Podolsky Rosen Paradox," *Physics 1* (1964): 195–200.

33. A. Aspect, J. Dalibar, and G. Roger, "Experimental Test of Bell's Inequalities Using Time-varying Analyzers," *Physical Review Letters* 49 (1982): 1804–1806; J. A. Wheeler, "Law without Law," in *Quantum Theory and Measurement,* eds. John A. Wheeler and Wojciech H. Zurek (Princeton, N.J.: Princeton University Press, 1984).

34. J. A. Wheeler, "Information, Physics, Quantum: The Search for Links," in *Complexity, Entropy and the Physics of Information,* Wojciech H. Zurek, ed. (New York: Perseus Books, 1990).

35. August Stern, *Matrix Logic* (Amsterdam: Elsevier Science, 1988).

36. R. Penrose, *Shadows of the Mind: A Search for the Missing Science of Consciousness* (Oxford: Oxford University Press, 1966).

37. J. Sarfatti, *Super Cosmos* (Bloomington, Ind.: AuthorHouse Publishing, 2005).

38. M. Pitkanen, *Topological Geometrodynamics* (Frome, U.K.: Luniver Press, 2006).

39. H. Wesselman, *Visionseeker: Shared Wisdom from the Place of Refuge* (Carlsbad, Calif.: Hay House, 2001).

40. D. Lewis-William and D. Pearce, *Inside the Neolithic Mind* (London: Thames and Hudson, 2005).

41. A. Hastings, *With the Tongues of Men and Angels: A Study of Channeling* (Fort Worth, Texas: Holt, Rinehart and Winston, 1991); S. Riordan, "Channeling: A New Revelation?" In *Perspectives in the New Age,* James R. Lewis and Gordon J. Melton, eds. (New York: State of New York Press, 1992).

42. Ibid.; J. Klimo, *Channeling: Investigations on Receiving Information from Paranormal Sources* (Los Angeles: Jeremy P. Tarcher, 1988).

43. B. D. Josephson, "The Discovery of Tunneling Supercurrents," *Reviews of Modern Physics* 46 (1974): 251–54.

44. J. Jaynes, *The Origin of Consciousness in the Breakdown of the Bicameral Mind* (Boston: Mariner Books, 2000).

45. J. D. Bakst, "Journey to the Secret City of Luz: Ladder to the Face of God" (2007), available on www.chazonhatorah.org, under "Learning Center."

46. Ibid.

47. R. Strassman, *DMT: The Spirit Molecule.*

48. S. Nasar, *A Beautiful Mind: The Life of Mathematical Genius and Nobel Laureate John Nash* (New York: Simon and Schuster, 2001).

49. J. Narby, *The Cosmic Serpent: DNA and the Origin of Knowledge* (New York: Tarcher/Putnam Books, 1998).

CHAPTER 8. HOW CAN SHAMANS TALK WITH PLANTS AND ANIMALS?

1. M. Pitkanen, *Topological Geometrodynamics.*

2. C. Backster, "Evidence of a Primary Perception in Plant Life," *International Journal of Parapsychology* 10 (1968): 329–48.

3. R. N. Miller, "The Positive Effect of Prayer on Plants," *Psychic* 3 (1972): 24–25.

4. M. Vogel, "Man-plant Communication," in *Psychic Exploration,* ed. John White (New York: Tarcher/Putnam, 1974).

5. Ibid.

6. F. Loehr, *The Power of Prayer on Plants* (Garden City, N.Y.: Doubleday, 1959).

7. M. Hoffman, "Tomaten Belohnen Zuwendung. 'Grüner Daumen' der Gärtner Bewiesen," *Garten Organisch* 7 (1992): 20–23.

8. A. Saklani, "Preliminary Tests for Psi Ability in Shamans of Garhwal Himalaya," *Journal of Society for Psychical Research* 55 (1988): 60–70; A. M. Scofield and D. R. Hodges, "Demonstration of a Healing Effect in the Laboratory Using a Simple Plant Model," *Journal of the Society for Psychical Research* 57 (1991): 321–43.

9. R. Shapiro and J. Rapkins, *Awakening to the Plant Kingdom* (San Rafael, Calif.: Cassandra Press, 1991).

10. A. Kinkade, *Straight from the Horse's Mouth: How to Talk to Animals and Get Answers* (New York: Crown Books, 2001).

11. J. V. Iovine, "A Dog Biscuit for Your Thoughts," *New York Times,* July 22, 2001.

12. Ibid.

13. S. Hameroff, *Ultimate Computing* (Amsterdam: North-Holland, 1987).

14. M. Tegmark, "Importance of Quantum Decoherence in Brain Processes," *Physical Review E: Statistical Physics, Plasmas, Fluids, and Related Interdisciplinary Topics* 61 (2000): 4194–206.

15. V. Jones, "Hecke Algebra Representations of Braid Groups and Link Polynomials," *Annals of Mathematics* 126 (1987): 335–88.

16. E. Witten, "Quantum Field Theory and the Jones Polynomial," *Communications in Mathematical Physics* 121 (1989): 351–99.

17. A. Kitaev, "Quantum Error Correction with Imperfect Gates," in *Quantum Communication and Computing and Measurement,* O. Hirota et al., eds. (New York: Plenum, 1997).

18. P. Parsons, "Dancing the Quantum Dream," *New Scientist* 2431 (2004): 31–34.

19. P. W. Anderson, *A Career in Theoretical Physics* (Hackensack, N.J.: World Scientific Publishing Company, 2005).

20. M. Pitkanen, *Topological Geometrodynamics.*

21. G. Collins, "Computing with Quantum Knots," *Scientific American* 294 (2006): 57–63.

22. P. Stamets, *Mycelium Running: How Mushrooms Can Help Save the World* (Berkeley, Calif.: Ten Speed Press, 2005).

23. T. McKenna, *The Archaic Revival: Speculations on Psychedelic Mushrooms, the Amazon, Virtual Reality, UFOs, Evolution, Shamanism, the Rebirth of the Goddess, and the End of History.*

24. M. Pitkanen, *Topological Geometrodynamics.*

CHAPTER 9. CLOSE ENCOUNTERS OF THE ANCIENT KIND

1. M. Winkelman, *Shamanism: The Neural Ecology of Consciousness and Healing.*

2. Mikra'ot Gedolot, *Rabbinic Bible* (Jerusalem: Hamoor, 1990).

3. M. Agrest, "The historical evidence of paleocontacts," *Ancient Skies: Official Logbook of the Ancient Astronaut Society* 20, no. 6 (1994): 1–3.

4. I. Shklovsky and C. Sagan, *Intelligent Life in the Universe* (Garden City, N.Y.: Doubleday, 1980).

5. E. Von Däniken, *Chariots of the Gods? Unsolved Mysteries of the Past* (New York: Penguin, 1987).

6. Z. Sitchin, *The 12th Planet* (Rochester, Vt.: Bear and Company, 1991).

7. M. Heiser, *The Meaning of the Word* Nephilim: *Fact vs. Fantasy,* at www .thedivinecouncil.com/nephilim.pdf (2005a).

8. M. Heiser, "Deuteronomy 32:8 and the Sons of God," *Bibliotheca Sacra* 158 (2001): 52–74.

9. Z. Sitchin, *Divine Encounters: A Guide to Visions, Angels, and Other Emissaries* (Rochester, Vt.: Bear and Company, 2002).

10. S. Mithen, *After the Ice: A Global Human History 20,000–5000 BC* (Cambridge, Mass.: Harvard University Press, 2006).

11. R. Strassman, *DMT: The Spirit Molecule.*

12. M. Harner, *The Way of the Shaman.*

13. R. Dawkins, *The Selfish Gene* (Oxford: Oxford University Press, 1976).

14. F. Crick and L. Orgel, "Directed Panspermia," *Icarus* 19 (1973): 341–46.

15. R. Strassman, *DMT: The Spirit Molecule.*

16. H. Wesselman, *Spiritwalker: Messages from the Future* (New York: Bantam Books, 1996); H. Wesselman, *Medicinemaker: Mystic Encounters on the Shaman's Path* (New York: Bantam Books, 1999); H. Wesselman, *Visionseeker: Shared Wisdom from the Place of Refuge* (Carlsbad, Calif.: Hay House, 2001).

17. M. Heiser, *The Nachash and His Seed: Some Explanatory Notes on Why the "Serpent" in Genesis 3 Wasn't a Serpent,* at www.thedivinecouncil.com/nachashnotes.pdf (2005b).

18. J. Pasachoff and A. Filippenko, *The Cosmos: Astronomy in the New Millennium* (Fort Worth, Texas: Harcourt College Publishers, 2001).

19. M. Kaku, *Parallel Worlds: A Journey Through Creation, Higher Dimensions, and the Future of the Cosmos* (Garden City, N.Y.: Doubleday, 2004).

20. Jim DeKorne, *Psychedelic Shamanism: The Cultivation, Preparation and Shamanic Use of Psychotropic Plants.*

21. J. D. Bakst, *Fallen Angels and Cosmic Fallout: The Secret of the Nefilim,* www.chazonhatorah.org/journeys-subpage-2.htm.

CHAPTER 10. HYPNOSIS, PAST LIFE REGRESSION, MEDITATION, AND MORE

1. J. E. Mack, *Abduction: Human Encounters with Aliens* (New York: Ballantine Books, 1997).

2. Intruders Foundation, www.intrudersfoundation.org.

3. J. E. Mack, *Passport to the Cosmos* (New York: Three Rivers Press, 2000).

4. Dan Curtis, director, Barry Oringer and Tracy Tormé, teleplay, *The Intruders* (Osiris Films, 1992).

5. G. Hancock, *Supernatural: Meetings with the Ancient Teachers of Mankind* (New York: The Disinformation Company, 2006).

6. R. L. Thompson, *Alien Identities: Ancient Insights into Modern UFO Phenomena* (Alachua, Fla.: Govardhan Hill Publishing, 1995).

7. Chakravarthi V. Narasimhan, trans., *Mahabharata* (New Delhi: Motilal Banarsidass, 1999).

8. B. Weiss, *Many Lives, Many Masters* (New York: Fireside, 1988).

9. B. Weiss, *Same Soul, Many Bodies* (New York: Free Press, 2004).

10. H. Wesselman, *Spiritwalker: Messages from the Future.*

11. G. Renard, *The Disappearance of the Universe* (Carlsbad, Calif.: Hay House, 2004).

12. G. Renard, *Your Immortal Reality* (Carlsbad, Calif.: Hay House, 2006).

13. S. Ray and L. Orr, *Rebirthing in the New Age* (Berkeley, Calif.: Celestial Arts, 1983).

14. N. D. Walsh, *Communion with God* (New York: Penguin Putnam, 2000).

15. A. C. Bhaktivedanta Swami Prabhupada, *Easy Journey to Other Planets* (Boston: Iskon Press, 1970).

CHAPTER 12. THE SACRED VOYAGE: BEYOND SCIENCE FICTION?

1. Andy Wachowski and Larry Wachowski, directors; Andy Wachowski and Larry Wachowski, screenplay, *The Matrix* (Groucho II Film Partnership, 1999); Richard Linklater, director; Richard Linklater, screenplay, *Waking Life* (Fox Searchlight Pictures, 2001); David Cronenberg, director; David Cronenberg, screenplay, *eXistenZ* (Alliance Atlantis Communications, 1999).

2. George Lucas, director; George Lucas, screenplay, *Star Wars* (Lucasfilm, 1977); Andy Wachowski and Larry Wachowski, directors; Andy Wachowski and Larry Wachowski, screenplay, *The Matrix* (Groucho II Film Partnership, 1999); Paul Verhoeven, director; Ronald Shusett, Dan O'Bannon, and Gary Oldman, screenplay, *Total Recall* (Tristar Pictures, 1990); Vicenzo Natali, director; André Bijelic, Vincenzo Natali, and Graeme Mason, screenplay, *Cube* (Cube Libre, 1997); Alex Proyas, director; Alex Proyas, Lem Dobbs, and David S. Goyer, screenplay, *Dark City* (Mystery Clock Cinema, 1998).

3. E. Pagels, *Beyond Belief: The Secret Gospel of Thomas* (New York: Random House, 2003).

4. Alejandro Amenábar, director; Alejandro Amenábar and Mateo Gil, screenplay, *Abre los ojos* (Canal + España, 1997).

5. Harold Ramis, director; Danny Rubin and Harold Ramis, screenplay, *Groundhog Day* (Columbia Pictures, 1993); Darren Aronofsky, director; Darren Aronofsky, screenplay, *The Fountain* (Warner Bros. Pictures, 2006).

6. S. Lem, "Lymphater's Formula," in *The Book of Robots* (Warsaw: Iskry, 1961).

7. S. Lem, *The Futurological Congress: From the Memoirs of Ijon Tichy* (Kraków: Wydawnictwo Literackie, 1971).

8. P. K. Dick, *Ubik* (New York: Vintage, 1991).

9. Paul Verhoeven, director; Ronald Shusett, Dan O'Bannon, and Gary Oldman, screenplay, *Total Recall* (Tristar Pictures, 1990).

10. *A Course in Miracles* (Mill Valley, Calif.: Foundation for Inner Peace, 1992).

11. G. Renard, *The Disappearance of the Universe.*

12. Richard Linklater, director; Richard Linklater, screenplay, *Waking Life* (Fox Searchlight Pictures, 2001).

13. David Cronenberg, director; David Cronenberg, screenplay, *eXistenZ* (Alliance Atlantis Communications, 1999).

14. André Bijelic, Vincenzo Natali, and Graeme Mason, screenplay, *Cube* (Cube Libre, 1997).

15. Alex Proyas, director; Alex Proyas, Lem Dobbs, and David S. Goyer, screenplay, *Dark City* (Mystery Clock Cinema, 1998).

16. Dalai Lama, *A Flash of Lightning in the Dark of Night: A Guide to the Bodhisattva's Way of Life* (Boston: Shambhala Publications, 1994).

17. H. Wesselman, *Spiritwalker: Messages from the Future.*

18. G. Renard, *Your Immortal Reality: How to Break the Cycle of Birth and Death.*

recommended reading

Arntz, William, Betsy Chasse, and Mark Vicente, directors; William Arntz, Betsy Chasse, Matthew Hoffman, and Mark Vicente, screenplay, *What the Bleep Do We Know?* Lord of the Wind, 2004.

Callaway, J. C., D. J. McKenna, C. S. Grob, G. S. Brito, L. P. Raymon, R. E. Poland, E. N. Andrade, et al. "Pharmacokinetics of Hoasca Alkaloids in Healthy Humans." *Journal of Ethnopharmacology* 65 (1999): 243–56.

del Castillo, G. *Observaciones sobre la intoxicación provocada en el hombre por la ingestión de la Ayahuasca.* Bachelor's thesis, Universidad Nacional Mayor de San Marcos, Lima, 1962.

Goldman, I. *The Cubeo: Indians of the Northwest Amazon.* Urbana: University of Illinois Press, 1963.

Harner, M. *The Way of the Shaman.* San Francisco: HarperSanFrancisco, 1990.

Hirota, Osamu, Alexander S. Holevo, and Carlton M. Caves, eds. *Quantum Communication, Computing and Measurement.* New York: Plenum Press, 1997.

Karsten, R. "Studies in the Religion of the South American Indians East of the Andes." In A. Runenberg and M. Webster, eds., *Societas Scientiarum Fennica. Commentationes Humanarum Litterarum* XXIX, 1964.

Kounen, Jan, director; Cassidy Pope, screenplay. *Renegade.* A.J.O.Z. Films, 2004.

Langdon, E. J. "Dau Shamanic Power in Siona Religion and Medicine." In *Portals of Power: Shamanism in South America.* E. Jean Matteson Langdon and Gerhart Baer, eds. Albuquerque: University of New Mexico Press, 1992.

Leloup, J. Y. *The Gospel of Mary Magdalene.* Rochester, Vt.: Inner Traditions, 2002.

———. *The Gospel of Philip: Jesus, Mary Magdalene, and the Gnosis of Sacred Union.* Rochester, Vt.: Inner Traditions, 2004.

Luna, L. E. "A Barquinha: Una nueva religión en Río Branco, Amazonía Brasileña." *Acta Americana* 3(2) (1995): 137–51.

Luna, L. E., and P. Amaringo. *Ayahuasca Visions: The Religious Iconography of a Peruvian Shaman.* Berkeley, Calif.: North Atlantic Books, 1991.

McKenna, D. J., L. E. Luna, and N. H. Towers. "Biodynamic Constituents in Ayahuasca Admixture Plants." In *Ethnobotany—The Evolution of a Discipline.* R. E. Schultes and S. Von Reis, eds. Portland, Ore.: Timber Press, 1995, 349–61.

McKenna, D. J., C. S. Grob, and J. C. Callaway. "The Scientific Investigation of Ayahuasca: A Review of Past and Current Research." *Heffter Review of Psychedelic Research* 1 (1988): 65–77.

McKenna, T., and D. J. McKenna. *The Invisible Landscape: Mind, Hallucinogens, and the I Ching.* San Francisco: HarperSanFrancisco, 1975.

McKenna, T. *The Archaic Revival.* San Francisco: HarperSanFrancisco, 1991.

Ott, J. *Ayahuasca Analogues: Pangaean Entheogens.* Kennewick, Wash.: Natural Products Co., 1994.

Pagels, E. *The Gnostic Gospels.* New York: Vintage, 1989.

Penrose, R. *Shadows of the Mind: A Search for the Missing Science of Consciousness.* Oxford: Oxford University Press, 1996.

Roe, P. G. *The Cosmic Zygote: Cosmology in the Amazon Basin.* New Brunswick, N.J.: Rutgers University Press, 1982.

Starhawk. *The Fifth Sacred Thing.* New York: Bantam, 1993.

Stolaroff, M. *The Secret Chief: Conversations with a Pioneer of the Underground Psychedelic Therapy Movement.* Ben Lomond, Calif.: Multidisciplinary Association for Psychedelic Studies, 1997.

About the Authors

Rick Strassman, M.D., a native of Los Angeles, obtained his B.S. in biology from Stanford University and his medical degree from Albert Einstein College of Medicine of Yeshiva University. His training in adult psychiatry took place at the University of California Davis and in clinical psychopharmacology research at the University of California San Diego. He was on the full-time faculty in the Department of Psychiatry at the University of New Mexico between 1984 and 1995, where he performed human melatonin research, as well as the first new U.S.-government-approved and -funded clinical research with psychedelic drugs in more than twenty years.

Currently associate professor of psychiatry in the University of New Mexico School of Medicine, Dr. Strassman has published thirty peer-reviewed scientific papers and serves as a reviewer for several psychiatric research journals. He has been a consultant to the US Food and Drug Administration, National Institute on Drug Abuse, Veterans Administration Hospitals, Social Security Administration, and other state and local agencies. He lives and practices community psychiatry in northern New Mexico and is cofounder and president of the Cottonwood Research Foundation (www.cottonwoodresearch.org). Dr. Strassman's website is www.rickstrassman.com.

Slawek Wojtowicz, M.D., was born and grew up in Gdansk, Poland. After graduating from the Medical School of Gdansk in 1990, he immigrated to the United States. He completed his internal medicine internship and residency at Henry Ford Hospital in Detroit and a medical oncology fellowship at Georgetown University in Washington, D.C. Dr. Slawek lives in

New Jersey with his wife and two children and works full time as a medical oncologist in the pharmaceutical industry.

Dr. Slawek started drawing and painting science-fiction images at age fifteen after an accident that almost cost him his eyesight, and continues to create art to this day. His work can be found online at www.slawcio.com.

His science-fiction website won multiple awards, including *USA Today's* Hot Site award in 1998. He has illustrated numerous books, book covers, CD covers, magazine covers, and products such as Rifts Collectible Card Game. His art was used in the 2002 movie *In the Neighborhood*. He is the author of *Daydreaming—The art of Slawek Wojtowicz*, as well as of multiple professional publications in the field of medical oncology.

Luis Eduardo Luna, Ph.D., was born in Florencia, in the Colombian Amazon region, in 1947. He studied philosophy and literature in Madrid and taught at Oslo University. He received his Ph.D. from the Institute of Comparative Religion of Stockholm University in 1989 and an honorary degree from St. Lawrence University in Canton, New York, in 2002. A Guggenheim fellow and fellow of the Linnean Society of London, he is the author of *Vegetalismo: Shamanism among the Mestizo Population of the Peruvian Amazon* and, with Pablo Amaringo, *Ayahuasca Visions: The Religious Iconography of a Peruvian Shaman*. He is also co-editor—with Steven F. White—of *Ayahuasca Reader: Encounters with the Amazon's Sacred Vine*. In 1986 with Pablo Amaringo he cofounded the Usko-Ayar Amazonian School of Painting of Pucallpa, Peru, and served as its director of International Exhibitions until 1994. He was professor of anthropology at the Federal University of Santa Catarina, Brazil, from 1994 to 1998, has lectured about Amazonian shamanism and modified states of consciousness worldwide, and has curated exhibitions of visionary art in several countries. He is the director of Wasiwaska—Research Centre for the Study of Psychointegrator Plants, Visionary Arts, and Consciousness in Florianópolis, southern Brazil (its website is www.wasiwaska.org.). He is also a senior lecturer at the Swedish School of Economics and Business Administration, in Helsinki.

Ede Frecska, M.D., is chief of psychiatry at the National Institute of Psychiatry and Neurology in Budapest. He received his medical degree in 1977 from the Semmelweis University in Hungary and his psychologist certification from the Department of Psychology at Lorand Eotvos University in Budapest, after which he completed his residency training in psychiatry both in Hungary (1986) and in the United States (1992). He is a qualified psychopharmacologist (1987) of international merit with fifteen years of clinical and research experience in the United States at Mount Sinai School of Medicine in New York, State University of New York at Stony Brook, and the University of Florida at Gainesville. Dr. Frecska has published more than sixty peer-reviewed scientific papers and book chapters as an invited contributor in research on schizophrenia and affective illness. His recent experimental work includes studies on psychedelic drugs and psychointegrative techniques. He is specifically interested in the neurobiological mechanism of initiation ceremonies and healing rituals using ayahuasca preparation. Dr. Frecska has participated in several pharmaceutical industry–sponsored Phase II and Phase III drug safety and efficacy trials and has received a variety of grants and awards, including from the National Alliance for Research on Schizophrenia and Depression and the National Institute of Alcohol Abuse.

index